A Canyon through Time

A Canyon through Time

Archaeology, History, and Ecology
of the Tecolote Canyon Area,
Santa Barbara County, California

Jon M. Erlandson, Torben C. Rick,
and René L. Vellanoweth

The University of Utah Press
Salt Lake City

The Defiance House Man colophon is a registered trademark
of the University of Utah Press. It is based on a four-foot-tall,
Ancient Puebloan pictograph (late PIII) near Glen Canyon, Utah.

12 11 10 09 08   1 2 3 4 5

LIBRARY OF CONGRESS CATALOGING-IN-PUBLICATION DATA

Erlandson, Jon.
    A canyon through time : archaeology, history, and ecology of the
Tecolote Canyon area, Santa Barbara County, California / by Jon M.
Erlandson, Torben C. Rick, and René L. Vellanoweth.
        p.   cm.
    Includes bibliographical references and index.
    ISBN 978-0-87480-879-7 (pbk. : alk. paper)   1. Paleo-Indians—
California—Tecolote Canyon.   2. Chumash Indians—California—Tecolote
Canyon—Antiquities.   3. Indigenous peoples—Ecology—California—
Tecolote Canyon.   4. Excavations (Archaeology)—California—Tecolote
Canyon.   5. Tecolote Canyon (Calif.)—History.   6. Tecolote Canyon
(Calif.)—Antiquities.   I. Rick, Torben C.   II. Vellanoweth, René L.,
1965–   III. Title.
    E78.C15E72 2008
    979.4'91—dc22   2008021796

Cover photo courtesy of Jon M. Erlandson.
Printed and bound by Sheridan Books, Inc., Ann Arbor, Michigan.
Interior printed on recycled paper with 50 percent post-consumer content.

We dedicate this volume to the Chumash people of Hel'apunitse and their ancestors, who lived in the Tecolote Canyon area for millennia. It is also dedicated to Chumash elder John Thothokanayoh Ruiz for his extraordinary efforts to preserve the history of Tecolote Canyon and the broader Santa Barbara Channel area.

Finally, we are deeply grateful to Mr. Alvin Dworman, owner of the Bacara Resort and Spa and the Tecolote Preserve, for his commitment to preserving the rich history on his property and for his financial support of our work to protect and interpret that history.

Contents

Figures

Tables

Preface

I first learned about the fascinating history of Tecolote Canyon in 1979 as an undergraduate anthropology student and fledgling archaeologist working at the Office of Public Archaeology at the University of California–Santa Barbara (UCSB). Born and raised in Santa Barbara, I had long thought of myself as a native Barbarian. In my youth I knew little of the long history of my home, however, especially the more than 13,000 years Native Americans had lived in the area. This hidden history, which dwarfed that of my own European ancestors in America, was not taught in public schools. Santa Barbara celebrated its Spanish heritage with annual parades and architectural codes, but the Chumash Indians were a largely invisible presence.

My ignorance of this deep history began to change in 1974, when I went to Santa Barbara City College and later UCSB to study archaeology. I volunteered at the Santa Barbara Museum of Natural History and the Santa Barbara Presidio. In 1977–1978, I took a year off from college to work for the County of Santa Barbara as one of two archaeologists and several Chumash tribal members surveying county-owned lands for archaeological sites. In this job, I gained valuable experience in archaeology and local history. More important, I began working with Chumash Indian descendants on a daily basis and came to understand their deep connections to the landscape and history of the Santa Barbara area.

Back at UCSB in 1979, I codirected an archaeological study for a housing project proposed for the beachfront property at Tecolote. In a few months working in this beautiful canyon, I learned more about its natural and cultural history than I could ever have imagined as a boy surfing at what we then called Haskell's Beach. When our report was completed in 1980, I had no idea that archaeological and historical studies would continue in the Tecolote Canyon area for much of the next 25 years—conducted by a variety of university and corporate teams—or that I would be the common thread that linked them together. In the 1980s I moved from Santa Barbara to southeast Alaska and then to central Oregon, Seattle, Fairbanks, and Eugene. Throughout my migrations I returned regularly to Santa Barbara and Tecolote, however, touchstones that reminded me of where I came from and the amazing history of the land where I was born.

I returned to Tecolote Canyon year after year because of my commitment to Chumash friends who cared deeply about the history of this coastal landscape and the Chumash village sites and ancestors it contains. Federal, state, and local laws protect such sites, but their sacred and scientific contents are not appreciated by all. Tragically, they continue to be lost at an alarming rate—destroyed by development, damaged by agriculture and erosion, desecrated by vandals or looters—often before their history can be studied or written. Fortunately, Tecolote Canyon has had strong protectors, including the Chumash people, a conscientious archaeological community, owners and land managers committed to doing the right thing, and many others. From the beginning, the nature of the Bacara Resort and Spa was shaped by a commitment to preserve the history of Tecolote Canyon. Today, much of the archaeology of the lower canyon remains intact and better protected than it has been for a century or more.

Over the years, many people have helped protect and preserve the history and archaeology of Tecolote Canyon, but no one deserves more credit and recognition than the Chumash people themselves. First and foremost among these is John Thothokanayoh Ruiz, of the Coastal Band of the Chumash Nation, who has dedicated most of his life to the revival and restoration of Chumash culture and to protecting archaeological sites of the Santa Barbara area. For two decades—through the strength of his personality, his knowledge of preservation and construction processes, and his iron-willed perseverance and determination—John ensured that the archaeological sites of Tecolote Canyon survived and that the history of the canyon would be told. Along the way, he was helped by many members or friends of the Chumash community, including Deana Dartt, Aggie Garnica, Larry Garnica Jr., Larry Garnica Sr., Patsy Gomez, Victor Slo'w Gutierrez and John Sespe Gutierrez, Madelaine Tukoloc Hall, Darlene and Ray Hall, Marty "No. 7" Martin, Esther and J. C. Ruiz, Al White Bear Sulwasunaytset, and many others. Deana Dartt also created a wonderful interpretive display on the Chumash people and their history that can be seen in the store by the entry court at Bacara.

Although I directed much of the archaeological work reported on in this book, I was helped by many talented individuals who worked with me in the field or the lab. To these colleagues, and many other crew members too numerous to name individually, I am deeply grateful: Richard Carrico, Ted Cooley, Anne DuBarton, Mike Glassow, Bill Glover, Patsy Gomez, Darlene Hall, Leeann Haslouer, Kristina Horton, Mike Imwalle, John Johnson, Dustin Kay, Marcel Kornfeld, Julia Knowles, Marc Linder, Charles Locke, Rob Losey, Mike McEttrick, Jerry Moore, Sandra Day Moriarty, Joe Pjerrou, Melissa Reid, Torben Rick, Tom Rockwell, Kristy Rotermund, Loren Santoro, Izaac Sawyer, Jeff Serena, Bob Sheets, Stacy Smith, Pan-

dora Snethkamp, Megan Stansbury, Harry Steele-Moyer, Bruno Texier, Mark Tveskov, Andrea Van Schmus, René Vellanoweth, Phil Walker, and Chris Webb. I also want to thank Tom Fuller and Greg King of UCSB's Public History Program, who wrote a 1980 summary of the history of Tecolote Canyon on which I have relied heavily. Similar thanks go to Chester King for his 1980 summary of previous archaeological research at Tecolote Canyon. I am also grateful to Mr. Paul Bush, who lived in one of the homes on the western terrace as a child and shared his knowledge about the function of some of the historic structures on the property.

Another important aspect of our work was the study of existing archaeological collections from the Tecolote Canyon area. David Banks Rogers's collections are housed at the Santa Barbara Museum of Natural History, where John Johnson, Jan Timbrook, Linda Agren, and Ray Corbett facilitated our research. Other collections are housed at UCSB, where Mike Glassow, Jim Cassidy, Peter Paige, and Sarah Abraham were extremely helpful. I am also grateful to the staff of the UCSB Maps and Imagery Library who helped me access historical maps and photos of the Tecolote Canyon and Goleta Valley area.

Clearly, this volume is a product of the support and commitment of many people. As much as possible, we have written it in a style we hope is accessible to a wide range of readers, and have included a glossary of technical terms at the end of the book. We are indebted to Patricia Erlandson, Jeff Grathwohl, John Herbert, anonymous reviewers, and the editorial staff at the University of Utah Press for helping bring this vision to fruition. For their help with illustrations, Deana Dartt, Julia Knowles, Melissa Reid, and Eric Carlson also deserve special recognition. I am especially grateful to my coauthors, Torben Rick and René Vellanoweth, who helped supervise much of the analysis of the Tecolote collections, and to Melissa Reid and Rob Losey, who assisted in our analysis, compiling data tables, and other essential tasks. Without the help of René, Torrey, Rob, and Melissa during several critical years, I would surely have gone insane.

Finally, I thank several individuals who contributed significantly to our work in Tecolote Canyon over the years. From 1986 to 1998, John Tynan of the Tynan Group was extremely helpful in complicated consultations among representatives of the landowner, state and county agencies, engineers, contractors, and others involved in the planning and construction of the Bacara Resort and Spa. John Hunt, longtime manager and resident of the Embarcadero Ranch, was extremely gracious and helpful in arranging access to ranch facilities, solving myriad problems, and providing assistance from ranch employees. Although our relationship was stormy at times, Ilyne Mendelson of ADCO provided invaluable administrative assistance during the hectic days of hotel construction. Finally, we thank Alvin Dworman for helping preserve the history of Tecolote Canyon and his financial support of our work.

Jon M. Erlandson

A Canyon through Time: An Introduction

Jon M. Erlandson

Histories are written both large and small. For countless generations, our histories were recorded as stories carefully memorized, passed from one generation to the next while sitting around a fire in a cave or earthen lodge. In more recent times they have been written on clay tablets, on scrolls, or in books, recorded in photographs, audiotapes, compact disks, and other media. Much older histories, many lost from memory and more difficult to decipher, are found in the ruins of archaeological sites that mark the locations of former villages and towns occupied at various points in human history. Still older lessons are recorded in the landscape, in the bedrock beneath us, in the fossils that weather from such rocks, in the pollen grains layered in the sediments exposed in creek banks, and in the up-lifted marine terraces that mark our dynamic coast-lines and the shifting boundaries between land and sea. All of these varied histories have something im-portant to tell us about who we are, where we come from, the world we live in, and our relationships to one another and the natural environments that sur-round us.

In this volume, we record the long history of the Tecolote Canyon area along the southern Cali-fornia Coast, an area known as Owl Canyon to the Spanish who first settled here less than 250 years ago and as Hel'apunitse (Guitarfish) to the Barba-reño Chumash Indians who lived here for mil-lennia prior to the coming of Europeans. Located along the Santa Barbara Coast on the western edge of the city of Goleta, Tecolote Creek flows for only about 8 km (5 mi), from the southern flanks of the Santa Ynez Mountains to the emerald waters of the Santa Barbara Channel and the Pacific Ocean. Walking the bed of Tecolote Creek from the sea to the mountains takes just a few hours, but the rocks, and ruins, and recent history encountered on that short walk tell a fascinating story of southern Cali-fornia landscapes and cultures, a history that spans more than 60 million years. In a universe formed 18 billion years ago, on a planet spinning for five bil-lion years or more, the history of Tecolote Canyon may appear to be a short story. Compared with our everyday lives, however, it is a remarkable story of colliding continents, dramatic landscape changes, Native American cultures spanning more than 13,000 years, the clash of cultures that resulted when Europeans first colonized these golden shores, and the rapidly changing faces of California as the multiethnic communities and increasingly global economies of the Spanish, Mexican, and American periods emerged and expanded.

THE TECOLOTE CANYON ARCHAEOLOGICAL PROJECT

Our story grew out of 25 years of archaeologi-cal and historical studies in the Tecolote Canyon area. As a boy growing up in Santa Barbara in the 1960s, I surfed in the waves off the beach we called Haskell's, located at the mouth of Tecolote Canyon in front of what is now the Bacara Resort. Basking in the sun on the beach, I had no idea of the history that surrounded me. In 1979, as an anthropology student at the University of California–Santa Barbara, I was asked to help direct fieldwork on the 70-acre parcel of land immediately behind Haskell's Beach. Working with descendants of the Chumash Indians, our job was to map the boundaries of archaeological sites on the property, assess their significance according to California laws that protected such sites, and evaluate the potential impacts of a proposed housing development (see Kornfeld et al. 1980). Within a few short months in 1979 and 1980, I learned a great deal about the history of Tecolote Canyon—including the fact that it had been occupied by Native people for more than 5,000 years. At the time, I had no way of knowing that I would be engaged in research on this beautiful canyon for much of the next 25 years or how much I would eventually learn about its long history.

As many developers and corporate officers can tell you, Santa Barbara County is a difficult place to build in. California has relatively strict environmental laws, especially along the coast. Enforcement of many of these laws falls primarily to individual cities or counties and has been mixed, but Santa Barbara County has historically been one of the most zealous in trying to protect its natural and cultural resources. In the planning and review process for construction in Tecolote Canyon, environmental studies identified a number of potential problems, including the presence of several large and highly significant village sites of the Chumash Indian people. For a variety of reasons, the proposed residential development in Lower Tecolote Canyon was never built. In the mid-1980s, however, the landowner teamed with Hyatt Hotels to propose a resort complex for the property, initiating another round of environmental and archaeological studies. Working with members of the Coastal Band of the Chumash Nation (CBCN), I helped develop a plan that would avoid the destruction of most significant archaeological remains ("cultural resources") on the property and salvage information from those areas that could not be avoided (see Erlandson 1986).

My 1986 "Cultural Resources Management Plan" raised a series of questions and issues to be studied with archaeological data collected from sites investigated during the Tecolote Canyon Archaeological Project, including basic questions about the age, size, and contents of various sites within the project area. On a more general level, the research goals outlined for the project were to (1) reconstruct the history of environmental changes that occurred in the Tecolote Canyon area through time, as well as the effects of such changes on the canyon's human inhabitants; (2) document and explain changes in human settlement, subsistence, and technology in the area over time; (3) examine the development of local and long-distance trade or exchange networks within and beyond the Santa Barbara Channel region; and (4) explore the nature of cultural evolution and transitions in the Santa Barbara Channel area (Erlandson 1986: 27–32). As work on the project progressed and new data accumulated, additional topics and issues were developed that helped guide our research in the Tecolote Canyon area.

After a long process of planning, environmental review, and project revisions—including a list of over 100 conditions placed on the project by the County of Santa Barbara and the California Coastal Commission—the proposal to build a major resort at Tecolote Canyon was approved in 1988. Construction seemed imminent, and archaeological investigations related to the project continued sporadically until 1989, but financing for the construction of a large resort on the Santa Barbara Coast was difficult to obtain in the economic conditions of the time. Further archaeological studies were put on hold, and archaeological collections were placed in storage. With a freshly printed Ph.D. in hand, I moved on with my life, from an archaeological consultant living in Seattle, to a visiting professor of anthropology at the University of Alaska in Fairbanks, then to an assistant professor of anthropology at the University of Oregon. I began new projects in coastal Alaska, Oregon, and California, including a major research effort focused on the Channel Islands off the Santa Barbara Coast.

Early in 1997, however, I learned that financing for the construction of the Bacara Resort had finally been secured, grading and construction permits were being obtained, and I needed to assemble a team of archaeologists and Native Americans to protect or salvage sensitive sites during grading and construction. For much of the next three years, we worked closely with representatives of the landowner, architects and engineers, and agency and construction personnel as the Bacara Resort was built. Our work, conducted under the auspices of Hutash Consultants of the CBCN, included monitoring of grading operations and compliance with cultural resource conditions; salvage and documentation of archaeological materials exposed by various ground-disturbing activities; and the collection, cleaning, and cataloging of the recovered archaeological remains. In 1999, in consultation with Chumash representatives, the archaeological collections from the Tecolote Canyon area were transferred temporarily to the University of Oregon for final analysis, description, and the preparation of this report. In fall 2004, those collections—including almost 10,000 catalog entries, were returned to the Chumash people for long-term curation in a local museum facility.

In this volume, we synthesize what is known about the long and remarkable history of the Tecolote Canyon area. Because the project ultimately involved archaeological studies from a series of sites located in the vicinity of both Tecolote and Winchester canyons, these two drainages define our project area. There is an unintended and fortuitous logic to this definition, as the two canyons almost certainly were joined into a single larger drainage prior to about 6,000 years ago, when sea levels were significantly lower than they are today and the coastal plain was considerably wider.

Our work is the culmination of 25 years of periodic research in the area, but it also builds on a foundation of earlier studies that date to the late 1800s. Though most of our data comes from archaeological sites located in the immediate Tecolote Canyon and Winchester Canyon areas, we have also relied on information from other sites along the Santa Barbara Coast and the larger Santa Barbara Channel area to fill in the gaps or provide a broader context for the objects, events, developments, and patterns identified at Tecolote. As much as possible, we have designed and written this volume to provide a complete history of the

canyon, from remote geological times to the present. As archaeologists, however, our emphasis is on the human side of that long history. Given the almost 10,000 years of Native American history documented in the Tecolote area, our emphasis is also on the nature of lifeways prior to the arrival of Europeans in southern California less than 500 years ago. Although Tecolote Canyon has a fascinating history from the Spanish, Mexican, and American periods, not all these changes are well represented in the archaeological record. Wherever possible, however, we have tried to illustrate and integrate the more recent archaeology and history of the Tecolote area into our larger tale of a canyon through time. In writing this volume, we have also tried to avoid the jargon and dense prose that afflict so many scientific or technical reports, weaving together geological, archaeological, historical, and ecological data into a synthesis we hope is accessible to a wide range of readers.

THE CHUMASH IN HISTORICAL PERSPECTIVE

With a long and remarkable history spanning more than 13,000 years, California was one of the most diverse cultural landscapes in Native North America. Although California Indians raised dogs, grew tobacco, and actively managed the landscapes they lived in, they are classified by anthropologists as nonagricultural peoples—as hunters, gatherers, and fishers. Nonetheless, long before the arrival of Europeans, California was one of the most densely settled areas in North America. Among California's many tribes, one of the most populous and culturally complex was the Chumash (see Arnold 2001; Gibson 1991; King 1990; Landberg 1965), especially the maritime peoples who lived along the California Coast from Malibu to Morro Bay (Figure 1.1).

Not long ago, most anthropologists thought of hunter-gatherers as relatively primitive peoples with little of the social, political, or economic complexity typical of agricultural societies. It was known that some hunter-gatherers who lived in rich environments like California or the Pacific Northwest obtained higher population levels and greater social or cultural complexity, but these

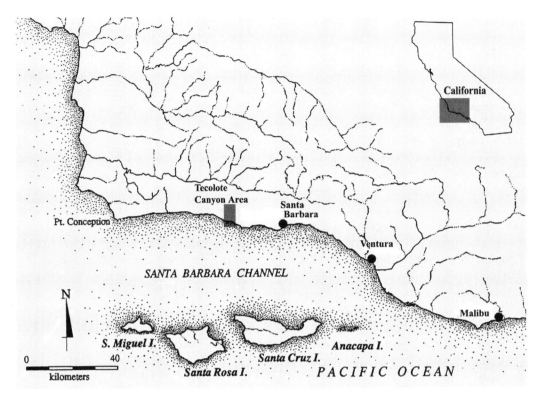

FIGURE 1.1. Location of Tecolote Canyon and the Santa Barbara Channel area.

groups were generally regarded as exceptions to the norm. Such views were supported by the fact that virtually all living hunter-gatherers, like the Kalahari San and Australian Aborigines, were relatively mobile peoples who lived in small social groups, had comparatively simple technologies, and were more or less isolated from the more "complex" cultures that surrounded them. In recent decades, this view has changed. Anthropologists realized that the ethnographic accounts of supposedly "pristine" contemporary hunter-gatherer societies came almost exclusively from marginal arid, forested, or arctic environments. Moreover, historical or ethnographic accounts of many other hunter-gatherers were not collected until such cultures had been devastated by a host of diseases, warfare, conquest, and other catastrophes that accompanied contact with the representatives of European colonial powers. Unfortunately, anthropological stereotypes about hunter-gatherers and other supposedly "primitive" peoples reflected broader historical attitudes among the Europeans who conquered much of the world in the past 500 years, leading to tremendous suffering among California Indians and other indigenous peoples around the world.

Archaeology has played an important role in revising our views of hunter-gatherer peoples and the concepts of cultural primitiveness or complexity. In recent decades, archaeologists have shown that many hunter-gatherer cultures displayed traits supposedly found only among agricultural societies: traits such as high population densities, sedentary living in large villages or towns, craft specialization and intensive trade, ranked or socially stratified class structure, intensive warfare, and political complexity. Today, we know that complexity was much more widespread among hunter-gatherers than previously believed. We also know from the archaeological record that relatively high population densities and cultural complexity among hunter-gatherers correlated closely with proximity to rich coastal or riverine environments. When European explorers first navigated North Pacific waters in the sixteenth, seventeenth, and eighteenth centuries,

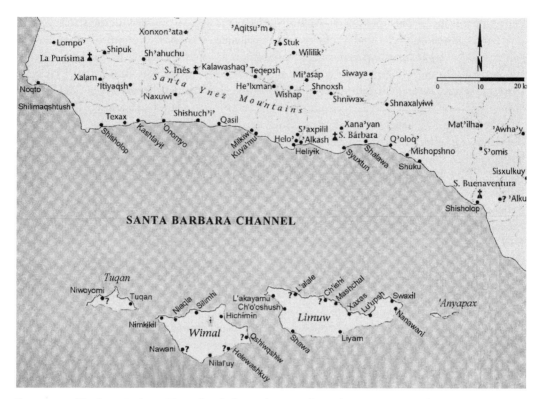

FIGURE 1.2. The Santa Barbara Channel and Chumash geography in the Mission period (adapted from McLendon and Johnson 1999).

virtually the entire Pacific Coast of North America was occupied by relatively sedentary and complex hunter-gatherers (see Lightfoot 1993; Moss and Erlandson 1995). Considerable archaeological research has been focused in recent years on documenting the development of social, economic, and political complexity among the maritime societies of the Pacific Coast.

At the time of European contact some of the most complex societies of the Pacific Coast lived within the boundaries of what we now call California. More than any other California tribe, the Chumash impressed early Spanish explorers with their industriousness, their organization in craft guilds, their extensive trade networks, their artistic accomplishments, and their elaborate maritime technology (see chapter 3). In the 235 years since the Spanish settlement of Alta California, the richness and diversity of Chumash culture have captivated antiquarians, art collectors, historians, ethnographers, archaeologists, and many others.

The political and economic core of Chumash

territory was centered on the Santa Barbara Channel, especially the Santa Barbara mainland coast and the Northern Channel Islands. Nurtured by a relatively mild and productive environment (see chapter 2), the maritime Chumash lived in numerous coastal towns and villages (Figure 1.2), some with as many as 800 to 1,000 residents. Chumash society was governed by a complex web of social, economic, religious, and political codes and institutions. Many Chumash artisans were organized into guilds based on craft specialization. They produced elaborate tools and art objects, studied the stars and the heavens (Hudson and Underhay 1978), participated in widespread trade with neighboring towns and tribes, and lived in hierarchical societies governed by political and religious leaders. When, how, and why this complex culture developed are just some of the many questions that continue to captivate scholars working in Chumash territory today.

Since the late 1800s, archaeological studies in the Santa Barbara Channel area have played an important role in documenting the material culture, developing chronologies, and reconstructing culture histories for California's precontact coastal cultures (e.g., Orr 1968; Rogers 1929; Schumacher 1875). In the early 1900s, most anthropologists believed that North America had been occupied for only a relatively short amount of time and that little evidence for cultural change should be expected in regions like California. The publication of David Banks Rogers's (1929) pioneering culture history for the Santa Barbara Coast helped change such notions by establishing a long history of human occupation and culture change in the area. Rogers's work in the Santa Barbara Channel area during the 1920s also laid the foundation on which many broader—and still widely used—regional chronologies are based. Recently, Santa Barbara Channel archaeologists have also contributed to a growing body of theory on the initial peopling of the Americas, the evolution of maritime adaptations, and the development of cultural complexity among hunter-gatherers (e.g., Arnold 2001; Erlandson 1988a, 1988b; Erlandson and Jones 2002; Glassow and Wilcoxon 1988; Glassow et al. 1988; Kennett et al. 2007; King 1990; Lambert 1993; Rick, Erlandson, and Vellanoweth 2001).

These and other issues are the subject of this volume, which describes the results of our investigations at a series of archaeological sites located in the Tecolote Canyon area. These sites, the subject of archaeological and paleoecological investigations related to the development of the Bacara Resort, span much of the past 9,000 years. In the following chapters, we summarize the past and present environments of the Tecolote Canyon area, provide an overview of the long history of the Santa Barbara Channel area and the Chumash people who inhabited it (and still do) for thousands of years, and describe the results of our archaeological research for four major time periods—the Early, Middle, and Late Holocene and the "Historic" period following European contact. In the process, we summarize the results of a variety of analyses of the diverse archaeological and paleoecological materials recovered from Tecolote Canyon sites—the tangible objects from which our knowledge of history is reconstructed. A more detailed synthesis of the archaeology of the western Santa Barbara Coast is presented in the final chapter, followed by an appendix of related data, a glossary of technical terms used in the text, and a list of the references cited. We hope that our archaeological and ecological history of the Tecolote Canyon area will encourage a more profound understanding of the importance of studying the past (paleoecology, archaeology, and history), a deeper respect for the Chumash and other people who lived and died along the Santa Barbara Coast for millennia, the historical processes that forged California's multiethnic communities, and the importance of preserving the remarkable landscapes and resources of the Santa Barbara Channel area.

2

A Landscape History
for the Tecolote Canyon Area

Jon M. Erlandson

Reconstructing past environments is crucial to understanding the lives and adaptations of ancient peoples, the dynamic ecological conditions in which they lived, and the effects they had on their natural environments. Among hunter-gatherers, in particular, the distribution of physical and biological resources strongly influences where, why, and how people live. At a time when many of California's natural ecosystems have been severely disrupted, and many Americans are deeply concerned with restoring and managing our dwindling natural resources wisely, archaeological data can provide invaluable information about the nature of California environments prior to the devastating human impacts of the past century or two. Thus, archaeological sites contain a wealth of information on the historical ecology of the California Coast, information that provides important baselines for protecting and restoring our natural ecosystems.

In this chapter, I describe the modern environmental setting of the Santa Barbara Channel and Tecolote Canyon areas, briefly summarize the geological history of the area, and introduce some of the environmental dynamics that have altered the geography of the area and affected the lives of the people who lived in the area for millennia. Wherever possible, I focus on aspects of the natural environment that were significant to the people who lived in the area at various times in the distant and recent past.

SANTA BARBARA
CHANNEL GEOGRAPHY

Santa Barbara is situated at about 34° north latitude, roughly equivalent to the latitudes of Tokyo, Beirut, Sydney, and Cape Town. The Santa Barbara Channel encompasses an area about 125 km from east to west and 75 km north to south. It is bounded by the Northern Channel Islands on the south, Point Dume to the east, the Santa Barbara Coast to the north, and Point Conception on the west. Located about 160 km (100 mi) north of Los Angeles, the Santa Barbara Coast trends from east to west, a scenic shoreline where the mountains rise relatively abruptly from the sea, where waves move through emerald ocean waters to break on sandy beaches and lap against the base of tall white sea cliffs made of tilted shales and porcelainites.

The area has a Mediterranean climate, with cool wet winters and warm dry summers. Local climates are moderated by the vast Pacific Ocean and by the barrier the Santa Ynez Mountains pose to the more extreme temperatures of the interior. On the coast, air temperatures average 56°F in winter and 63°F during summer (Smith 1976). Average annual rainfall is about 45 cm (18 in) along the coast, increasing to about 75 cm (30 in) at the crest of the Santa Ynez Mountains. Rain falls primarily from October to April, but morning fog often shrouds the channel in summer. By late summer, many coastal streams have dried up or retreated underground.

Like much of California, the Santa Barbara area is susceptible to periodic droughts, El Niño events accompanied by heavy storms and rains, and occasional earthquakes and wildfires.

Rising rapidly from the ocean to an elevation of over 1,000 m (~3,300 ft), the Santa Ynez Mountains are a local manifestation of the east–west-trending Transverse Ranges. Formed by the collision of crustal plates, the entire region is tectonically active, and much of the Santa Barbara Channel area is slowly rising from the sea.

The Santa Barbara Coast is characterized by a relatively narrow coastal plain that stretches more or less continuously from Point Conception on the west to Rincon Point on the east, a distance of about 80 km (50 mi). Never more than about 10 km wide, the coastal plain pinches out to nearly nothing in places, while in others it is punctuated by large estuaries like the Goleta or Carpinteria sloughs. West of Goleta, no productive estuaries exist along the Santa Barbara Coast today. The coastal plain is dissected by numerous small streams that flow south from the Santa Ynez Mountains to the sea, and many of these have small freshwater or brackish marshes at their mouths.

Assembling the Santa Barbara Landscape

The evolution of California's coastal landscape was a dynamic geological process spanning tens of millions of years. It involved nearly unimaginable forces, from the collision of tectonic plates to the tearing apart of a continent, migrating terranes, monumental earthquakes, mountain building, and massive erosion. Spanning at least the past 165 million years, the geology of the western Transverse Ranges is predominantly marine in origin. Portions of Santa Barbara County contain rocks associated with the Franciscan Formation, a chaotic "mélange" or mix of rock types created in a subduction zone where the Pacific Plate was forced under the North American Plate. The Franciscan Formation, dated between about 165 and 50 million years ago, contains a variety of deep-sea sediments, undersea lava flows, and metamorphic rocks scraped off the Pacific Plate and welded onto the western edge of North America. Norris and

Webb (1990:307) suggest that the tectonic forces that created the Franciscan Formation in the Santa Barbara area ended in the late Cretaceous period, about 75 million years ago.

The Tecolote area remained beneath the sea, however, where thick wedges of sediment were deposited along the ancestral continental margin. The rugged south slopes of the Santa Ynez Mountains are made up of these sedimentary rocks, with thousands of feet of compressed clays, silts, and sands dropped at varying distances from the shore. These sediments were buried and lithified and then later uplifted and dissected as the mountains were pushed up from the sea. From the crest of the Santa Ynez Mountains to the beach, the rocks underlying the Tecolote Canyon area become progressively younger. The canyon cuts through masses of sandstone and shale uplifted and steeply tilted by tectonic forces. Many of the peaks are capped with massive marine sandstones of Eocene age that are erosion resistant and form highly visible escarpments or outcrops. One of the most prominent formations, the Coldwater sandstone, formed near an ancient shoreline and is studded with fossil oyster shells roughly 40 million years old. Between about 39 and 25 million years ago, the ancestral California Coast appears to have remained near the Tecolote area (Norris and Webb 1990). To the east, a broad coastal plain existed, on which the distinctive reddish sands and gravels of the Sespe Formation were deposited by rivers flowing from nearby highlands. West of Tecolote, as much as 2,000 ft of marine sands were deposited in nearshore environments. Roughly 25 million years ago, the sea advanced across the area, leaving the Vaqueros sandstone, which is studded with large scallop fossils deposited along an ancient shoreline.

Also about 25 million years ago, some of the fundamental forces shaping the modern southern California Coast came into play. These include the creation of the San Andreas Fault system, along which much of the southern and central California Coast is moving slowly but relentlessly northwest relative to the rest of California. This shearing along the western margin of North America has moved some distinctive geological formations west of the San Andreas Fault more than 160 km (100 mi) from sources in the eastern Los Angeles Basin (Schoenherr 1992:321). The Santa Ynez Mountains and the broader Transverse Ranges are situated on a large bend in the San Andreas Fault. Compressional forces that accumulated in this area rotated the Transverse Ranges roughly 90° clockwise, created a network of east–west-trending faults, caused intensive tectonic uplift and volcanic activity in some areas, and helped assemble the diverse landscape we now call the Santa Barbara Channel area.

At the beginning of the Miocene, some 23 million years ago, the Santa Barbara area was flooded by relatively deep ocean waters (Norris and Webb 1990:308). Fine clays and silts were first deposited in offshore waters as the soft shales of the Rincon Formation—over 500 m (~1,700 ft) thick—that now underlie the grassy foothills just north of the coastal plain. These were followed by almost 1,000 m (~3,000 ft) of thinly bedded shales and cherts known as the Monterey Formation. Visible in many of the white, tan, or buff sea cliffs of the Santa Barbara Coast, the bedrock of the Monterey Formation underlies the coastal plain in the Tecolote Canyon area. These steeply tilted beds are composed largely of the tiny skeletons of marine microorganisms—calcareous foraminifera and siliceous radiolarians. Individual beds of the Monterey Formation contain varying amounts of silica, from nearly pure cherts to porcelainites (cherty shales) and soft calcareous shales. Cobbles of these materials can still be found on the beach today, along with occasional fossil whale bones. Between about 10 million and five million years ago, marine silts, clays, and muds continued to be deposited in the area. These relatively soft sediments of the Sisquoc Formation, up to 1,000 m (3,200 ft) thick (Norris 2003:65), are now submerged beneath the sea just off Tecolote.

During the Pliocene and Pleistocene, beginning about five million years ago, these forces caused an extended period of orogeny (mountain building) that continues to this day. Tectonic uplift raised the predominantly marine rocks of the Santa Barbara Coast out of the sea to create the Santa Ynez Mountains. As they rose, the mountains were carved by erosion. Freshwater running off their south flank cut a series of canyons—

including Tecolote—with creeks flowing southward to the sea. Starting about 1.8 million years ago, the Pleistocene was also marked by a series of global cycles of alternating glacial and interglacial conditions. Although no glaciers were found along the California Coast, sea levels rose and fell dramatically as the amount of water locked up in glacial ice around the world fluctuated. During high sea stands, marine erosion truncated the relatively soft shales of the Rincon, Monterey, and Sisquoc formations, just as the ocean is currently eroding sea cliffs in the area today. The Pleistocene history of the Santa Barbara Coast is still written, in part, in a flight of raised marine terraces visible in the Tecolote area. The best preserved of these terraces is the coastal plain on which the Bacara parking lot is built, cut during a high sea stand of the Last Interglacial between about 135,000 and 125,000 years ago. The truncated beds of the Monterey Formation are still visible in sea cliffs and railroad cuts in the area today, as is the ancient sea cliff, which rises toward the foothills at the edge of the coastal plain north of Highway 101.

As glacial conditions returned and sea levels dropped, coastal streams deposited relatively coarse sediments on the subtidal platform that underlies the coastal plain today, leaving a blanket of Pleistocene sediment that sometimes produces the remains of wooly mammoths, saber-tooth cats, or other extinct mammals of the famous Ranchola-brean fauna. During the height of the last glacial, which lasted until roughly 20,000 years ago, sea level was about 120 m (~400 ft) lower than it is today, a much broader coastal plain existed along the Santa Barbara Coast, and the current mouth of Tecolote Canyon was probably located roughly 6 to 8 km (4–5 mi) from the sea. Adjusting to the lower sea level and a more distant shoreline, Tecolote and Winchester creeks cut deeper and wider canyons, which probably merged into a single large canyon, remnants of which still extend offshore.

After the end of the last glacial, sea level rose rapidly, and the modern conformation of the Tecolote Canyon area gradually emerged. First, however, the rapid rise of sea level flooded the lower reaches of many canyons along the Santa Barbara Coast, creating numerous productive estuaries that attracted some of the earliest humans in the area (Erlandson 1994). From a geological perspective, such estuaries are often relatively short-lived, prone to infilling by sediments carried by the streams that empty into them. Such was the case with many estuaries along the western Santa Barbara Coast, which seem to have largely disappeared by about 6,000 years ago, although remnants of some larger estuaries such as the Goleta Slough still exist to the east. The filling of coastal estuaries also allowed more stream sediments to reach the coast and, along with intensified coastal erosion (Inman 1983), may have contributed to the development of more extensive sandy beach habitats. Sometime during the last 2,500 years or so, however, coastal habitats along much of the Santa Barbara Coast may have taken on a more or less modern character.

As sea levels and shorelines fluctuated, local creeks went through erosional and depositional phases. In depositional times, stream terraces formed at various levels in coastal canyons as a result of periodic flooding. Erosional periods, when streams were downcutting and flooding no longer occurred, are often marked by buried soils (paleosols) dating to the Holocene. In the Tecolote Canyon area, the result is a terraced coastal landscape, with old marine terraces forming flattened ridges that flank Tecolote and Winchester canyons, several lower alluvial terraces paralleling the creeks in canyon bottoms, and a series of intermediate slopes between terraces. In general, surface soils formed on the coastal plain or higher ridges flanking the upper canyon areas tend to be relatively old and stable. Such canyon-rim locations were often the focus of permanent settlements along the Santa Barbara Coast, especially during the Early and Middle Holocene. Many stream terraces in the canyon bottoms were much less stable, which discouraged year-round settlement by early peoples. Archaeological sites are sometimes found deeply buried in these stream terraces, however, as we will see in chapter 5.

The geological formations that make up the Santa Ynez Mountains, the foothills, and the coastline provide a number of mineral resources used by the Chumash and other peoples for millennia. Local sandstones were used by Native Americans to make ground-stone tools such as mortars and pestles and for building materials by Europeans and Euro-Americans after the establishment of the Spanish missions. The Chumash made a variety of tools from local Monterey cherts and siliceous shales, as well as quartzite, igneous, and Franciscan chert cobbles weathered from the Sespe Formation. Many of these rock types are distributed widely in beach, stream, and marine terrace deposits of the western Santa Barbara Coast. Most high-quality Monterey and Franciscan cherts, along with other exotic materials such as obsidian, fused shale, and soapstone, however, were acquired by trade with neighboring groups. Also locally available were ochers (iron oxides) used as pigments and the asphaltum (tar or bitumen) that has washed ashore on Santa Barbara beaches for millennia and was used as a glue or sealant by the Chumash. Later, local tar and oil seeps—as well as the underground reservoirs they come from—were exploited commercially as sources of paving materials, energy, and other petrochemical products, just as they continue to be used by oil and gas companies today.

FLORA AND FAUNA

One of the reasons the Chumash attained the population densities and cultural complexity they did was the diversity and productivity of food resources available along the Santa Barbara Coast. On land, the diversity of plants and animals is related, in part, to the "stacking" of habitats between the mountains and the sea, where differences in elevation, rainfall, aspect, landform, and bedrock combine to create a diverse array of microenvironments (Lantis et al. 1973:186). In addition to terrestrial diversity, the Santa Barbara Coast contains a variety of aquatic habitats, from streams and estuaries to the open ocean. Coastal habitats are particularly diverse, including sandy, rocky, and muddy intertidal or nearshore communities, extensive and highly productive kelp forests, and pelagic or deepwater zones (Figure 2.1). The juxtaposition of land and sea provided a wealth of subsistence options for the Chumash and their ancestors, especially those people who lived along the coastal mainland.

The unusual productivity of food resources along the Santa Barbara Coast was, and is, related

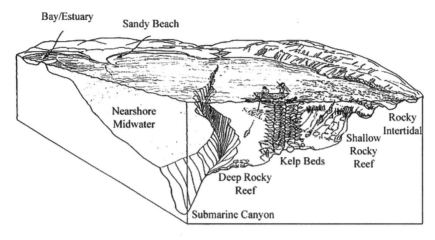

FIGURE 2.1. Major marine habitats of the California Coast (adapted from Salls 1988).

to several factors. Strong upwelling currents bring nutrient-laden waters from the ocean floor to feed the rich marine food webs of the Santa Barbara Channel. Large estuaries on the eastern Santa Barbara Coast (the Goleta Slough, El Estero, Las Salinas, Carpinteria Slough) also added nutrients to the ocean and provided nursery habitats for many aquatic animal species. Kelp forests stimulate both marine and terrestrial productivity and shelter a diverse array of marine animals. The mild winter climate and high marine productivity attract a variety of migratory species to the area seasonally. For humans, however, the most important trait of all may have been the protected nature of the Santa Barbara Coast, which allowed reliable and year-round access to the wealth of marine resources found in Santa Barbara Channel waters.

The Chumash used over 100 types of plants for food, construction materials, medicines, or other purposes. Information about economically important plants has been summarized by a number of authors (King 1967; King and Rudolph 1991; Landberg 1965; Timbrook 1990; Timbrook et al. 1982; and others). Plants that provided important foods for the coastal Chumash include acorns or nuts from live oak (*Quercus agrifolia*), walnut (*Juglans californica*), and piñon (*Pinus monophylla*) trees. A number of smaller seeds were also important food sources, especially chia (*Salvia columbariae*) and other sage (*Salvia* sp.) varieties, redmaids (*Calandrinia breweri*), and pigweed (*Amaranthus* sp.).

Edible berries were gathered from toyon (*Photinia arbutifolia*), islay (*Prunus ilicifolia*), blackberry (*Rubus* sp.), and elderberry (*Sambucus* sp.) plants. The roots or bulbs of yucca (*Yucca whipplei*), wild onions (*Allium* sp.), blue dicks (*Brodiaea* sp.), cattails (*Typha* sp.), and tules (*Scirpus* sp.) also were eaten, as were the fruit of the prickly pear cactus (*Opuntia* sp.), mushrooms, and at least one type of seaweed (*Porphyra perfosta*).

These and many other plant foods provided diversity to the Chumash diet, along with a ready supply of carbohydrates, vitamins, and minerals to complement the protein-rich meats provided by animals of the land and sea. Most of the edible plants on the Santa Barbara Coast were available during the spring, summer, or fall, but many could be stored for consumption during the winter. Economically, the most important plant foods for the Barbareño Chumash may have been acorns and small seeds like chia and redmaid, which were locally abundant and were especially rich sources of carbohydrates, fats, and energy. Many other plants such as willow (*Salix* sp.), tules, and sea grass (*Phyllospadix torreyi*) provided valuable materials for construction purposes. Still others (*Nicotinia* sp.) were used as tobacco or, like the toloache plant (*Datura meteloides*), for medicinal and ceremonial purposes.

Landberg's (1965) summary of ethnographic and archaeological evidence is still the most complete account of the animals used by the Chumash.

His summary has been supplemented by numerous excavations of Santa Barbara Channel sites, however, as well as additional data gleaned from the ethnographic notes of anthropologist John Peabody Harrington. Prior to European settlement, the land mammals found along the Santa Barbara Coast—listed roughly from largest to smallest—included California grizzly bears (*Ursus horribilis*), mule deer (*Odocoileus hemionus*), coyotes (*Canis latrans*), domestic dogs (*Canis familiaris*), bobcats (*Lynx rufus*), raccoons (*Scapanus latimanus*), badgers (*Taxidea taxus*), gray foxes (*Urocyon cinereoargenteous*), striped skunks (*Mephitis mephitis*), ringtail cats (*Bassaricus astutus*), brush rabbits (*Sylvilagus bachmani*), western gray squirrels (*Sciurus grisevs*), wood rats (*Neotoma fuscipes*), pocket gophers (*Thomomys bottae*), long-tail weasels (*Mustela frenata*), Pacific kangaroo rats (*Dipodomys agilis*), California moles (*Scapanus latimanus*), several types of bat (*Chiroptera*), and several species of mice (*Peromyscus* and *Microtus*). Also found along the Santa Barbara Coast are a variety of reptiles, amphibians, and insects. The remains of virtually all these animals have been found in Chumash sites, although some of them may be of natural rather than cultural origin. The Chumash are thought to have used snakes and pond turtles (*Clemmys marmorata*), however, and possibly grasshoppers (Landberg 1965).

The Santa Barbara Channel area also supports one of the most diverse avian faunas in North America. According to Landberg (1965:76), at least 128 species of birds breed within Chumash territory. Other species are transient or seasonal visitors to the area. Many of the resident birds are very small songbirds that are unlikely to have been important economically, but the Chumash reportedly took a variety of larger birds such as ducks, geese, quail (*Lophortyx californicus*), doves, hawks, and eagles (*Haliaeetus leucocephalus*), as well as cormorants (*Phalocrocorax* sp.) and other seabirds (see Guthrie 1980). Despite the diversity of birds available in the Santa Barbara area, archaeological data suggest that they were rarely an important source of food, although their bones and feathers were used for a variety of purposes.

Before the widespread commercial decimation of marine mammals in historic times, the waters of the Santa Barbara Channel sheltered at least 24 species of marine mammals. These included eight types of whales, nine dolphins and porpoises, six seals and sea lions, and the sea otter (*Enhydra lutris*). According to Heizer (1974), whales were not hunted by the Chumash, but the flesh of beached whales was consumed, and whale bones were used for a variety of purposes. Judging from Chumash coastal middens, the most common sea mammals taken probably were California sea lions (*Zalophus californianus*), harbor seals (*Phoca vitulina*), Guadalupe fur seals (*Arctocephalus philippii*), and sea otters, but the bones of northern fur seals (*Callorhinus ursinus*), Steller sea lions (*Eumatopias jubatas*), and elephant seals (*Mirounga angustirostris*) are also found.

Santa Barbara Channel waters also support diverse and productive fish populations. Pedro Fages, a member of the Portola Expedition who visited the Santa Barbara Coast in AD 1769, wrote that "the fishing is so good, and so great is the variety of fish…that this industry alone would suffice to provide sustenance to all the settlers which this vast stretch of country could receive" (Priestley 1937:35). California's kelp beds are particularly productive, supporting more than 125 fish species (Landberg 1965:68–69), including many varieties of rockfish (*Sebastes* sp.), croakers (Sciaenidae), and surfperch (Embiotocidae), halibut (*Paralichthys californicus*), and sheephead (*Semicossyphus pulcher*). Glassow and Wilcoxon (1988:44) have estimated that Santa Barbara Channel kelp forests contain up to 859 kg (1,890 lbs) of fish per hectare. Other productive fishing habitats included estuaries, bays, and pelagic zones. These contained a wealth of sardines (*Sardinops sagax*), anchovies (Engraulididae), and other small schooling species, as well as the much larger tuna (e.g., *Thunnus albacares*, *Euthynnus pelamis*) and bonitos (*Sarda chiliensis*) that feed on them. Large sharks, swordfish (*Xiphias gladius*), and sun fish (*Mola mola*) were once common in the pelagic waters of the Santa Barbara Channel, where they were hunted by the Chumash. Anadromous steelhead (*Oncorhynchus gairdnerii*) still spawn in some perennial streams along the Santa Barbara Coast (Mulroy et al. 1984), and they may have been much more abundant prior to the damming of many area streams and other historical habitat disruptions.

Finally, a variety of marine shellfish are also found in the intertidal communities of the Santa Barbara Channel. Prior to European contact, the most productive habitats were probably the large estuaries in the Goleta, Santa Barbara, and Carpinteria areas on the eastern Santa Barbara Coast. These contained a wealth of clams (e.g., *Chione undatella, Sanguinolaria nuttalli, Saxidomus nuttalli, Tresus nuttalli, Protothaca staminea*), cockles (*Clinocardium nuttalli*), bay mussels (*Mytilus edulis*), oysters (*Ostrea lurida*), and other quiet-water species. Rocky intertidal habitats are also locally productive, supporting mussels (*Mytilus californianus, Septifer bifurcatus*), abalones (*Haliotis* sp.), and a variety of chitons, limpets, and other rock-perching shellfish. Generally somewhat less productive but sometimes locally important were high-energy sandy beaches, where Pismo clams (*Tivela stultorum*) thrive, and semiprotected bay shores rich in littleneck clams (*Protothaca staminea*). Because of the mosaic nature of intertidal communities along the Santa Barbara Coast, many site locations afforded access to multiple shellfish habitats. Although shellfish were used primarily as a source of food, several types of marine shells, including California mussels, red and black abalones (*Haliotis rufescens, H. cracherodii*), small olive snails (*Olivella biplicata*), and keyhole limpets (*Megathura crenulata*) were extensively used by the Chumash to make fishhooks, beads, ornaments, and other artifacts.

Tecolote Canyon: Local Setting

Many plants and animals of the larger Santa Barbara Channel area were available to the occupants of the Tecolote area, but the local environment provided a somewhat more restricted suite of food resources. Tecolote Canyon is located about 42 km (26 mi) east of Point Conception and 21 km (13 mi) west of Rincon Point. The Santa Barbara Coast is relatively straight in this area, running generally east to west, with only shallow bays and less-than-prominent points. Small freshwater marshes exist at the mouths of some local drainages, but no productive estuaries are found in the immediate vicinity. The mouth of the extensive Goleta Slough is located about 6 km to the east, however, and associated estuarine habitats would have been even closer by traveling over land in the past. The shoreline in the area is made up primarily of sand or sandy cobble beaches. In places, the sand veneer is relatively transient, accumulating during the summer and moving offshore during winter, and covers a bedrock platform cut by recent wave erosion. A few rocky outcrops located in the vicinity support small populations of mussels and other rock-perching shellfish, but these are limited in extent.

The shoreline in the site vicinity is flanked by sheer sea cliffs up to 30 m high, punctuated by occasional canyons. The coastal canyons were important sources of freshwater for the Chumash and provided access to the shoreline and the sea. In the Tecolote Canyon area, the relatively level coastal plain is less than a kilometer wide (Figure 2.2), with the foothills of the Santa Ynez Mountains rising relatively rapidly to the north. By local standards, Tecolote Canyon is a relatively large drainage. The canyon mouth is roughly 350 m wide where it enters the sea. Just to the east and also falling within the project area, Winchester (aka Bell) Canyon is even larger, draining both Winchester and Ellwood canyons to the sea. Both Tecolote and Winchester contain perennial streams, which would have provided more or less permanent water sources for people who lived in the area.

The Tecolote Canyon area contains five principal native plant communities: marine, coastal strand, oak woodland, riparian woodland, and coastal sage scrub (see Smith 1976). The first of these provided habitat for a major Chumash fishery, and the last three were all sources of important plant foods. The distribution and character of terrestrial plant communities in the area have been heavily altered in historic times by a combination of livestock grazing, fire suppression, development, and exotic plant introductions that have disrupted native ecosystems. Still, it is possible to reconstruct the general distribution of native plant communities in the site vicinity. Offshore forests of the rapid-growing giant kelp (*Macrocystis pyrifera*), sometimes referred to as the redwoods of

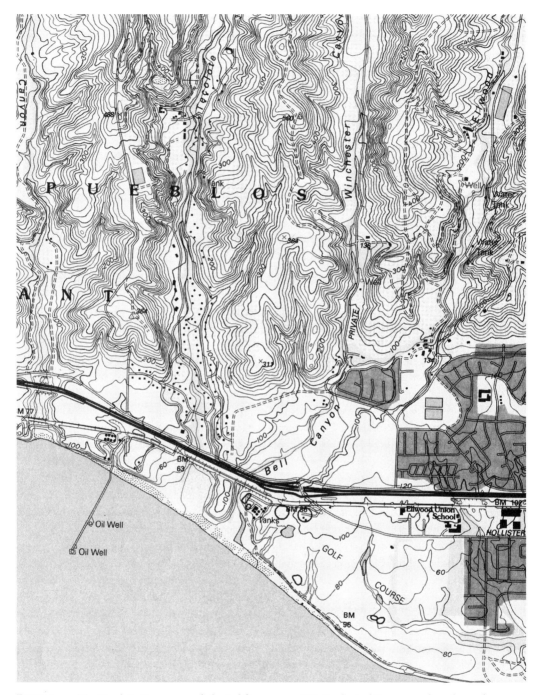

FIGURE 2.2. The Tecolote Canyon area (adapted from a 1995 U.S. Geological Survey quadrangle map).

the sea, attach to rocky holdfasts in cool coastal waters up to 30 m (100 ft) deep. Kelp forests provide a three-dimensional habitat that supports a wide array of fish, shellfish, and other marine organisms. Their general distribution, at least for the past 2,000 to 3,000 years, may have been similar to today, although they were probably more abundant and more productive in the past (Kinlan et al. 2005). As is the case today, coastal strand habitats would have been closely associated with sand dunes located around the mouths of Tecolote and Winchester canyons and nearby drainages. Coastal sage scrub vegetation was probably found mostly on the slopes of Tecolote Canyon and the adjacent foothills. Oak woodlands would have been limited to stable and well-drained stream terraces and the coastal plain. Finally, riparian woodlands would have been found on either side of Tecolote and Winchester creeks, extending for several kilometers inland from the canyon mouths.

In general, the diversity and productivity of food resources in the Tecolote Canyon area were probably quite high. A variety of terrestrial and aquatic habitats are found within a radius of 5 to 10 km of the canyon mouth, although resource-use patterns may have been more restricted than this because of competition with groups living in nearby villages. Fishing in nearshore and pelagic waters, hunting sea and land mammals, and gathering shellfish and plant foods were all important activities prior to European contact, although the relative importance of these activities changed through time (see chapter 3). The productivity of any particular subsistence activity is governed by the abundance and availability of resources, the number of people to be fed, the technologies used, and the effects of humans on local ecosystems, as well as natural environmental fluctuations on a variety of scales.

Environmental Change, Humans, and History

With its natural beauty and relatively benign climate, its wealth of biological and physical resources, and the shelter it provides to maritime peoples, the Santa Barbara Channel has attracted humans for more than 13,000 years. Once they col-onize an area, humans tend to leave an increasingly heavy imprint on local environments, especially as populations grow and their technologies become more sophisticated. For millennia, the natural wealth of the Santa Barbara Coast supported the growth and development of Native American populations who lived off the land and the sea. These cultural developments culminated in the maritime Chumash—among the most populous and complex hunter-gatherers known to human history. A variety of evidence suggests that even the natural abundance of the Santa Barbara Channel area had limits, however, and that population growth and environmental changes sometimes caused resource shortages and social stress that affected Chumash society. Like the effects the Chumash had on local ecosystems, however, the impact these changes had on the Chumash paled in comparison to the cultural and ecological impact wrought by the colonization of the area by representatives of Europe's emerging colonial empires.

As we have seen, coastal ecosystems are highly dynamic, changing in response to a variety of geological, biological, climatic, or cultural factors. These changes have important implications for human populations, past and present. In the past 18,000 years, sea levels have risen about 120 m, flooding large tracts of a once broad coastal plain. Productive estuaries were created, matured, and largely disappeared. Sea level rise has also fueled coastal erosion, historically measured at annual rates of 10–15 cm (4–6 in) along the Santa Barbara Coast (Norris 1968), which further reduced the coastal plain and still threatens many oceanfront properties in the Santa Barbara area. Postglacial warming caused shifts in vegetation communities, including a northward retreat of coniferous forests that once were common along the Santa Barbara Coast (see Axelrod 1967; Heusser 1978). A long pollen sequence from the Santa Barbara Basin analyzed by Heusser (1978) indicates that a shift toward more arid vegetation occurred in the Santa Barbara Channel area during the Middle Holocene, and there may have been epic droughts associated with the Medieval Climatic Anomaly, between about AD 850 and 1300 (Jones et al. 1999). Such environmental changes, if they affected the western Santa Barbara Coast, may have disrupted the lives of the people who lived in the Tecolote Canyon area for more than 9,000 years.

One of the challenges facing archaeologists and other scientists is trying to establish clear connections between cultural and environmental changes. For years archaeologists interpreting archaeological assemblages from the Chumash area compared their findings with a paleoecological study of offshore Santa Barbara Basin sediments by Pisias (1978, 1979). Analyzing changes in the microorganisms in the finely laminated sediments, Pisias (1978) argued that sea temperatures fluctuated significantly during the past 8,000 years, including periods of very warm water that may have decimated kelp forests and significantly reduced marine productivity in the area. Using Pisias's data, Arnold (1992a) proposed that a period of warm sea temperatures and reduced marine productivity in the Santa Barbara Channel between about AD 1150 and 1300 caused major changes in the organization of Island Chumash society (see also Arnold et al. 1997; Colten 1993). Based in part on data from Tecolote Canyon, Walker and Lambert (1989:210; Lambert and Walker 1991:971) also suggested that a period of climatic instability, severe droughts, and unusually warm ocean waters contributed to elevated resource stress, health problems, and violence among the coastal Chumash between about AD 500 and 1100. In studying a stratified Chumash site several miles west of Tecolote Canyon,

however, I found little evidence for warm-water conditions or reduced marine productivity (see Erlandson 1993). Since that time, analysis of new Santa Barbara Basin cores has changed key aspects of Pisias's oceanographic reconstructions, causing a reevaluation of some of the linkages between climate and culture change in the Santa Barbara Channel area (see Kennett 1998; Kennett and Kennett 2000).

Questions about the human and environmental impacts of climate and oceanographic changes over the past 2,000 years are particularly relevant to our study, for Tecolote Canyon appears to have been intensively occupied by the Chumash during much of this time. Such questions are also relevant to understanding the dynamics of modern ecosystems in the Santa Barbara Channel area, the recent collapse of several major fisheries, and the potential effects of drought or El Niño events and other climate changes on the modern residents of the area. In the chapters that follow, we examine the development of the cultures and environments of the Tecolote Canyon area over the past 9,000 years, using animal remains from archaeological sites to reconstruct changes in local ecosystems through time. In the process, we will return to questions about how environmental changes affected the occupants of the area, how these people affected local ecosystems, and some of the relationships among human population growth, technological change, and environmental variation on a variety of scales.

3

The First Californians

Jon M. Erlandson

The Santa Barbara Channel area has a long, rich, and varied human history. This history plays an important role in the modern culture of the Santa Barbara area, with its Spanish-style architecture, numerous historical attractions, laws that protect archaeological and historical sites, and a multi-ethnic community that reflects a series of cultural transitions and influences spanning the millennia. As we will see, the Tecolote Canyon area has a cultural history that spans at least 9,000 years, but the first people entered the area even earlier, probably between about 15,000 and 13,000 years ago. In recent years, archaeological sites of the Santa Barbara Channel area have played an important role in our understanding of the initial colonization of the Americas, as well as the development of cultural complexity among maritime peoples like the Chumash.

Today, evidence collected by archaeologists and physical anthropologists provides much of what we know about Santa Barbara Channel cultures prior to the zenith of Chumash society. Antiquarians and archaeologists have worked in the Santa Barbara Channel area since the 1870s. The earliest "scientific" explorations, sponsored primarily by museums in Europe and the eastern United States, amounted to little more than organized looting. The Rev. Stephen Bowers plundered numerous Chumash village and cemetery sites during the late 1800s, for instance, and sold much of his collections to the highest bidder (Benson 1997;

Smith 1983). Work by other early antiquarians—stimulated by the mistaken notion that Native American cultures would soon be extinct—also focused primarily on Chumash cemeteries and was poorly documented.

The first attempts to reconstruct a deep cultural history of the Santa Barbara Channel area did not take place until the 1920s, when David Banks Rogers (1929) of the Santa Barbara Museum of Natural History, Ronald Olson (1930), and other pioneering archaeologists first applied the principles of stratigraphic excavations to reconstructing the archaeological history of the area. Rogers's cultural sequence provided a foundation for almost every subsequent chronological scheme proposed for the archaeology of the southern and central California Coast (Figure 3.1).

Invaluable sources of information about traditional Chumash society also reside in historical documents recorded at California's Spanish missions and the notes of early scholars who interviewed Chumash elders about life before and after Spanish colonization. Mission records tell us much about the social organization of the Chumash, including a wealth of data on the names of Chumash people, their villages or towns of origin, and often the dates they were baptized, married, and died. Such data provide a variety of insights into Chumash contact history, demography, marriage patterns, and other social interaction (see Johnson 1988). Scholars have also mined the extensive body

Date	Rogers (1929)	Orr (1943)	Wallace (1955)	Harrison (1964)	Warren (1968)	King (1990)	Geological Time
AD 2000	Historic Chumash	Historic Chumash	Historic Chumash	Historic Chumash		Historic Chumash	
AD 1500	--------------	-----------------	---------------	------------------------	-----------------	Late Period	
AD 1000	Canaliño	Late Canaliño	Late Prehistoric	Late Canaliño	Chumash Tradition		Late Holocene
AD 500							
AD 0	------?------	--------?---------		-----------------------	------------------	Middle Period	
500 BC		Middle Canaliño	-------?---------	Middle Canaliño			
1000 BC					Campbell Tradition		
1500 BC	Hunting People	--------?--------- Early Canaliño	Intermediate	------------------------ Rincon Phase			
2000 BC		--------?---------		------------------------			
2500 BC		Hunting		El Capitan Phase	?		Middle Holocene
3000 BC	------?------ hiatus?	--------?---------	-------?---------	Extranos Phase		Early Period	
3500 BC				------------------------			
4000 BC		Oak Grove		?	Encinitas Tradition		
4500 BC				------------------------			
5000 BC	Oak Grove		Milling Stone	Goleta Phase			
5500 BC				---------?---------			
6000 BC		--------?---------					Early Holocene
6500 BC		?		?			
7000 BC	------?------		-------?---------				
7500 BC							
8000 BC						----?-------	
9000 BC			Early Man				Terminal Pleistocene
9500 BC							
10000 BC							

FIGURE 3.1. Chronological sequences for the Santa Barbara Channel and southern California Coast.

of information shared with anthropologists by Chumash elders, publishing numerous books and articles on the cosmology, material culture, healing practices, and other aspects of Chumash society (see Blackburn 1975; Hudson and Blackburn 1982, 1983, 1985, 1986, 1987; Hudson and Underhay 1978; Hudson et al. 1978; Librado 1979, 1981; Walker and Hudson 1993).

SUMMARY OF SANTA BARBARA CHANNEL ARCHAEOLOGY

Origins

During the last glacial, about 20,000 years ago, much of northern North America was covered with vast glaciers, and world sea levels were over 100 m lower than they are today. At the time, Asia and North America were connected by a low-lying land bridge more than 1,000 km wide in what is now the Bering Straits. For decades, most archaeologists believed that the Americas were settled by late Upper Paleolithic peoples from northeast Asia, who marched across the plains of Beringia through a long and narrow "ice-free corridor" that led them into the heartland of North America. The earliest evidence for this migration was thought to be from Clovis "Paleoindian" peoples, whose economies focused primarily on the hunting of large land mammals found on the Great Plains and in the valleys of the intermontane west. Only later, according to this view, did early peoples follow river valleys to the coast, where they gradually adapted to life by the sea. In this scenario, the Pacific Coast—and the sea in general—was thought to be peripheral to the peopling of the New World until about 7,000 to 8,000 years ago (Erlandson 2001, 2002).

Recently, this orthodoxy has been challenged by evidence that humans settled the hinterlands of coastal Chile a thousand or more years prior to Clovis; by questions about the availability and viability of the "ice-free corridor" as an early migration route; by the discovery of several Clovis points along the California Coast; and by the dating of numerous early shell middens from Alaska, California, and Peru to between about 11,000 and 9,000 years ago. As a result, an alternative "coastal migration theory" is now widely accepted in debates about the peopling of the Americas, and the archaeology of the Pacific Coast has been elevated from periphery to center stage. This transition has been fueled in part by discoveries from the Santa Barbara area, where evidence suggests that Paleoindian peoples settled the Channel Islands by boat at least 12,000 to 13,000 calendar years before present (cal BP).

Controversial claims have been made for much earlier occupations of the area (see Berger 1982; Orr 1968; Orr and Berger 1966)—including the Tecolote Canyon area (Carter 1980a)—but the first humans to settle the Santa Barbara Coast were probably Paleoindian or Paleocoastal peoples who arrived between about 15,000 and 13,000 years ago. Not surprisingly, archaeological evidence for these early peoples in the Santa Barbara Channel area is sparse. The search for the earliest sites is hampered by low archaeological visibility of what must have been very small and widely scattered populations. Paleocoastal sites also may have been lost to rising sea levels and coastal erosion or obscured by sediments accumulating near the coast.

Despite such problems, tantalizing clues have emerged about the origins and adaptations of early peoples of the Paleocoastal Tradition (Moratto 1984:104). These include a fragment of a Clovis-like fluted point found on the coastal plain of Hollister Ranch west of Santa Barbara (Erlandson et al. 1987), the terminal Pleistocene sites of Arlington Springs and Daisy Cave on the Northern Channel Islands, and several early shell middens on the islands and mainland coast dated in excess of 9,000 years old. The fluted point fragment, like several others found near the California Coast, is not well dated but suggests that Paleoindian hunters roamed the area as much as 13,000 years ago. At Arlington Springs on Santa Rosa Island, a few bones of a woman who died between about 12,000 and 13,000 years ago were found in the 1960s (Johnson et al. 2002; Orr 1968). These bones demonstrate that Paleoindian peoples used boats to explore the Channel Islands at a surprisingly early date. From a roughly 11,000-year-old stratum at Daisy Cave, a few stone tools and a midden (refuse) deposit of abalone, mussel, and other marine shellfish further testify to the maritime capabilities of these early Santa Barbara Channel residents (Erlandson et al. 1996). A remarkable assemblage of artifacts and faunal remains from Daisy Cave strata dated between about 10,000 and 8,500 years ago also shows that early islanders were fishing in kelp forest and other nearshore habitats (Rick, Erlandson, and Vellanoweth 2001), collecting a variety of shellfish, hunting sea otters and other marine mammals, manufacturing cordage and basketry from sea grass fibers, and making beads from *Olivella* shells (Erlandson 2007).

Milling Stone (Oak Grove) Peoples

Along the mainland coast, we know very little about how Paleoindian or Paleocoastal peoples lived. Given what we know from the earliest island sites and the wider range of plants and animals available on the mainland, it seems likely that they lived near the coast, utilized a variety of marine and terrestrial resources, and traveled occasionally to and from the islands. The low archaeological visibility of these earliest mainland peoples creates a major gap in our knowledge of the human history of the Santa Barbara Coast.

By about 8,500 years ago, a number of sites along the mainland coast are known to have been occupied, and our knowledge of early peoples and environments is much better documented. About 9,000 years ago, a "new" adaptation emerged, with the widespread appearance of assemblages dominated by manos and metates. These grinding tools, or milling stones, are thought to have been used mostly for processing small seeds and other plant foods. Their widespread use suggests a broadening of the economy and technology by what archaeologists call Milling Stone peoples. Over the years, some scholars have attributed this change to the local development of Paleocoastal cultures, whereas others believe that it may mark the westward migration of desert peoples (Gallegos 1991; Kowta 1969). Milling Stone sites are not found on the Northern Channel Islands, probably because of the low diversity of seed-producing plants.

Whatever their origins, Milling Stone peoples appear to have focused primarily on gathering plant foods and shellfish (Erlandson 1991; Wallace 1955; Warren 1968). Except for manos and metates, and the core hammers used to make and maintain them, projectile points and other formal tools are relatively rare in early Milling Stone sites. Artifact and faunal assemblages from numerous sites show that these early people hunted and fished, but these activities were probably of secondary economic importance. Shell beads and other ornaments are relatively rare compared with their numbers in later sites, evidence for craft specialization is virtually nonexistent, and Milling Stone societies were probably relatively egalitarian. There is evidence for long-distance trade by early Milling Stone peoples of the Santa Barbara Coast (Erlandson 1994). Artifacts made from obsidian, a volcanic glass whose nearest sources are in the Sierras about 300 km from Santa Barbara, have been found at CA-SBA-1807, an 8,500-year-old Mill-

ing Stone site located west of Gaviota. Shell beads from the California Coast have also been found in early Great Basin sites (Bennyhoff and Hughes 1987; Fitzgerald et al. 2005).

Settlement during Milling Stone times was probably relatively sedentary. Almost all known sites are located on knolls or other elevated landforms of the coastal plain or coastal foothills. Many sites are relatively large, and some contain burials or even substantial cemeteries. These patterns led Glassow et al. (1988:68) to suggest that all known Milling Stone sites of the Santa Barbara Channel served as base camps. Recent research has shown, however, that short-term campsites also existed and that there is considerable diversity in their constituents (Erlandson 1991). Along the western Santa Barbara Coast, Milling Stone sites appear to cluster around canyon mouths where small estuaries existed during the Early Holocene (Erlandson 1994).

In some parts of southern California, Milling Stone adaptations seem to have persisted until relatively recent times. In Chumash territory, the distinctive aspects of Milling Stone assemblages—the dominance of grinding tools and the dearth of hunting and fishing equipment or food remains—appear to have gradually developed into a more elaborate and diversified lifestyle about 5,000 years ago. A few Milling Stone sites in the area have been dated between about 4,000 and 3,000 years ago, however, showing that basic Milling Stone economies persisted in some areas. Some early investigators viewed this adaptive variability as evidence that two separate cultures coexisted along the Santa Barbara Coast for a time (Harrison 1964), but it seems more likely that these later Milling Stone sites—with their abundance of manos and metates—reflect the continuing importance of small seeds in certain areas where they were abundant and alternative resources (acorns, cattails, etc.) were not.

The Hunting People

Between about 6,000 and 5,000 years ago, significant technological and economic changes are evident in some archaeological sites of the Santa Barbara Channel area, as well as the broader southern and central California Coast. One of these changes is the appearance of mortars and pestles, a new class of grinding tools thought to be associated with the processing of acorns and other pulpy plant foods. In Hunting period sites, mortars and pestles appear to gradually replace manos and metates over the next few millennia, but both types of equipment continued to be used into historic times. Projectile points are also more common in many sites, including side-notched dart points beginning about 6,000 years ago and contracting-stem varieties a millennium or two later.

Not surprisingly, an increase in the number of projectile points seems to correlate with an increase in the amount of animal bone found in many sites, suggesting that the importance of hunting increased during this period (Rogers 1929). Prominent among the animal remains are the bones of seals, porpoises, dolphins, and sharks, evidence for the existence of a more diversified maritime adaptation (Harrison and Harrison 1966). These economic changes appear to indicate a progressive broadening of human subsistence to incorporate the intensified use of a wider range of resources and habitats. This intensification was probably related to the need to feed growing numbers of people as Santa Barbara Channel populations grew.

In favored areas like the Goleta Slough, Hunting period sites are often very large, with dense accumulations of midden refuse (Glassow 1997; Harrison and Harrison 1966; Rogers 1929). Such sites are also quite numerous, suggesting that a substantial population lived in relatively sedentary villages. Along the western Santa Barbara Coast, however, many of the known Hunting period sites are smaller and more diffuse. Most of these sites have shellfish assemblages dominated by outer coast species such as Pismo clams and California mussels, suggesting that the estuaries that sustained early Milling Stone groups had disappeared by the Middle Holocene.

As is the case for the Paleocoastal and Milling Stone peoples that preceded them, there has been no consensus about the origin of the Hunting people. Rogers (1929) and Harrison (1964) both thought the Hunting people were intrusive immigrants. Harrison suggested that they were maritime peoples who migrated to the Santa Barbara Channel from the coast of western Alaska, in part because similar types of large side-notched points found in both areas. Today we know that such points appeared across a vast area of North America between roughly 6,000 and 4,000 years ago, however, and most archaeologists believe that the Hunting people descended from Milling Stone ancestors. During the roughly 3,000 years that Hunting period sites existed along the Santa Barbara Coast, there was a further elaboration and diversification of material culture that marks an evolution into the Chumash or Canaliño culture.

The Chumash or Canaliño

During the last 3,000 to 4,000 years, the emergence of a series of cultural traits in the Santa Barbara area appears to signal the development of the distinctive Canaliño or Chumash people who lived in the larger Santa Barbara Channel area at the time of European contact. First defined by David Banks Rogers (1929:367–419) and later refined by Orr (1943), the concept of a highly developed Canaliño culture is sometimes extended beyond the boundaries of Chumash territory to encompass Tongva (Gabrielino) peoples of the Los Angeles Coast and the Southern Channel Islands. The height of Canaliño culture was reached among the Chumash, however, particularly among the populous groups of the Santa Barbara Coast. By the time of European contact, the maritime Chumash are widely considered to have had population densities and an elaborated culture as sophisticated as any hunter-gatherers on earth (Moratto 1984:118).

Along the Santa Barbara Coast, the Barbareño Chumash lived in towns with as many as 1,000 residents. In each province, there were principal towns in which most social, political, and religious leaders lived (Gibson 1991:48). These leaders, drawn from the ranks of the nobility or upper class, governed the economic and spiritual lives of their people. They reportedly regulated the use of resource areas, governed the accumulation and distribution of food stores, administered ceremonial feasts, participated in regional councils, and were responsible for warfare and defense. Access to the nobility and leadership was governed by rules of heredity, but *wots* (captains, who could be either male or female) reportedly had to be approved by the people they governed (Landberg 1965:33).

Well-organized Chumash communities reportedly contained streets, rows of domestic houses, cemeteries, communal play or dance grounds, and ceremonial *temescals* or sweat houses. The Chumash lived in large semisubterranean multifamily dwellings that Pedro Font described as the finest houses the Spaniards saw during the exploratory de Anza Expedition in AD 1775–1776:

> They are round in form, like a half-orange, very spacious, large and high. In the middle of the top they have an aperture to afford light and to serve as a chimney, through which emerges the smoke of the fire which they make in the middle of the hut. Some of them also have two or three holes like little windows. The frameworks of all of them consist of arched and very straight poles, and the walls are of very thick grass interwoven. At the doors there is a mat which swings toward the inside like a screen, and another one toward the outside which they ordinarily bar with a whalebone or stick [Hudson and Blackburn 1983:324].

Based on the appearance of what are thought to be boat drills and related paraphernalia, the Chumash plank boat (*tomol*) may have been developed about AD 500 (Hudson et al. 1978). This invention greatly impressed the Spanish and undoubtedly facilitated ocean fishing, maritime trade, and travel to the Channel Islands. Another technological innovation that probably took place about this time was the introduction of the bow and arrow, which may have revolutionized hunting and warfare among the Chumash and their neighbors. Commerce, artistry, and occupational specialization were also well developed among the Chumash, as noted by Fages in AD 1775:

> The occupations and ordinary pursuits of these people is limited; some of them follow fishing, others engage in their small carpentry jobs; some make strings of beads, others grind red, white, and blue clays…. They make variously shaped plates from the roots of the oak and

the alder trees, and also mortars, crocks, and plates of black stone, all of which they cut out with flint, certainly with great skill and dexterity. They make an infinite number of arrows. The women go about their seed-sowing, bringing the wood for the use of the house, the water and other provisions. They skillfully weave trays, baskets, and pitchers for various purposes [King 1990:58–59].

Chumash assemblages also include a variety of artistically wrought projectile points, fishing and sea mammal–hunting tackle, bowls and pestles, *comals* (soapstone cooking slabs), digging stick weights, ornaments, charm stones, animal effigies, hairpins, whistles, and many other artifact types. Finely made utilitarian objects were often inlaid with shell beads. The elaborate and sophisticated technologies of the Chumash inspired over 2,000 pages in the five volumes of *The Material Culture of the Chumash Interaction Sphere* compiled by Hudson and Blackburn (1982, 1983, 1985, 1986, 1987). Unfortunately, the artistry of Chumash material culture also led to an illegal market for Chumash antiquities and the looting of numerous Chumash burial sites—an activity that is anathema to archaeologists and Chumash descendants.

The elaboration of Canaliño society is evident, in part, in the numbers and variety of beads and ornaments used (King 1990). A diverse array of ornaments was made from *Olivella*, abalone, limpet, clam, cowrie, *Dentalium*, and other shell types, as well as stone and bone. Some of these were decorated with elaborately serrated edges, incised or painted designs, or shell bead inlay. Some bead and ornament styles changed relatively rapidly and are sensitive chronological markers. Chester King (1990) believes that beads and ornaments served several functions in Chumash society, from personal adornment, to status markers, the accumulation of wealth, and as a form of money that facilitated Chumash trade. In AD 1792, the Spaniard Longinos Martinez noted that

> these Indians are fond of traffic and commerce. They trade frequently with those of the mountains, bringing them fish and bead-work, which

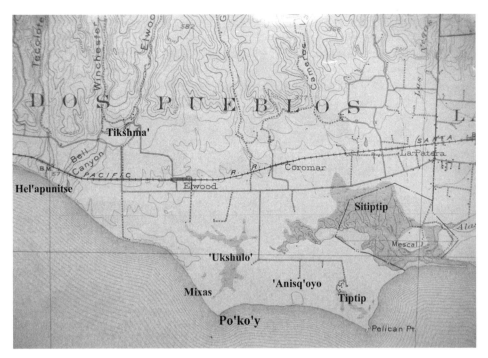

FIGURE 3.2. A 1903 map of the Goleta Valley and Tecolote Canyon area, showing Chumash place-names in the vicinity (courtesy of the University of California–Santa Barbara Maps and Imagery Library; photo by Jon Erlandson).

they exchange for seeds and shawls of foxskin, and a kind of blanket made from the fibers of plant which resembles cotton…. When they trade for profit, beads circulate among them as if they were money, being strung on long threads [King 1990:59].

Shell bead currencies may have first appeared between about AD 500 and 1300 in the midst of the Canaliño cultural florescence. Money beads were manufactured primarily by the Island Chumash (Arnold 1992b; Gibson 1991:42; King 1971) from the callus portion of purple olive (*Olivella biplicata*) shells, a small marine snail commonly found along area beaches.

When the Spaniards first explored the California Coast, they described the Chumash as a thriving, highly populous, and industrious people. Tragically, within a few short decades of the Spanish colonization of California, much of the traditional framework of Chumash society was laid to waste by the effects of European contact.

CHUMASH PLACE-NAMES IN THE TECOLOTE AREA

During the late 1800s and early 1900s, early American scholars worked with a number of Chumash elders to record voluminous amounts of information on the nature of traditional Chumash culture. John Peabody Harrington alone collected over 200 boxes of notes on the Chumash during the early 1900s, much of which is available on microfilm or has been published in a variety of books on Chumash culture. Among the information recorded were numerous place-names that record the social and natural geography of the Chumash world.

Several Barbareño Chumash place-names are known for the Tecolote Canyon area (Figure 3.2), although scholars have not always agreed on the precise location or nature of some of these. According to Applegate (1975:29), the name for the Tecolote Canyon area, or possibly a village located at the mouth of the canyon, was Hel'apunitse (Guitarfish; see Figure 3.3), while Ellwood Canyon just to the east was known as Tikshma' (Ear of the Rabbit). Eagle Canyon, the next major canyon west of

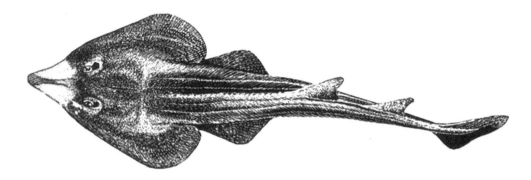

FIGURE 3.3. The *hel'apunitse* or shovelnose guitarfish (*Rhinobatos productus*), from which the Chumash name for the Tecolote Canyon area derives (adapted from Eschmeyer et al. 1983).

Tecolote, reportedly was known as Huspat hulki-lik (Nest of the *Kilik* Bird). In the vicinity of Dos Pueblos Canyon, about 5 km (3 mi) west of Teco-lote Canyon, there are four Barbareño Chumash place-names, two for the large historic villages of Mikiw (On the Other Side) and Kuyamu (mean-ing unknown). Applegate (1975) also noted that a rock just offshore of the Dos Pueblos area was called Chqoshi (meaning unknown), while Las Varas Canyon just beyond Dos Pueblos was known as Mimehme'y (Place of Reeds).

Barbareño Chumash place-names are also known for three geographic features located near Coal Oil Point, located about 4 km (2.5 mi) southeast of Tecolote. According to Johnson et al. (1982:28), the Chumash name for the point itself is Po'ko'y (meaning unknown), while the fresh-water or brackish lagoon just west of it is 'Ukshulo' (Stinking Water). The sand dunes located around the mouth of this lagoon, an area known to local surfers as Sands for decades, was known to the Chu-mash as Mixas (Place of Sand) or Mihas (Applegate 1975; Johnson et al. 1982:28). A bit farther afield, there are also Barbareño Chumash place-names re-corded for the old Goleta Slough (Sitiptip, "The Place of Much Salt"); for the lagoon at the Uni-versity of California–Santa Barbara (UCSB; Tip-tip, "Much Salt") and for the mesa ('Anisq'oyo', "At the Manzanita") west of these lagoons where the UCSB campus and the community of Isla Vista are now located; and for several villages located around the margins of the Goleta estuary.

EUROPEANS IN CALIFORNIA

Landberg (1965:11) has divided the era of Chu-mash contact with Europeans into four periods: the Spanish Exploration period (AD 1542–1769), the Mission period (AD 1769–1834), the Mexican Rancho period (AD 1834–1849), and the American period (AD 1849–the present). Today, most archae-ologists refer to the period of Spanish exploration as the Protohistoric period, a time when contacts between Europeans and the Chumash were spo-radic, written historical accounts are rare, and the effects of contact on Chumash culture are often presumed to have been minor.

In AD 1542, a Spanish expedition led by Juan Rodriguez Cabrillo wintered in the Santa Barbara Channel, the first recorded contact between Eu-ropeans and the Chumash. Cabrillo himself died that winter and is believed to have been buried on the Channel Islands. For the next 227 years, inter-action with Europeans was relatively limited un-til the land-based Portola Expedition marched through southern California in AD 1769. Ironically, Portola's party reportedly was welcomed through-out Chumash territory, a fact that probably accel-erated the formal colonization that devastated the Chumash. Permanent Spanish settlement of the Santa Barbara Channel area occurred in AD 1782, when the Santa Barbara Presidio was established. The Santa Barbara Mission was built in AD 1786; La Purisima near Lompoc, in 1787; and Mis-sion Santa Ines near Solvang, in 1808 (Landberg 1965:13). The Tecolote Canyon area was among vast landholdings placed under the jurisdiction of the mission fathers, supposedly held in trust for the Chumash people.

The Chumash were integrated into the mission system gradually over several decades. Many converted to Christianity and moved to the mission compounds. Unable to feed all their Chumash converts, however, the missionaries allowed some Chumash people to spend part of the year hunting and gathering in their traditional territories (Landberg 1965:20–21). People from the Chumash villages of the western Santa Barbara Coast were baptized primarily at the Santa Barbara, La Purisima, or Santa Ines missions (Johnson 1988:84). There they were introduced to Western technology, religion, agriculture, and diseases. Ultimately, missionization broke down or weakened many aspects of the Chumash economic and sociopolitical systems. By the early 1800s, most Chumash coastal villages were nearly abandoned, and the Chumash themselves had been decimated by European diseases. In AD 1824, the severe beating of an Indian at Mission Santa Ines galvanized the Chumash into open rebellion at the Santa Ines, La Purisima, and Santa Barbara missions (Gibson 1991:77–78). The rebellion was harshly suppressed, and many Chumash, deciding not to return to the missions, stayed in the backcountry where they had fled during the revolt.

In AD 1834, the newly independent Mexican government secularized the missions. Gradually, they fell into disrepair, and most were abandoned. The Chumash survivors dispersed into a foreign society, taking jobs in towns or on ranches. Ironically, many Chumash who learned ranching or farming skills at the missions found work on large estates like Rancho Los Dos Pueblos, made up of lands that belonged to the Chumash people just a few years earlier.

Alta California was the destination for a growing flood of American settlers who were increasingly at odds with and isolated from the Mexican government. During the 1840s, the United States engaged in a series of conflicts with Mexico over territorial issues in California, Arizona, and New Mexico. Known as the Mexican War, this conflict was ultimately won by the United States. As a result of the AD 1848 Treaty of Guadalupe Hidalgo, control of Alta California was ceded to the United States. Within two years, a flood of gold-seeking immigrants gave California the population and political clout to become the thirty-first state of the union (Gibson 1991:84).

In AD 1850, the California legislature passed a law that essentially legalized slavery for many California Indians:

This law declared that any Indian, on the word of a White man, could be declared a vagrant, thrown in jail, and have his labor sold at auction for up to four months with no pay. This indenture law further said any Indian adult or child with the consent of his parents could be legally bound over to a White citizen for a period of years, laboring for subsistence only. These laws marked the transition of the Indian from peonage to virtual slavery; they gave free vent to the exploitative ethos of Americans who soon took advantage of the situation [Castillo 1978:108].

During the second half of the nineteenth century, the Chumash and other California Indians became wards of the U.S. government with few legal rights. For many Chumash, the tragedy of dispossession and discrimination continued for decades under American administration.

In AD 1901, a small reservation was established in the Santa Ynez Valley, a community that now operates a highly successful casino and serves as an important nexus of Chumash cultural revival. In recent decades, several groups of Chumash descendants—including the Coastal Band of the Chumash Nation and the Chumash Maritime Association—have taken dramatic steps to reclaim aspects of their heritage and traditional culture. A significant component of this revival has been active participation in protecting the archaeological sites that are an important part of their heritage. Working with archaeologists in the field and laboratory, the Chumash today play a crucial role in protecting and learning from the archaeological sites that are a tangible connection to their past.

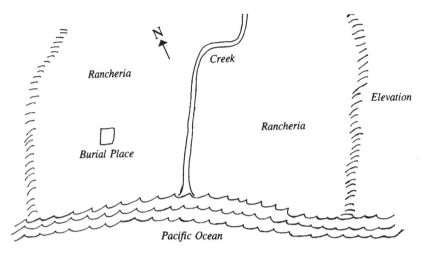

FIGURE 3.4. Bowers's 1877 map of Haye's (Tecolote) Canyon (adapted from Benson 1997).

A BRIEF HISTORY OF ARCHAEOLOGY IN THE TECOLOTE CANYON AREA

As noted in chapter 1, antiquarians and archaeologists have been engaged in the study of Chumash archaeological sites since at least the 1870s. The first 50 years of archaeology in the area were dedicated primarily to the pillaging of cemeteries and display-quality artifacts for European or East Coast museums. Most of these antiquarians focused on excavating cemetery plots associated with coastal villages or towns, where the finest artifact specimens generally were concentrated. Within the Santa Barbara Channel area, much of this early work was conducted by men such as Paul Schumacher and the Rev. Stephen Bowers, both affiliated (loosely in Bowers's case) with the Smithsonian Institution. Such collectors unsystematically plundered scores of Chumash cemeteries, carting off thousands of skeletons and tons of artifacts for sale or storage. Some of the earliest of these antiquarians noted that relic hunters had preceded them at many sites.

The first known excavations in the Tecolote Canyon area appear to have been by the Methodist minister Stephen Bowers in August 1877. Bowers was a notorious and tireless relic hunter much maligned by local historians for his destruction of numerous important archaeological sites. Benson (1997) generously refers to him as an archae-

ologist, but Bowers plundered scores of sites and cemeteries throughout Chumash territory and then sold the fruits of his labors to the highest bidder (Smith 1983). He kept cursory notes of his activities and published some short scientific papers on Chumash artifacts, but his collections are now dispersed in museums and private collections around the world. Despite the enormous destruction he wrought in Chumash sites, little information remains on the origins or provenience of the materials he collected.

Previous accounts of the archaeology of Tecolote Canyon (see King 1980; Rogers 1929) have not mentioned Bowers's work in the area. In *The Noontide Sun*, however, Arlene Benson published Bowers's field diary for August 7 and 8, which describes an expedition to "Haye's Canyon." Between 1872 and 1875, Tecolote Canyon was owned by Thomas and Daniel Hayes (see chapter 7), and Bowers's field map (Figure 3.4) strongly resembles the mouth of the canyon. Unfortunately, Bowers's field notes for this two-day "archaeological" expedition are limited to the following passages:

> August 7. Went to Haye's Canyon today. I examined a burial place at the mouth of the canyon near the sea. We found a great many skeletons but few implements. We obtained a beautiful mortar, several arrowheads, a serpentine bead and some asphaltum ornaments.

August 8. Finding no more specimens we returned home [Benson 1997:104].

The field map published by Benson suggests that Bowers excavated in a cemetery plot on the west side of Tecolote Creek, in a *ranchería* or village site now known as SBA-73.

In AD 1908 a renowned anthropologist from the University of California–Berkeley, Frederick Ward Putnam, also worked at SBA-73 (Table 3.1). Putnam found two intact burials in a heavily disturbed cemetery, probably the same cemetery Bowers looted some 30 years earlier. Putnam reportedly split his finds with the landowners of the time, Mr. and Mrs. Thomas Bishop, and portions of the small collection ended up in the Lowie (now Hearst) Museum in Berkeley and in the Santa Barbara Museum of Natural History (King 1980:24).

In 1926, David Banks Rogers of the Santa Barbara Museum of Natural History conducted extensive excavations in the Tecolote area. Rogers excavated three major villages (SBA-71, SBA-72, and SBA-73) at the mouth of Tecolote Canyon and two more (SBA-69 and SBA-70) on the east rim of Winchester Canyon, and he also first described several other sites (SBA-68, SBA-74, SBA-75, SBA-106) in the vicinity. Like his predecessors, Rogers focused his excavations primarily on cemetery areas, but he also explored some residential areas and worked to roughly determine the boundaries of each site (King 1980:24). In his *Prehistoric Man of the Santa Barbara Coast*, Rogers (1929:181–201) published a lengthy description of his work at Tecolote Canyon and incorporated some of his results into a summary of his Canaliño culture. He excavated all or part of five cemeteries at SBA-71, SBA-72, and SBA-73, exhuming more than 300 Chumash skeletons (King 1980). Rogers considered the two major villages (SBA-72 and SBA-73) flanking Tecolote Creek to be portions of one large village, with a parallel organization of residential areas, cemeteries, dance floors, and sweat houses (temescals).

Chester King (1980) completed a relatively thorough analysis of Rogers's notes and collections, which are still housed at the Santa Barbara Museum of Natural History, and incorporated

some of these results into his 1990 book *Evolution of Chumash Society*. A key component of King's analysis is his study of the chronological implications of the beads, ornaments, and other artifacts found by Rogers. In this study, King suggested that various loci near the mouth of Tecolote Creek had been occupied sequentially, from at least 3,500 years ago until about AD 1500, a sequence that has largely been confirmed by radiocarbon (^{14}C) dating. More detailed descriptions of Rogers's work in the Tecolote Canyon area as well as King's (1980) interpretations will be left to individual site summaries presented in the chapters that follow.

After a long hiatus, archaeological research in the Tecolote area accelerated in the 1970s and subsequent decades. This work began in 1971 with an archaeological field school at SBA-71 that was directed by two prominent California archaeologists, Claude Warren and Tom King. Warren and King excavated about 45 test pits and 26 backhoe trenches scattered widely across the site. The results of this work, never fully published, were briefly summarized by King (1980) and more extensively reviewed in a master's thesis by Anne DuBarton (1991) of the University of Nevada, Las Vegas.

In the early 1970s, Travis Hudson of the Santa Barbara Museum of Natural History began a study of archaeological materials found submerged off the southern California Coast, with a focus on objects found in the Santa Barbara Channel area. In 1976 he published a booklet that describes the results of his research in cataloging and analyzing the distribution of such underwater finds, including two stone bowls found off the mouth of Tecolote Canyon in waters 9–12 m (30–40 ft) deep. The exact locations where these artifacts were found are not known, but Hudson (1976:10, 46) has associated them with SBA-71 and suggests that they may indicate the presence of a submerged village site offshore.

With the rapid development of the Goleta Valley area during the 1960s and 1970s, pressure to develop the beachfront property in Tecolote Canyon grew. As a result of various development proposals, and legal requirements that the potential effects of development projects on historical resources be evaluated, a series of archaeological studies focused

TABLE 3.1. History of Investigations at Tecolote Canyon Area Archaeological Sites

Investigator(s)/ Affiliation(s)	Year(s)	Site(s)	Type of Investigation	Reference(s)
Stephen Bowers, relic hunter	1877	SBA-73	Looting of "a great many skeletons but few implements"	Benson 1997:104
Frederick W. Putnam, University of California–Berkeley	1908	SBA-73	Excavation of two burials in badly disturbed (by Bowers?) cemetery	King 1980
David Banks Rogers, Santa Barbara Museum of Natural History	1926	SBA-71, -72, and -73	Extensive excavation in several cemeteries and village areas	DuBarton 1991; King 1980
Claude Warren, University of Nevada–Las Vegas, and Tom King, University of California–Los Angeles	1971	SBA-71	Extensive excavation associated with archaeological field school	DuBarton 1991; Kornfeld et al. 1980
Dee Travis Hudson, Santa Barbara Museum of Natural History	1976	SBA-71? (offshore)	Described discovery of stone bowls on seabed off Tecolote Canyon	Hudson 1976
Pandora Snethkamp, University of California–Santa Barbara	1979–1980	SBA-71, -72, -73, -1673, and -1674	Survey of lower canyon, limited excavation at five sites to determine boundaries and significance	Kornfeld et al. 1980
	1982	SBA-73	Limited excavation along pipeline route through northern site area	Moore et al. 1982
	1984	SBA-75	Surface survey and collection, small excavation in three site areas to determine boundaries and significance	Erlandson 1997a; Erlandson et al. 1988
Jon Erlandson, QRA, University of California–Santa Barbara, and WESTEC/ERCE	1986–1988	SBA-71, -72, -73, -1326, -1673, and -1674	Limited excavations for boundary definition and data recovery	Erlandson 1986; Erlandson and Cooley 1988a, 1988b, 1988c
Michael Macko, Macko Inc.	1987	SBA-69 and -70	Reconnaissance and small-scale test excavation	Macko 1987
Lorene Santoro, ISERA Group	1994	SBA-2499	Reconnaissance and limited test excavation	Santoro et al. 1995
David Stone, Science Applications International Corporation	1995, 1997	SBA-69, -70, and -2499	Reconnaissance, limited testing, and construction monitoring	Anderson and Stone 1999; Hess and Stone 1997
Jon Erlandson, René Vellanoweth, and Torben Rick, University of Oregon, Hutash Consultants	1997–2004	SBA-70, -71, -72, -73, -74, -106, -1326, -1673, and -1674	Reconnaissance, surface collection, excavation in several sites, construction monitoring, and extensive dating and research	Erlandson and Rick 2002; Rick et al. 2002; Vellanoweth 2001; Vellanoweth and Erlandson 2000, 2004

around the mouth of Tecolote Canyon was conducted by UCSB archaeologists beginning in 1979. All these projects were conducted under the overall direction of Pandora Snethkamp of the Office of Public Archaeology at UCSB. The first involved various background studies, a systematic survey of the 70-acre beachfront property and a proposed water system extending into the Upper Tecolote Canyon area, and limited excavations to determine the boundaries and significance of archaeological sites located on the property. This project recorded four new sites in the area (SBA-1671, SBA-1672, SBA-1673, and SBA-1674) and provided the first quantitative data for artifact and faunal samples from the area (Kornfeld et al. 1980), the first detailed summary of the postcontact history of the Tecolote area (Fuller and King 1980), and the first relatively secure chronology for the occupation of the canyon (King 1980), including the first radiocarbon dates. The discovery and dating of a shell midden lens buried almost 3 m below the surface in the Tecolote Creek bank also extended the antiquity of known human occupation in the area back to approximately 5,000 years (see chapter 5).

In 1981, UCSB archaeologists followed up their 1979–1980 study with excavations near the northern margin of SBA-73, work related to the construction of an ARCO pipeline from Bell Canyon to Eagle Canyon (Moore et al. 1982). This work involved the excavation and analysis of materials from seven 1-×-1-m-wide test units running across the site from east to west. The materials recovered from these peripheral site deposits include over 2,600 chipped-stone artifacts (the vast majority consisting of tool-making debris) and a small assemblage of shellfish and vertebrate remains associated with Chumash occupation. Also recovered were various historical materials—concrete, glass, iron, ceramics, and others—related to oil and other industrial development in the lower canyon area from the 1930s to the 1950s.

In 1984, further work by UCSB archaeologists determined the boundaries and significance of SBA-75, a large shell midden located on the west rim of Tecolote Canyon north of Highway 101. My colleagues and I (Erlandson et al. 1988) have summarized this work, including radiocarbon dates showing that this site was occupied on several occasions between about 5,200 and 4,900 years ago (see also Erlandson 1997a). A summary of the archaeology of SBA-75, including new radiocarbon dates, is presented in chapter 5.

In 1986, representatives of ADCO and Hyatt Hotels engaged me to prepare a cultural resources management plan for a hotel and resort project proposed for the beachfront parcel at the mouth of Tecolote Canyon. As principal investigator, I worked with archaeological teams from UCSB, WESTEC or ERCE Inc., and Hutash Consultants to meet a series of requirements placed on the proposed project by the County of Santa Barbara and the California Coastal Commission. Archaeological studies related to what eventually became the exclusive Bacara Resort were suspended from 1989 to 1997 and then reactivated under the direction of René Vellanoweth and me, and we supervised a team of archaeologists and Native Americans working for Hutash Consultants, the cultural resources arm of the Coastal Band of the Chumash Nation. After completion of fieldwork and preliminary laboratory work in 2000, the collections were moved to the University of Oregon for final analysis. The results of that work, including additional surface reconnaissance, subsurface testing, and monitoring of construction activities, are documented in this volume.

Also relevant to an understanding of the archaeology of the larger Tecolote Canyon area are three investigations of sites located on the east rim of Winchester Canyon. These three studies were related to the extension of Cathedral Oaks Road and the Winchester Commons housing development just north of Highway 101 and east of Cathedral Oaks. The first was conducted by Michael Macko (1987) and involved reconnaissance work and small-scale testing of peripheral portions of SBA-69 and SBA-70. Further work on the margins of these two sites was later done by archaeologists from Scientific Applications International Corporation, including additional subsurface testing and the first radiocarbon dating of these important sites (Anderson and Stone 1999). Finally, in another project related to the extension of Cathedral Oaks Road, archaeologists from the ISERA Group conducted test excavations at SBA-2499 on the east rim of Winchester Canyon (Santoro et al. 1995). As part of their study, they obtained a ^{14}C date that suggests that SBA-2499 was occupied as much as 7,900 years ago (see chapter 4). In the following chapters, we summarize the results of these archaeological studies in the Tecolote Canyon area and synthesize what is currently known about the archaeology, history, and dynamic environments of the Tecolote Canyon area from at least 9,000 years ago to the present.

4

Early Settlement:
10,000 to 7,000 Years Ago

Jon M. Erlandson

In chapter 3, I briefly explored issues related to the origins of the first Americans and the earliest peoples of the Santa Barbara Coast. Among archaeologists and other scholars, questions about when humans first entered the Americas, what route (or routes) they took, and when and how they reached the California Coast are still actively debated. Early theories focused on an interior migration by terrestrial hunting peoples trekking through Alaska and Canada to reach America's heartland, who gradually spread from sea to shining sea. As noted earlier, archaeological evidence from the Santa Barbara Channel region has played an important role in revising this scenario. Evidence for the maritime settlement of the Northern Channel Islands by at least 12,000 to 13,000 years ago has lent credence to the coastal migration theory that proposes that some of the earliest Americans were maritime peoples who traveled around the North Pacific in boats and moved rapidly into California and the Channel Islands (Erlandson 2002). If the coastal migration theory is ultimately proven correct, then the first Americans would have been maritime peoples fully comfortable in coastal settings.

Because the earliest evidence we currently have for a human occupation of the Tecolote Canyon area dates back "only" about 9,000 years, we cannot effectively address questions about the origins of the very first peoples of the Santa Barbara Channel area. Found just 48 km (30 mi) west of Tecolote, however, a fragment of a fluted stone projectile point is similar to Paleoindian Clovis points found in both interior and coastal areas across the continent, points generally dated to roughly 13,000 years ago (Erlandson 1994; Erlandson et al. 1987). This artifact, along with early sites on Santa Rosa and San Miguel islands, suggests that people roamed the Santa Barbara Coast—including the Tecolote area—at least 3,000 years prior to the earliest tangible evidence from the canyon. Traces of these earliest occupants may now lie offshore, submerged by rising postglacial seas, buried in thick accumulations of sediment in the lower canyon bottoms, or undiscovered on ridges or terraces that are still undeveloped.

Settlement Locations

Despite the vagaries of archaeological preservation and discovery, evidence for occupation by people the Chumash reportedly referred to as the "Mol Mol 'ique" or "ancient, ancient ones" (Rogers 1929: 342) comes from at least six sites in the Tecolote and Winchester Canyon area: SBA-69, SBA-70, SBA-71, SBA-75, SBA-1326, and SBA-2499. Unfortunately, although we know that coastal peoples occupied these sites between about 9,000 and 7,500 years ago, we have only limited or blurry images of the nature of these earliest peoples and how they lived. Three of the earliest sites in the project area (SBA-71, SBA-75, and SBA-1326) may have been occupied briefly during the Early Holocene, with the evidence mixed with the debris from later and more substantial occupations. Three of the sites (SBA-69, SBA-70, and SBA-71) were excavated by David Banks Rogers in the 1920s, but archaeological methods at the time were relatively crude, and only limited documentation exists for these collections. Tragically, most of another early site (SBA-2499) was destroyed recently after only limited archaeological study, when the County of Santa Barbara completed the western extension of Cathedral Oaks Road and approved the construction of a nearby housing development.

Fortunately there are a number of reasonably well-documented sites of similar age located along the Santa Barbara Coast. After the data from the Tecolote Canyon area are summarized, these can be used to reconstruct a more complete picture of these early peoples. The Tecolote sites, or at least what we currently know about their earliest occupations, are described in the following sections, beginning with the oldest.

SBA-69

Located on the east rim of Winchester Canyon some distance from the coast, SBA-69 is situated on a knoll overlooking the lower canyon. D. B. Rogers, the first archaeologist to investigate the site, described its "striking situation, since the land drops away abruptly on all sides" except for a narrow ridge to the south (1929:178–179). Because Rogers excavated "a large number of test pits, driven into various parts of this village," we have some knowledge of the general structure and contents of the site. However, because his methods were crude by modern standards and subsequent investigations have been very limited, much could still be learned from a careful study of the site. More recent studies of the site (Anderson and Stone 1999; Macko 1987), associated with nearby developments, have focused on peripheral deposits along the southern site boundary.

Rogers described the "extreme boundaries" of SBA-69 as extending about 91 m (300 ft) north to south and 43 m (140 ft) east to west. In the central site area, Rogers noted archaeological soils an average of about 90 cm (36 in) deep where the black "Indian soil…contained very little of the camp refuse in its original form. The heavier parts of the more massive sea shells were still to be seen, although much decomposed, but little trace was left of the

more fragile debris" (1929:178). Rogers found no evidence of houses or other structures but identified an elliptical cemetery area about 15 × 12 m (50 × 40 ft) wide, where he found the remnants of 14 fragmentary human skeletons encased in a hard calcareous crust. Other than "crumbling manos and metates," Rogers reported no artifacts associated with these skeletons. Elsewhere in the site, however, he noted the presence of numerous milling stones, hammer stones, and large "flint" (chert) chips showing little evidence of modification or use. In concluding, Rogers notes that SBA-69 was a village "that served for ages as a home for the Oak Grove People" (1929:179), where not one artifact typical of later cultures was found.

More recently, the southern portions of SBA-69 were the subject of two archaeological investigations associated with planning studies for a housing development and the extension of Cathedral Oaks Road (Anderson and Stone 1999; Macko 1987). These studies showed that the site is considerably larger than estimated by Rogers, who paid little attention to peripheral site areas where artifacts were rare. Macko (1987) excavated 15 50-×-50-cm-wide test pits within the Cathedral Oaks right-of-way and documented the presence of shallow and sparse cultural deposits well south of Rogers's site boundary. Macko's work shows that SBA-69 is probably more than 200 m long and at least 90–100 m wide (see also Anderson and Stone 1999). In the southern site area, Macko found very small amounts of marine shell and animal bone but noted the presence of sandstone manos, chipped-stone tool-making debris, and utilized flakes made from Franciscan chert, Monterey chert, quartzite, and fused shale. No radiocarbon dates were obtained, but the artifacts recovered are consistent with Rogers's Oak Grove (Milling Stone) attribution, suggesting an occupation prior to about 3,500 years ago.

In the 1990s, archaeologists from Science Applications International Corporation (SAIC) excavated five more 1-×-1-m-wide test units in the same southern site area and then monitored grading of the area for the construction of Cathedral Oaks Road and an adjacent housing tract (Anderson and Stone 1999). The SAIC work confirmed the presence of low-density archaeological materials in the area. A total of 241 chipped-stone artifacts were recovered in the SAIC test units, dominated by toolmaking debris ($n = 235$) made from local materials such as Franciscan chert (64 percent), Monterey chert (33 percent), and quartzite (1 percent). One piece of exotic obsidian from the Coso Volcanic Field in eastern California was recovered, however, as were six possible chipped-stone tools: a biface midsection, two retouched flakes, and three utilized flakes. Five ground-stone tools also were recovered, four manos and one metate fragment. Small amounts of plant remains were also found at SBA-69, including nine types of plant seeds. All the seeds are unburned, however, and are probably recent intrusions unrelated to Native American occupation of the site. Just four small fragments of undifferentiated fish bone and three small pieces of marine shell (two Venus clam fragments, one undifferentiated shell) were recovered during the excavation. With 51 bone fragments, land animals are better represented, but these are dominated by small mammals such as rabbits, ground squirrel, pocket gopher, and wood rat. Some of these species might be natural intrusions in the site soils, but the fact that roughly 70 percent of the bones are burned suggests that many of them are cultural in origin.

Significantly, Anderson and Stone also report the first ¹⁴C dates for SBA-69, one of 1630 ± 70 RYBP on soil organics from the 20–40 cm level of Unit 103 and another of 2890 ± 60 RYBP for soil organics from the 40–55 cm level of the same unit. After calibration to calendar years, these dates suggest that SBA-69 was occupied approximately 1,500 and 3,000 years ago, raising the possibility of a Late Holocene occupation of the site. There is little evidence, however, that the soil organics selected for dating by SAIC archaeologists were associated with human occupation at SBA-69. Anything more than an ephemeral occupation of the site during the Late Holocene, in fact, currently seems at odds with the artifact assemblages and other evidence recovered by Rogers, Macko, and SAIC.

In 2000, I visited the remnants of SBA-69 with Chumash tribal member John Ruiz to try to resolve the age of the site occupation. The central site

area remained essentially intact except for numerous gopher tailings. Surface exposures contained a relatively dense scatter of marine and estuarine shells, some heavily weathered and others relatively well preserved. Such variation is typical of many shell middens of the Santa Barbara Coast, where shells gradually deteriorate in the more acidic upper soil levels but are well preserved in the lower levels where calcium carbonates tend to accumulate. A small assemblage (246 g) of shell fragments collected from the surface of the site's central area is dominated by Pismo clam (*Tivela stultorum*, 61.8 percent), with smaller amounts of Venus clam (*Chione* spp., 13.2 percent), Washington clam (*Saxidomus nuttalli*, 11.4 percent), horse clam (*Tresus nuttalli*, 5.2 percent), California mussel (*Mytilus californianus*, 3.8 percent), undifferentiated shell (2.8 percent), and other estuarine clams (*Protothaca* spp., *Sanguinolaria nuttallia*), scallop (*Argopecten* sp.), and oyster (*Ostrea lurida*). The abundance of *Tivela*, a clam that burrows in the sand on relatively stable and surf-swept sandy beaches, is typical of Middle Holocene assemblages in the area, but the abundance of estuarine shell (especially *Saxidomus*) is more typical of Early Holocene sites. Two ¹⁴C dates on single fragments of *Tivela* (~6470 cal BP) and *Saxidomus* (~8900 cal BP) appear to confirm these patterns and are more consistent with Rogers's site chronology and the artifact assemblage from the site.

These dates suggest that SBA-69 is a Milling Stone site occupied almost 9,000 years ago and again about 6,500 years ago. The estuarine shellfish remains may be associated primarily with the earlier site occupation, and the Pismo clam shell may be derived mostly from the Middle Holocene occupation. Although more recent occupation of the site cannot yet be ruled out, it seems likely that the Late Holocene dates obtained for the site by SAIC archaeologists reflect the continuing accumulation of plant organics long after the main occupations of the site ended. At present, it is not known for certain which occupation the cemetery is associated with, but Rogers's (1926) description of at least one skeleton buried in an extended prone position suggests that much of the cemetery may date to the Middle Holocene (Erlandson 1997a).

SBA-75

SBA-75 is a large site located on the west rim of Tecolote Canyon. Known primarily as a Middle Holocene site (see chapter 5; Erlandson et al. 1988), SBA-75 now appears to have been occupied on multiple occasions during the past 8,000 years. The first archaeologist to describe the site, which he lumped with SBA-74 located on the opposite rim of the canyon, was D. B. Rogers:

> A rather exhaustive superficial survey was made of them, but, owing to the presence of heavy crops at the time of our visit, no trenches could be put down. My conclusions in regard to these sites are somewhat uncertain. I am, however, positive that both the Oak Grove People and the Canaliño had occupied both of these sites for a considerable period, for ancient manos and oval metates were present in great numbers, as well as the more advanced products of the later race. Only systematic trenching could determine whether these were the remains of permanent settlements, or only those of camping places in times of the acorn harvest [1929:201].

The only systematic subsurface investigation of SBA-75 was done by archaeologists from the University of California–Santa Barbara Office of Public Archaeology in 1984 (Erlandson et al. 1988). This work, associated with the early planning phases of the Bacara Resort, found that SBA-75 once extended for at least 200 m north to south and about 300 m east to west, with at least three separate occupation areas (A, B, and C). As we will see in chapter 5, SBA-75 produced artifacts and faunal remains consistent with occupation primarily during the Middle Holocene, including numerous milling stones and shellfish remains dominated by Pismo clams and California mussels typical of sandy beach and rocky shore intertidal habitats of the outer coast. Among the artifacts recovered at SBA-75, however, is a fragment of a flat-rimmed or "flowerpot" mortar typically found in sites dating to the past 1,000 to 1,500 years. This sandstone mortar fragment supports Rogers's conclusion that both Oak Grove and Canaliño peoples used the site. Among the shellfish remains from the site, small amounts of estuarine shell were also recovered, however, including the remains of species such as Venus clam common in Early Holocene and Late Holocene sites in the Tecolote area (see chapter 6). To test whether these estuarine shells mark a later occupation of SBA-75, a clam fragment from Area C was submitted for ^{14}C dating. Analysis of this shell produced an uncorrected date of 7780 ± 80 RYBP, suggesting that the site also was occupied roughly 8,400 calendar years ago. Unfortunately, we know little about what was probably a relatively brief early occupation, one largely obscured by more intensive occupation during the Middle Holocene.

SBA-2499

Like SBA-69, SBA-2499 is located on the east rim of Winchester Canyon near the northern edge of the coastal plain. About 1.5 km from the modern coast, SBA-2499 was first documented in 1993 during an archaeological survey associated with planning for the construction of the western end of Cathedral Oaks Road. Surface reconnaissance and test excavations at the site by archaeologists from the ISERA Group revealed a low-density scatter of marine shell and stone tools 250–300 m long (along the canyon rim, northeast to southwest) and about 100 m wide (Santoro et al. 1995). Within this area, two concentrations of archaeological material were identified, one near the west end of the site and another toward the east.

Santoro et al. obtained three ^{14}C dates for SBA-2499, two on charcoal and one on California mussel shell. The charcoal samples, from the upper 50 cm of Units 4 and 6, both produced essentially modern dates that probably represent contamination by recent charcoal. The shell sample was dated to 7200 ± 80 RYBP, however, with a calibrated age of about 7850 cal BP, suggesting that the site was occupied during the Early Holocene.

Hess and Stone (1997) later excavated three 1-×-1-m test units along the southern margins of SBA-2499 for the Mountain View Residential Development just south of Cathedral Oaks Road. They recovered 308 chipped-stone artifacts, including five flake tools, four cores, one biface fragment, and 298 pieces of stone tool-making debris.

These artifacts were made primarily from Franciscan chert (47 percent), Monterey chert (43 percent), and other local materials, but Santoro et al. also recovered a few small obsidian flakes. Small amounts of animal bone (mostly undifferentiated fragments) were also recovered, along with a few pieces of marine or estuarine shell. Based on the early ^{14}C date and the limited width of hydration bands on the obsidian artifacts, Hess and Stone concluded that SBA-2499 was occupied on multiple occasions, once more than 7,000 years ago and again roughly 1,500 years ago.

In 2000, I visited SBA-2499 and found that much of the site had been destroyed. A sparse scatter of marine shell fragments and chipped-stone tool-making debris was still visible along the edge of Cathedral Oaks Road. Nearby I also found a recent cache of ground-stone tool fragments, including three large metate fragments and one piece of a flat-rimmed bowl or mortar. The three metates are generally consistent with an Early Holocene occupation, but the mortar fragment is more typical of sites dating between about 1,000 and 200 years ago. If all these ground-stone artifacts came from SBA-2499, which is not certain, they may support Hess and Stone's site chronology.

SBA-71

This large and complex site, located on the bluff overlooking the beach between the mouths of Tecolote and Winchester canyons, was occupied by Native Americans several times over the millennia. The site includes archaeological components dated to the Early, Middle, and Late Holocene. Of interest here is the earliest known occupation of the site, largely obscured by the accumulation of later occupational debris and disturbances related to human use of the landform before and after European contact.

SBA-71 was first investigated by D. B. Rogers, who believed the site had been occupied successively by his Oak Grove, Hunting, and Canaliño peoples. Rogers mapped the Oak Grove occupation as being localized in the southern site area adjacent to the sea cliff, covering an area about 46 m (150 ft) north–south and 38 m (125 ft) east–west. He noted that

even at that early date, the site had been occupied by man, for I found imbedded in this adhesive, stubborn subsoil, several worn manos and fragments of crumbling metates. I also found the vestiges of two very ancient burials, stretched at length, with no black soil in the graves; these had evidently been laid away before the black soil was formed. These evidences were very few and were restricted to a small area [1929:182].

Along the Santa Barbara Coast, human skeletons buried in a prone position are most often associated with Middle Holocene occupations (Erlandson 1997a). However, King (1980:30) has argued that most of the traits Rogers identified as characteristic of the Oak Grove culture were associated with an extensive occupation dated between about AD 1 and AD 400. Based on a few shell beads found during the 1971 and 1979–1980 excavations of the site, King (1980:38) also noted that an occupation of the southern site area appeared to predate 1200 BC, including a rock feature (Warren's Feature 4) he interpreted as a possible cooking area (see also King and Serena 1980:179). DuBarton (1991:160), who analyzed Warren's collection for her master's thesis at the University of Nevada, Las Vegas, confirmed that SBA-71 was occupied during the Early Holocene when she dated an abalone shell from this rock feature to 7080 ± 120 RYBP or about 7,700 years ago.

Unfortunately, because more extensive Middle and Late Holocene occupational debris is heavily mixed with these early materials (including Feature 4, which also produced a rectangular shell bead dated to c. 3,300 years ago), we can say little about the activities of these early peoples. What we know is that a group of people camped atop the ridge between Tecolote and Winchester canyons some 7,700 years ago. Some of the well-worn milling stones (manos and metates) found in the southern site area may be associated with this early occupation. Two cairn-like milling stone features found in the northern site area may also date to the Early Holocene. The abundance of such milling equipment suggests, in turn, that the early occupants of Tecolote were heavily dependent on small

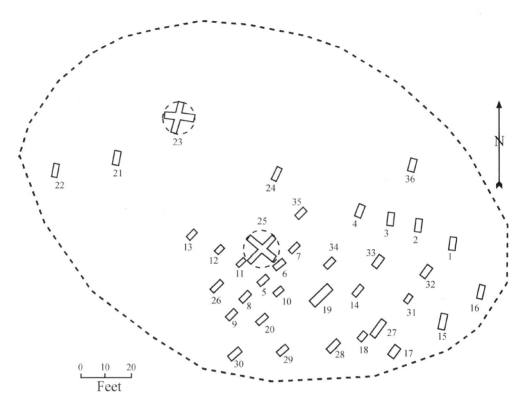

FIGURE 4.1. Map of D. B. Rogers's 1926 excavations at SBA-70 (redrawn by Julia Knowles).

seeds and other plant foods, as were their contemporaries along the Santa Barbara Coast (Erlandson 1991, 1994). Because materials associated with this early occupation appear to be found mostly near the current sea cliff and it has been estimated that such cliffs are retreating an average of about 15 cm (c. 6 in) per year, a substantial amount of this early site may have been lost to coastal erosion. Because sea level was roughly 15 m (~50 ft) lower than present about 7,700 years ago (Inman 1983), the geography of the Tecolote area was also quite different than it is today, a topic I return to later in this chapter.

SBA-70

Located on the east rim of Winchester Canyon, roughly 700 m from the modern coast, SBA-70 has been the subject of several archaeological studies, beginning with D. B. Rogers's work in the 1920s. Rogers described the site as a "great refuse heap" of black, mellow soil strewn with occasional shells and artifacts. He estimated that the site covered a roughly elliptical area about 61 m (200 ft) east to west and 46 m (150 ft) north–south (Figure 4.1). In the central site area, the archaeological deposit was generally between 91 and 107 cm (~36–42 in) deep, but it reached depths of nearly 1.5 m (5 ft) in some areas. According to Rogers:

Fragments of the heavier parts of the more massive sea shells were the only organic remains that had endured in the original form in the great refuse heap. None of the more delicate shells and no traces of bone were found in this discarded refuse. Flint chips, hammers, and oval manos were of fairly frequent occurrence. No vessels were encountered, probably because I failed definitely to locate the cemetery where these artifacts are commonly found. I did, however, find a few fragmentary human remains near the southern border of the site. These were partially fossilized and covered with a calcareous matrix. These fragments probably indicate the presence of the cemetery in the vicinity.

Traces of the stony, calcareous formation which is almost an invariable accompaniment of the deposits left by first culture occupancy were noted along the lower reaches of this heap.

At two points, I unearthed almost unmistakable evidence that partially subterranean, circular structures had existed here; one was approximately twelve feet, the other fourteen feet in diameter. The floor of each had been sunk twenty-four inches below the original ground surface [~60 in below the modern ground surface]. If these structures were maintained up to the close of the settlement, which is unlikely, they would have been almost entirely beneath the surface. The encircling walls of clay had, in each case, partially caved in. Thin beds of ashes marked the center of the floor level of each, the ashes of the larger enclosing a circle of small burned stones. Amidst the debris that filled the larger depressions were several small boulders that had evidently once lain on or very near the hut, for I assume from their size and from the absence of charcoal, that these ruins probably represent the remains of dwellings, rather than a sweat house.... I believe that we have at this site undisturbed remains of a settlement of the people of the first culture.... They lived unchanged to the end of their story, the final chapter of which was closed at such a remote time in the past that the materials of their refuse heap have largely reverted to the condition of mellow soil, and the skeletons of the ancient cemetery are now represented only by scattered fragments of semi-fossilized bones [1929:180].

For more than 50 years no further work was done by archaeologists at SBA-70. In the early 1960s, most of the central site area was graded into oblivion during an expansion of Highway 101. As far as we know, no archaeology was done at the time to salvage information from this important site. In 1987, Macko investigated remnants of SBA-70 identified north of Highway 101 to determine the site boundaries and condition relative to an extension of Cathedral Oaks Road and the Winchester Common Residential Development. He studied surface artifacts and excavated 15 50-×-50-cm-wide test units to determine the subsurface extent of the deposit, as well as the density and nature of any archaeological materials in the proposed development area. Macko identified low-density archaeological deposits in a truncated elliptical area extending about 61 m (200 ft) north of Calle Real Road and about 91 m (300 ft) east to west on the east rim of Winchester Canyon.

In 1995, SAIC archaeologists conducted salvage excavations in the same area tested by Macko and then monitored the destruction of this northern site area as most of it was graded away (Anderson and Stone 1999). SAIC archaeologists excavated three 1-×-1-m-wide test units and a total volume of 1.86 m^3. They also obtained three ^{14}C dates on soil organics from arbitrary levels in Unit 102. A sample from the 20–40 cm level produced a date of 2340 ± 60 RYBP, another from the 40–60 cm level was dated to 4110 ± 70 RYBP, and a third from the 60–80 cm level was dated to 3140 ± 60 RYBP. After calibration to calendar years, these dates are equal to roughly 2350, 4670, and 3360 cal BP. As is the case with the dates on soil organics from SBA-69, however, it is not clear if these dates are related to the age of the human use of the site. Recent dating of five shell fragments from SBA-70 strongly suggests that the site was occupied much earlier than the SAIC dates indicate.

It has long been assumed that SBA-70 did not extend south of the Highway 101 corridor. This area has been heavily developed over the years: the Southern Pacific Railroad, Hollister Avenue, and the Winchester 101 overpass all cut through the area; and commercial buildings have been built on the north side of Hollister Avenue, with oil-processing facilities and the Sandpiper Golf Course to the south. During grading of the entrance road to the Bacara Resort, however, a few chipped- and ground-stone artifacts were encountered by archaeological and Native American monitors. This led to the excavation of several shovel test pits on a narrow remnant of the east rim of Winchester Canyon between the railroad right-of-way on the north and the Bacara entrance road. These revealed the presence of a very low-density deposit of chipped-stone tool-making debris, typical of the extreme periphery of a more substantial archaeological site. After

TABLE 4.1. Radiocarbon Dates from SBA-70

LAB #	MATERIAL	PROVENIENCE	ADJUSTED $^{13}C/^{12}C$ AGE (RYBP)	CALENDAR AGE RANGE (CAL BP, 1δ)
Beta-82442	Soil organics	Unit 102: 20–40 cm	2340 ± 60	2490 (2350) 2180
Beta-82444	Soil organics	Unit 102: 60–80 cm	4110 ± 70	4810 (4670) 4450
Beta-82443	Soil organics	Unit 102: 40–60 cm	3140 ± 60	3450 (3360) 3270
OS-44641	California mussel	Surface	6730 ± 45	7085 (7000) 6920
OS-31799	Venus clam	Surface	6820 ± 45	7200 (7150) 7020
OS-31682	Estuarine shell	Surface	6890 ± 45	7250 (7210) 7150
OS-44642	California mussel	Surface	7010 ± 40	7360 (7310) 7260
OS-31681	Marine shell	Surface	7070 ± 50	7420 (7370) 7300

Note: Soil organic samples are of uncertain cultural origin; shell samples were single fragments of midden shell analyzed via accelerator mass spectrometry; all dates calibrated with CALIB 4.3 (Stuiver and Reimer 1993).

a ground-stone artifact was found during grading near the intersection of the Bacara entrance road and Hollister Avenue, I began to suspect that these artifacts might be associated with SBA-70, supposedly located about 150 to 200 m to the north. Carefully examining intact soil exposures between these two areas, I found remnants of shell midden deposits on the north and south sides of both Highway 101 and the railroad tracks. These deposits, all denser than any tested by Macko or SAIC in the northern site periphery, suggest that SBA-70 once covered a much larger area than originally described by D. B. Rogers. I also collected numerous fragments of marine and estuarine shell from these exposures and obtained five ^{14}C dates for the site (Table 4.1). These dates, ranging between about 7,400 and 6,900 years ago, provide a chronological picture that is consistent with Rogers's Oak Grove attribution, the dominance of estuarine shell at the site, the numerous Milling Stone artifacts recovered, and the lack of artifacts diagnostic of later time periods. If the architectural features described by Rogers also date to this time period, they are also the oldest houses yet reported for the Santa Barbara Channel area.

SBA-1673

On the high terrace west of Tecolote Creek, under what is now the main parking lot for the Bacara Resort, lies a large and low-density scatter of stone artifacts known as SBA-1673. First recorded in 1980, the site extends from the sea cliff on the south to the entrance road on the north, a distance of almost 175 m (~600 ft). Superimposed on top of this site were the scattered remains of residential debris from two houses occupied in the twentieth century (see chapter 7). Surface collections and subsurface excavations at SBA-1673 demonstrated that the density of Native American archaeological materials was highest near the south margin of the site and gradually declined to the north. Monitoring of grading associated with construction of the entry court for Bacara showed that densities also increased near the north margin, where materials from SBA-1673 overlapped with those from SBA-1326 (see chapter 5).

Most of the artifacts recovered from SBA-1673 are chipped-stone tools and tool-making debris that are not diagnostic of a particular time period. The few faunal remains recovered are poorly preserved and appear to come from imported soils or fill. As a result, no radiocarbon dates are available for SBA-1673, and the age and nature of the site remain something of a mystery. During the analysis of the chipped-stone artifacts from the site, however, a fragment of a chipped-stone crescent was identified. Such crescents are relatively rare along the California Coast and are generally thought to be between about 10,000 and 7,500 years old. Very few crescents have been found along the Santa Barbara Coast, but early investigators found a number of them on Santa Rosa and San Miguel islands

FIGURE 4.2. Mirror images of a chipped-stone crescent fragment from SBA-1673 (photo by J. Erlandson).

(Fenenga 1984), at least two are known from the Vandenberg area in northern Santa Barbara County, and one was found in an early site near Point Conception (Erlandson 1994:176). Along the southern California mainland coast, they are more common in early San Diego and Orange County sites located around the margins of large estuaries. The function of these unusual artifacts is not clear. Some "eccentric" crescents resemble animal effigies—one shaped like a bear is the official California state artifact—but most of them appear to have been utilitarian items. Many archaeologists believe that they served as "transverse" projectile points that were used to hunt waterfowl and seabirds.

The crescent from SBA-1673 consists of approximately one-half of a complete specimen and appears to be manufactured from Cico chert (Figure 4.2). The only known source of this chert is from the northeast coast of San Miguel Island, where another crescent made from Monterey chert was recently found in Early Holocene deposits at Daisy Cave. The fragment from SBA-1673 is also similar to some crescents found on the Northern Channel Islands (Fenenga 1984). At present, it is not clear if the crescent from SBA-1673 indicates that the entire site dates to the Early Holocene. It is possible that the crescent fragment represents a broken artifact lost during hunting or discarded when an early hunter was repairing equipment. However this unique artifact came to rest on the western terrace,

it provides further evidence that early peoples occupied the Tecolote area between about 10,000 and 7,000 years ago.

EARLY HOLOCENE GEOGRAPHY OF THE TECOLOTE AREA

To understand the adaptations of these early coastal peoples, we must also understand the natural environment of the Tecolote area during the Early Holocene, from about 10,000 to 7,000 years ago. As alluded to earlier, the environments of the Santa Barbara Coast were extremely dynamic at this time, changing dramatically in response to global transitions from glacial to interglacial conditions. During the last glacial, sea levels dropped as much as 125 m, extending the coastal plain by several kilometers and lengthening coastal drainages accordingly. In response, coastal streams cut deeply into their canyon bottoms to meet the lower sea level. Between about 18,000 and 7,000 years ago, rapidly rising seas flooded vast stretches of the once broader coastal plain, as well as the lower reaches of the canyons cut deeply through it. This process created a series of bays and estuaries along the Santa Barbara Coast, the extent of which depended on the size of individual canyons, the depth to which they had been cut, and the amount of sediment carried by their streams. Where the coastal plain was relatively wide, as in the Goleta Valley area, multiple streams flowed together and carved out large and relatively complex basins during the last glacial. Here, postglacial sea level rise created the large Goleta estuary, remnants of which have survived despite extensive human modifications, including the construction of the Santa Barbara Airport. In shorter and smaller canyons of the western Santa Barbara Coast, including Tecolote and Winchester, the bays and estuaries of the Early Holocene were considerably smaller and comparatively ephemeral geological features.

Between 13,000 and 8,000 years ago, a period when people clearly occupied the Santa Barbara area, sea levels rose by roughly 35 m, from about −50 to −15 m below present levels (Inman 1983). At the time, Tecolote and Winchester canyons almost certainly merged into a single larger canyon, the lower reaches of which have since been submerged. As sea levels rose, several kilometers of the coastal plain in the Tecolote area were probably inundated. An estuary, first formed several thousand years earlier in the submerged portions of the canyon, gradually expanded northward as the sea flooded the lower reaches of the canyons. We can reconstruct what such estuaries may have looked like using bathymetric charts, sea level curves, and estimated rates of coastal erosion (sea cliff retreat). By about 8,000 years ago, for instance, estimates from the southern California Coast tell us that sea level was roughly 15 m (50 ft) lower than it is today (Inman 1983). The location of the 15 m submarine contour on bathymetric charts suggests that the outer coast was situated roughly a kilometer south of the modern beach. The towering sea cliffs that now bracket and divide Tecolote and Winchester canyons probably did not exist then. Instead a broad and relatively flat coastal plain extended seaward to the ancient coast, where it probably terminated in a low cliff broken by a single canyon with a protected bay or estuary at its mouth (Figure 4.3). Freshwater sources, crucial to human survival, would have been found only at the head of such an embayment, where Tecolote and Winchester creeks flowed into it. Most environmental data suggest that climates were still slightly cooler and wetter during the Early Holocene, but vegetation communities appear to have been generally similar to those of today. Canyon-bottom landforms just upstream were highly dynamic at this time, adjusting to sea level rise and

the altered erosional and depositional regimes it caused. As a result, people who lived around such estuaries tended to settle on stable canyon-rim landforms close to freshwater—usually at the head of the estuaries rather than near the open coast.

These small estuaries appear to have supported a diverse and highly productive range of plants and animals. Within an hour's walk or paddle, the people of Tecolote could collect shellfish from estuarine and open-coast habitats; gather plant foods from chaparral, oak woodland, grassland, riparian, and other communities; hunt deer, sea mammals, and a variety of other game; and catch fish in estuary, rocky reef, kelp forest, and pelagic habitats. With human population densities considerably lower than they were at European contact—when the Spanish marveled at the abundance of Santa Barbara Channel environments—the Santa Barbara Coast must have been a truly bountiful paradise.

ARCHAEOLOGY OF THE TECOLOTE AREA IN THE EARLY HOLOCENE

Unfortunately, we still know relatively little about the earliest occupants of the Tecolote Canyon area. Although we know that the Santa Barbara Coast was settled by Native Americans at least 13,000 years ago, the earliest evidence of human occupation in the Tecolote Canyon area currently dates to about 9,000 years ago. At least six sites in the area were used or occupied between about 9,000 and 7,000 years ago. The nature of these early sites— and the people who left them behind—remains obscured, however, by the ephemeral nature of some occupations, the mixing of early materials with those from later and more substantial occupations, the destruction of large portions of several sites by historical developments, and the probable loss of others to coastal erosion. Because of such problems, substantive assemblages collected with modern archaeological techniques are unavailable from several early sites, the materials come from peripheral site areas, and the early materials are difficult to differentiate from those left by later peoples.

Despite these problems, the data available from the early sites of the Tecolote area seem generally consistent with patterns identified for other early

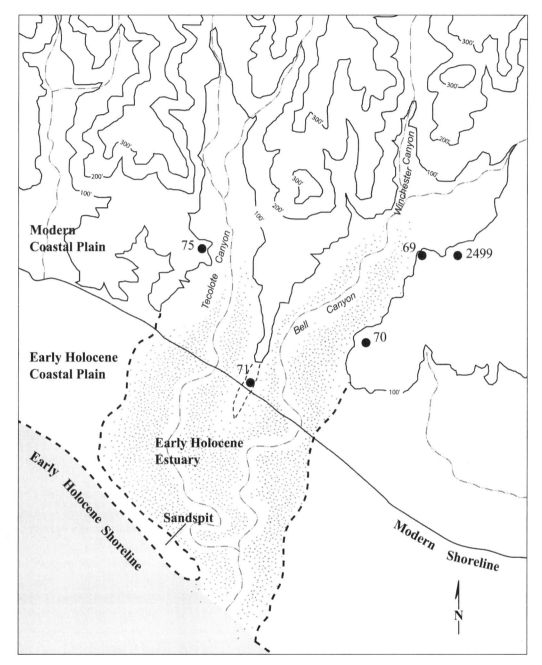

FIGURE 4.3. Reconstruction of the geography of the Tecolote Canyon area about 8,500 years ago, showing approximate locations of early sites (drawing by Eric Carlson).

sites along the Santa Barbara Coast. Some of the best data come from a series of sites in the Gaviota area that I studied in the 1980s (Erlandson 1988a, 1991, 1994; Rick and Erlandson 2000), as well as the Glen Annie Canyon site located on the northwest margin of the Goleta Slough, where portions of an early cemetery were excavated by University of California archaeologists in 1960 (Owen 1964; Owen et al. 1964).

Looking at the Santa Barbara Coast as a whole, early Milling Stone groups have been interpreted as semisedentary and relatively egalitarian peoples who thrived in the area for several thousand years (Erlandson 1994). Variation in the size, structure, and density of their sites suggests that they were occupied for differing amounts of time. Some clearly served as seasonal camps, but others were substantial villages occupied more permanently. If the house pits Rogers (1929:180) identified at SBA-70 are really 7,000 years old, they provide the first evidence of what the houses of early Milling Stone peoples looked like. To this picture we can add the presence of relatively abundant manos and metates, tool types generally assumed to have been used primarily to process small seeds and perhaps other plant foods. Chipped-stone tools and tool-making debris are relatively common in the Early Holocene sites, but most of these tools are informal or expedient types, with projectile points or other formal tool types being comparatively rare. The dearth of hunting equipment may result, in part, from a heavy reliance on shellfish collecting, which requires little or no specialized technology. All the sites produced the remains of shellfish collected from estuaries and other marine habitats, but they also contain smaller quantities of fish, mammal, and bird remains that suggest a relatively eclectic hunting and gathering economy. Dietary reconstructions for faunal remains recovered from several well-preserved sites suggest that these were maritime peoples who obtained most of their meat from shellfish and fish (Erlandson 1994; Rick and Erlandson 2000) but most of their calories from plant foods. The mixed reliance on the resources of the land and sea provided a relatively stable and productive subsistence economy that nurtured Native peoples of the area for millennia.

Local resources probably fulfilled most of their needs, but the presence of a few obsidian artifacts and other exotic goods suggests that the people of the Santa Barbara Coast participated in local and regional trade networks even at this early period. Shell beads were used as ornaments and traded to interior groups, but their lack of diversity or concentration (compared with later times) suggests that economic interaction between groups was more limited and social differences within groups were more restrained and informal. Although their spiritual life was probably complex, evidence for gender differences, economic specialization, social hierarchy, or elaborated ceremonialism is limited. With a wealth of resources and relatively few people on the landscape, however, the Early Holocene may have been an ideal time for the people of Tecolote and the Santa Barbara Coast, a time of relative abundance and limited territorial competition or social strife.

Although limited, the data from the Tecolote area are consistent with our more detailed knowledge of early environments and human adaptations along the broader Santa Barbara Coast. The cultural traditions of the Early Holocene appear basically conservative, with little evidence for significant cultural change during a roughly 3,000-year period. Although our knowledge is limited to some extent by the vagaries of preservation, there is also little evidence that the early peoples of the Tecolote Canyon area had the elaborated technologies, economies, social organization, craft specialization, and ceremonialism of the Chumash people who lived in the area during the past 2,500 years. In the chapters that follow, we explore how the geography of the Tecolote Canyon area changed through time and why the sophisticated and complex culture of the Chumash Indians evolved from such comparatively simple and egalitarian forebears of the Early Holocene.

5

The Middle Holocene:
7,000 to 3,500 Years Ago

JON M. ERLANDSON AND RENÉ L. VELLANOWETH

As we saw in chapter 4, at least six sites in the Teco-lote Canyon area were occupied more than 7,000 years ago. Several of these sites (SBA-69, SBA-71, and SBA-75) have also produced evidence for occu-pation between about 7,000 and 3,500 years ago, a time period referred to by many California archae-ologists as the Middle Holocene. Major cultural changes took place during the Middle Holocene, including the transition between what D. B. Rog-ers (1929) and William Harrison (1964) called the Oak Grove and Hunting peoples. This transition involved changes in local environments and human settlement, technology, subsistence, and demogra-phy. For the Santa Barbara Channel area, and the California Coast in general, the cultural changes of the Middle Holocene are not well understood (see Erlandson and Glassow 1997). This is related, in part, to the long emphasis of archaeologists on the larger coastal villages and towns of the Chumash, where relatively elaborate artifact assemblages could be found along with ample evidence for the cultural complexity that has long fascinated schol-ars. It is also related, however, to a strong interest in the earliest evidence for human occupation around the world, an emphasis on human origins that per-vades the field of archaeology.

The evidence for an Early Holocene occupation of the Tecolote Canyon area is widespread but rela-tively superficial, but we are fortunate to have two excavated sites in the area that date either primarily or entirely to the Middle Holocene. Altogether, we know that at least eight sites in the area were occu-pied during the Middle Holocene, and at least two of these (SBA-72 and SBA-75) appear to have been occupied on multiple occasions. Several nearby sites provide additional information that allows us to reconstruct a fairly detailed picture of the life-ways of the people who occupied the area, includ-ing their material culture, settlement and subsis-tence practices, and the dynamic environments they occupied. In the sections that follow, we pro-vide an overview of the known Middle Holocene settlements in the Tecolote Canyon area, includ-ing detailed evidence from SBA-72 and SBA-75, and then summarize what we know about this gen-eral time period along the western Santa Barbara Coast.

SETTLEMENT LOCATIONS

Erlandson (1997a:107–108) suggested that Middle Holocene peoples along the western Santa Barbara Coast were generally more mobile than those of the Early Holocene, with many village sites character-ized by large but relatively sparse midden deposits, including some that contained small cemeteries, and numerous smaller sites (campsites, process-ing sites, etc.) as well. He suggested that the greater mobility of Middle Holocene peoples in the area might be related to the declining productivity or disappearance of many of the small estuaries pres-ent in the area prior to about 6,000 years ago. Estu-aries are highly productive and protected habitats where the land meets the sea, freshwater and salt-water mix, and a diverse array of plants and animals can be found. These traits attracted humans for millennia, until sedimentation and the slowing of postglacial sea level rise spelled the end for the small estuaries of the western Santa Barbara Coast. We do not know precisely when the estuary at the mouths of Tecolote and Winchester canyons disappeared, but there is little evidence for estuarine shellfish in local sites dating to the later phases of the Middle Holocene.

Radiocarbon dates and diagnostic artifacts suggest that Native Americans occupied at least eight sites in the Tecolote Canyon area between about 6,500 and 3,500 years ago: SBA-68, SBA-69, SBA-71, SBA-72, SBA-74, SBA-75, SBA-106, and SBA-1326. As is the case with the Early Holocene sites in the area, several of these settlements were occupied multiple times over the millennia, with archaeological materials from different time periods mixed by burrowing animals, human occupation, and historical activities. Short summaries of what we know about the Middle Holocene occupation of several lesser-known sites are presented below, followed by more detailed descriptions of our investigations at SBA-72 and SBA-75.

SBA-68

High on the ridge between Tecolote and Winchester canyons, approximately 3 km from the sea, David Banks Rogers (1929:177–178) described a site he believed was occupied by his Oak Grove (Milling Stone) people. Rogers depicted the site as being located near a spring atop a knoll shown in the distance of a photo showing the location of SBA-69. He did not excavate SBA-68 but noted "dozens of manos and fragments of metates, many flint chips, and even traces of sea shells" on the site surface (1929:178). The precise location of this site has long been something of a mystery, and, to our knowledge, no subsequent work has been done at the site. As part of our background research on the history of the area, we quickly searched the knolls along this ridge, which is still being farmed. In 2003, we relocated what we believe is SBA-68 on a small knoll that had been freshly disked. Here we

found a few chipped-stone artifacts, two well-worn but heavily plow-scarred sandstone manos, and three or four small fragments of estuarine or marine shell. We collected the shell fragments, even though most are heavily weathered. All appear to be fragments of clams, and one of the better-preserved fragments is from a Venus clam (*Chione* spp.). We obtained a ^{14}C date of 6340 ± 45 RYBP for this estuarine shell fragment, suggesting that the site was occupied by Milling Stone peoples about 6,540 calendar years ago.

SBA-69

As described earlier, SBA-69 is located on the east rim of Winchester Canyon, more than 2 km from the coast. Rogers (1929:178–179) dug numerous trenches here, gathering general information about the site structure, contents, and chronology. His methods were crude by modern standards, and recent studies have been limited to the southern margins of the site (Anderson and Stone 1999; Macko 1987). In the central site area, Rogers found midden soil about 90 cm (36 in) deep. He reported that traces of "the more massive sea shells were still to be seen" (1929:178) but no evidence of houses or other structures was found. The large number of milling stones, hammer stones, and crude chert tools—along with a cemetery containing 14 poorly preserved human skeletons encased in calcium carbonate—suggested that SBA-69 was once a village of his Oak Grove people. Despite extensive excavation, Rogers found no evidence for more recent site occupation.

In his work on the southern edge of the site, Macko (1987) found nothing to contradict Rogers's chronology, but Anderson and Stone (1999) obtained two ^{14}C dates on soil organics that suggest much later occupations dating to roughly 2,900 and 1,600 years ago. To evaluate the very different chronology proposed by Anderson and Stone, we obtained ^{14}C dates for two well-preserved shell fragments from the surface of the central site area. These dates suggest that SBA-69 contains at least two discrete Milling Stone components, one dating to almost 9,000 years ago and another to about 6,500 years ago. These dates differ dramatically from those obtained by Anderson and Stone (1999), and it seems likely that their Late Holocene dates were contaminated by more recent soil organics, which continue to accumulate in surface sites long after they are abandoned.

As noted in chapter 4, distinguishing between the materials associated with the Early and Middle Holocene occupations of SBA-69 is difficult because many aspects of Milling Stone (Oak Grove) assemblages are very similar over thousands of years. A small sample of shellfish remains from the site surface is dominated by Pismo clam (*Tivela stultorum*, 61.8 percent), a species common in many Middle Holocene sites of the western Santa Barbara Coast. Estuarine shellfish (*Chione*, 13.2 percent; *Saxidomus nuttalli*, 11.4 percent; *Tresus*, 5.2 percent; and small amounts of *Protothaca*, *Sanguinolaria*, *Argopecten*, and *Ostrea*), more typical of Early Holocene sites in the area, are also well represented in the sample. The presence of at least one skeleton buried in an extended position in the tightly clustered cemetery also suggests a relatively intensive occupation during the Middle Holocene. Although SBA-69 seems to have been an important village about 6,500 years ago, only further investigation—including careful excavation and additional dating—will provide a more detailed picture of the age, structure, and contents of the site, as well as the lifeways of the people who lived there.

SBA-74 AND SBA-106

SBA-74 and SBA-106 are located on the flattened ridge between Tecolote and Winchester canyons, just north of the large cut for U.S. Highway 101, Calle Real, and the Southern Pacific Railroad. D. B. Rogers (1929:201, 257–259) first described these sites, but the area was reportedly being farmed at the time, preventing excavation. His comments are limited and somewhat generic because he described both SBA-74 and SBA-75 (see below) in a single paragraph. After a "rather exhaustive superficial survey," Rogers concluded that SBA-74 had been occupied by both "the Oak Grove People and the Canaliño." His conclusions are based on the presence of "ancient manos and oval metates…in great

numbers, as well as the more advanced products of the later race" (1929:201). Of SBA-106, Rogers had much more to say, believing the site to provide dramatic evidence for the great age of his Oak Grove culture.

The SBA-74 and SBA-106 area has been heavily affected by historical development, with much of the sites destroyed by the construction of the old Coast Highway, Calle Real, and Highway 101 (see chapter 7). What remains is largely covered with housing and unavailable for study. Although the remnants of SBA-74 and SBA-106 lie outside the Bacara property, we briefly examined them to learn more about the larger history of the Tecolote Canyon area. Small remnants of both sites were found exposed on public lands along the northern edge of the Calle Real/Highway 101 road cut. Here, we found a sparse scatter of chipped- and ground-stone artifacts, along with a few fragments of marine shell. The chipped-stone artifacts consist mostly of tool-making debris, but the ground-stone tools include two manos and a metate fragment (typical of Oak Grove or Milling Stone sites), as well as the distal end of a well-made sandstone pestle, more typical of a Canaliño or Late Holocene occupation. This small assemblage of tools appears to support Rogers's conclusion that the site was occupied during at least two discrete time periods. The few shell fragments found in the area are primarily from Pismo clams, one of which was collected for radiocarbon dating. Analysis of this shell fragment produced an uncorrected date of 6020 ± 80 RYBP, with a calendar age of ~6,200 years ago. This date supports Rogers's conclusion about an Oak Grove occupation of SBA-74 and fills a gap in the chronology of human occupation in the Tecolote Canyon area. Unfortunately, we know relatively little about the nature of this occupation.

What we know about SBA-106 may help flesh out this picture but also remains relatively limited. In his 1929 book, Rogers described the site as located on the northern edge of the old County Road that served as the coastal highway before Highway 101 was built. He discovered the site after a mud slide blocked the County Road, where he found a large metate in the debris being cleared away by a county

FIGURE 5.1. Photo of a Tecolote road cut in the 1920s, showing buried beach deposit (cobble bed) overlying light Rincon shale, where D. B. Rogers found ancient milling tools (courtesy of the Santa Barbara Museum of Natural History).

road crew. Rogers described his examination of the 50-ft-high road cut (Figure 5.1) in some detail:

At the base and rising about ten feet above the level of the road-bed is a ledge of cream-colored shale. The upper surface of this stratum appears to have been subjected to great and long-continued erosion, as though it had at some period lain close to sea level and been obliged to withstand the lash of the surf.... Lying unconformably upon this eroded surface, the next stratum above it consists of a twelve inch layer of loose, white sand, closely approaching beach sand in appearance. Above the sand is a tremendous jumble of gravel, clay and boulders,... detritus that has been torn from the nearby mountains in a time of terrific rain and flood. This structure is fairly constant in material, from the sand stratum to the top of the cut.... After long search, I found *in situ*, at the junction of the detritus and the sand, a typical well worn mano. There could be no mistake. It was, beyond any question, a result of human activities, but the location in which it was found imbedded was in my experience, unprecedented. It was between fifty and sixty feet back from the present walls of the canyon, and could not have been by any chance left in its present position by a recent landslide. The stratification alone is enough to provide that this artifact had lain undisturbed where I found it, since the first onrush of the flood of boulders.... Neither the mano nor the metate, both which I secured, showed any evidence of "water rolling," although they were very old and frail in texture [1929:257–258].

Although the exact location Rogers examined was destroyed by later development, the geological strata he described are still visible in road and railroad cuts that cross Lower Tecolote Canyon from east to west. Today, it is clear that the cream-colored shale and the overlying sands Rogers described are part of an ancient beach formed by high sea levels during the Last Interglacial period. There are several Last Interglacial beach deposits along the Santa Barbara Coast that date between about 130,000

and 88,000 years ago. If the grinding stones Rogers found were originally deposited atop the sand he described, they would place humans in the Americas at least 75,000 to 50,000 years earlier than most scholars currently believe. The eminent geographer George Carter (1980a) used Rogers's description from Tecolote Canyon to support his controversial claim that Milling Stone peoples lived along the southern California Coast since Last Interglacial times, about 125,000 years ago. Carter's claims are viewed skeptically by most scholars, although debate about when and how people first colonized the Americas remains highly charged.

Rogers knew little of this in the 1920s, but he clearly appreciated the potential antiquity and significance of the Tecolote locality now known as SBA-106. In describing the site, he noted:

I puzzled for days over this problem, without arriving at any solution. About three weeks after my first visit, after a heavy rain the night before, I again visited the cut. Again I found the roadway blocked with a landslide from the northern face. Again I carefully combed the exposure thus freshly laid bare, and found another ancient mano, imbedded in the boulder debris immediately above the white sand, not more than ten feet from where I discovered the first one. A week later I found a fragment of a metate not more than two feet from where the last mano was imbedded.... It lay directly upon the upper surface of the sand stratum, beneath a mass of boulders. These two objects, like the two previously taken, showed no trace of "water rolling." Only one explanation of the occurrence seems possible to me, namely, that at a period so distant that it staggers us, a primitive people were located somewhere in the vicinity of the present cut. A flood of extraordinary intensity overwhelmed them and buried their utensils upon the beach, or river bed, which is now marked by the stratum of white sand [1929:258–259].

George Carter and other advocates of a very ancient peopling of the Americas often criticize American archaeologists for not looking for

FIGURE 5.2. Pitted sandstone mano from SBA-106 (× .84; drawing by Deana Dartt).

artifacts in sediments older than about 13,000 years, supposedly ensuring that they find only what they expect to find. Since the 1980s, however, we have repeatedly searched the Pleistocene sediments exposed in Lower Tecolote Canyon for evidence of SBA-106 or other deeply buried and very ancient archaeological remains. Careful examinations of the railroad cut through Tecolote Canyon proved negative in the 1980s. In the 1990s, careful monitoring of grading associated with the construction of the Bacara entrance road through the high terrace east of Tecolote Canyon produced evidence of deeply buried soils, ancient wildfires, and a Last Interglacial beach overlying the Miocene shale bedrock. No trace was found, however, of buried artifacts (Vellanoweth and Erlandson 2000:86). Most of our search was conducted on the south side of the old County Road, however, raising the possibility that all traces of SBA-106 had been destroyed by highway construction or that they were restricted to the north side of the highway cut.

Our examination of SBA-74 provided a final opportunity to search for the remnants of Rogers's deeply buried Milling Stone site. Surprisingly, when we least expected it, we found it. In 1997, while walking down an erosional gully north of Calle Real Road, Erlandson found several well-worn grinding stones in the arroyo bottom and another fully encased in a dense clay, sand, and boulder deposit immediately overlying the Miocene shale. On this and several subsequent visits, we collected 12 manos and 14 metate fragments from a 30 m stretch of this arroyo. Most of these were found in the ravine bottom, but five well-preserved manos were found firmly embedded in the semicemented alluvium, two immediately above the bedrock and three 50 to 100 cm above it. Most of the grinding tools are heavily modified by human use (Figure 5.2), with clearly pecked, faceted, and polished surfaces. As Rogers (1929:59) noted, their geological context suggests that the grinding tools have been redeposited by running water, but none are visibly waterworn. Significantly, none bears the scratches or plow scars typical of such artifacts found in surface sites in the area. All are virtually identical, however, to manos and metates found in Early and Middle Holocene sites in the area. Unfortunately, no datable organic remains (shell, charcoal, etc.)

have been found associated with these tools. Near the base of the gully wall, in the same alluvium that contained ancient manos and metates, however, we also found a piece of rusted iron cable that hints at the recent mixing of cultural materials in these deposits.

Aerial photos from the 1930s suggest that this ravine once cut through the north bank of the old coastal highway and may have been the source of the landslide that blocked Rogers's vehicle. If so, the landslide track examined by Rogers and the ravine we discovered may be parts of the same archaeological site. Our investigation of SBA-106 confirms Rogers's description of milling tools deeply buried in alluvium just above a Last Interglacial beach. Where he found no sign of gullying or stratigraphic mixing, however, we found the opposite. We believe that the milling tools were probably derived from a Middle Holocene site (SBA-74) located immediately above the ravine. We can no longer evaluate the stratigraphic context of Rogers's original finds, but aerial photographs suggest that the tools he found atop the ancient beach deposit were probably also embedded in alluvial sediments redeposited by cyclical arroyo cutting and filling during the Holocene. Unless future studies—including the discovery and dating of organic remains associated with the buried grinding tools at SBA-106—alter our conclusions, Carter's (1980a) claim for the presence of a Milling Stone site at Tecolote Canyon dating to the Last Interglacial will continue to be highly unlikely.

SBA-1326

SBA-1326 is a relatively ephemeral scatter of chipped- and ground-stone tools flanking the railroad tracks on the terrace west of Tecolote Creek. Originally recorded by University of California–Santa Barbara (UCSB), archaeologists in 1976, it was believed to be limited to a narrow slice of intact landform bounded on the north by the railroad tracks and on the south by the old frontage road that now services the Bacara property and the Ellwood oil pier just to the west. In 1987, as part of the Bacara planning studies, archaeologists from WESTEC Services excavated 14 shovel test pits and six 50-×-100-cm-wide test units at SBA-1326

(Erlandson and Cooley 1988a). As a result, the site boundaries were expanded to encompass portions of the landforms to both the north and south. During construction of the resort in the late 1990s, all grading or other ground disturbances in the area were carefully monitored by archaeologists and Chumash representatives from Hutash Consultants. Impacts to the northern site area were minimal, so archaeological excavations were limited, and the number of artifacts recovered is relatively small. Excavation of several test pits and careful monitoring of grading in portions of the southern site area provided an opportunity to examine a broader swath of the site. A number of ground-stone tools and other artifacts were collected in this area, but no shell, charcoal, or other datable organic remains were associated with them. Without ^{14}C dates, and with most of the site destroyed by railroad and road construction, we can only speculate about the age, structure, and function of SBA-1326.

Excavations in the late 1980s were located on the north and south sides of the current Bacara entrance road (Figure 5.3). At the time, we also established that a sparse scatter of artifacts extended north of the railroad tracks, in intact soils capping a narrow sliver of land preserved between the graded corridors for the railroad and U.S. Highway 101. Our investigations indicate that SBA-1326 extends for about 150 m east to west, covering the relatively level terrace located between Tecolote and a small unnamed drainage to the west. The depth of the site appears to be defined primarily by the extent of active rodent burrowing, which stops at a dense clay layer underlying the topsoil (A-horizon). In the southern site area, in fact, most ground-stone tools were found at the base of this A-horizon, where they had probably been transported downward by the activity of gophers and other burrowing animals (see Erlandson and Rockwell 1987; Johnson 1989). The sinking of these larger and more conspicuous artifacts may help explain why earlier archaeologists did not recognize that SBA-1326 extended south of the Bacara entrance road.

In this southern area, artifacts associated with SBA-1326 overlap with the northern margins of site SBA-1673. Compared with most other sites in the project area, the density and diversity of

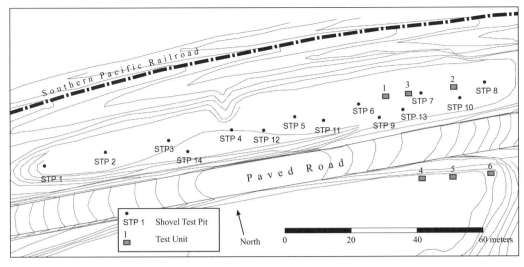

FIGURE 5.3. Map of SBA-1326 showing the location of shovel test pits and test units (drafted by Julia Knowles).

archaeological remains at SBA-1326 are very low. The site consists mostly of chipped-stone artifacts, with a small number of manos and metates also represented. No animal remains—shell or bone—were found associated with these tools, and no features (fire hearths, artifact concentrations, or structural remains) were found during our examinations of extensive soil profiles exposed in road and railroad cuts through the site or in the grading of portions of the southern site area.

Of the 137 artifacts recovered from SBA-1326 (including northern SBA-1673), 48 are ground-stone artifacts made from local sandstones. Almost 90 percent of these are manos and metates typical of Milling Stone sites along the Santa Barbara Coast (see Table A.1). The ground-stone tools also include three mortar and two pestle fragments, artifacts generally found in local sites only after about 6,000 years ago. The chipped-stone artifacts from the site consist mostly of tool-making debris of local cherts and quartzites but also include a handful of tools, including a hammer stone, a core, a core/chopper, a biface, an undifferentiated projectile point fragment, and several retouched or utilized flake tools. The dearth of bifaces and projectile points at SBA-1326 is also typical of Milling Stone sites along the Santa Barbara Coast. Overall, the artifacts recovered from the site suggest that

it most likely dates to between about 6,000 and 4,000 years ago.

Because of the massive disturbance of landforms in the vicinity, understanding the original size or nature of SBA-1326 is difficult. Grading associated with the construction of Highway 101 removed a roughly 50-m-wide swath of the coastal terrace that once existed between the remnants of SBA-1326 on the north side of the Southern Pacific Railroad corridor and the truncated southern boundary of Area A at SBA-75. Given what we now know about the extent of many of the Tecolote Canyon sites, SBA-1326 may represent the southern margin of SBA-75. If this is true, then most of the archaeological materials recovered at SBA-1326 probably are between about 5,500 and 5,000 years old.

The artifacts from SBA-1326 and northern SBA-1673 generally support this connection, especially in the dominance of manos and metates within the ground-stone assemblages from both sites and the presence of some mortar and pestle fragments as well. As with the "flowerpot" mortar fragment from SBA-75, SBA-1326 also produced one large and highly symmetrical pestle that may date to the Late Holocene. If the two sites are portions of what was once a larger Middle Holocene site, then the broader adaptations of the people who left the artifacts at SBA-1326 can be better understood by taking a closer look at the archaeology of SBA-75.

SBA-75

SBA-75 is a large site located on the west rim of Tecolote Creek a few hundred meters from the sea. Situated about 30 m above sea level, the site provided a commanding view of the lower canyon and still overlooks the ribbon of riparian habitat that flanks Tecolote Creek. As noted earlier, the site was first described by Rogers (1929:201), who did no digging but found artifacts on the site surface he considered diagnostic of his Oak Grove and Canaliño cultures. In the 1980s, the site was proposed for development as part of a hotel and resort complex, plans that led to reconnaissance and excavations by UCSB archaeologists (Erlandson et al. 1988). The 1984 work, designed to determine the site boundaries and evaluate its significance, found that SBA-75 encompassed an area spanning more than 300 m east to west and at least 200 m north to south. Unfortunately, large portions of the southern site area were destroyed by the construction of Highway 101 and Calle Real Road. In the 1990s, the County of Santa Barbara also allowed significant parts of the southeastern site area to be destroyed without archaeological investigation.

The 1984 study was directed by Pandora Snethkamp, with fieldwork supervised by Joe Pjerrou. After the fieldwork was completed, Erlandson was asked to oversee the analysis of the recovered materials and the writing of a final report (Erlandson et al. 1988). Field studies began with an intensive surface reconnaissance and systematic surface collections to help define the boundaries and structure of the site. Eighty-one shovel test pits (STPs; about 30 cm in diameter) were then excavated at roughly 10-m intervals to document the subsurface distribution of archaeological materials. This work identified three discrete clusters at SBA-75 (Areas A, B, and C) separated by archaeological deposits of much lower density. To explore these clusters, five 1.0-×-1.0-m test units were excavated near their centers, with two each in Areas A and C and one in Area B. Unfortunately, all the soils from the exca-

vated STPs and test units were screened over ¼-in mesh, which leads to the loss of smaller and more fragile site constituents (fish bones, shell beads, small shell fragments, etc.). To help compensate for this problem, Erlandson later collected three small "column samples" (2,000 cm^3) from Unit 2 in Area C, with the soils processed over 1/16-in screen.

The 1984 investigations provided a wealth of information on the archaeology of SBA-75, but much more could be learned from further careful work. What follows is a summary of what we currently know about the site, including updated information on the site chronology and the relationship of SBA-75 to other Middle Holocene sites in the Tecolote Canyon area. For a more detailed account of the 1984 excavations, readers can consult Erlandson et al. (1988). As we will see, the artifacts recovered in 1984—including a fragment of a flat-rimmed or flowerpot mortar typical of Chumash sites dating to the past 1,500 years—are largely consistent with the site chronology proposed by Rogers, with evidence for occupation by both his Oak Grove and Canaliño peoples. However, we also identified an early Oak Grove or Milling Stone occupation at SBA-75 dated to about 8,400 years ago (see chapter 4).

Site Structure, Stratigraphy, and Chronology

Although SBA-75 is large, the 1984 study showed that each of the three site clusters consisted of a relatively low-density shell midden associated with sparse scatters of chipped- and ground-stone tools. Archaeological deposits in each cluster were less than a meter thick, but this depth appeared to be determined primarily by the depth of burrowing by gophers and other animals. Three ^{14}C dates for single shells from each cluster suggest that the three residential areas may have been occupied sequentially from north to south between about 5,700 and 5,200 years ago (Erlandson et al. 1988:42). The relatively sparse nature of the site deposits, along with this evidence for multiple occupations over a period spanning 500 years or more, might suggest that each cluster represented a seasonal campsite occupied for a limited period of time. Remarkably, however, test units excavated near the center of each

TABLE 5.1. Radiocarbon Dates from Three Clusters at SBA-75

AREA	LAB #	MATERIAL	PROVENIENCE	MEASURED ^{14}C AGE (RYBP)	ADJUSTED ^{13}C/^{12}C AGE (RYBP)	CALENDAR AGE RANGE (CAL BP, 1δ)
A	Beta-137615*	Littleneck clam	Unit 3: 20–40 cm	4560 ± 60	5000 ± 60	5200 (5020) 4910
A	Beta-8297	Pismo clam	Unit 1: 40–60 cm	4990 ± 80	5420 ± 80	5630 (5570) 5470
B	Beta-8299	Pismo clam	Unit 5: 40–60 cm	4780 ± 90	5210 ± 90	5450 (5310) 5250
B	Beta-137616*	Littleneck clam	Unit 5: 0–20 cm	4550 ± 60	4970 ± 60	5060 (4970) 4860
C	Beta-8298	Pismo clam	Unit 4: 40–60 cm	5080 ± 80	5510 ± 80	5730 (5630) 5570
C	Beta-137617	Washington clam	Unit 2: 20–40 cm	7780 ± 80	8210 ± 80	8540 (8410) 8360

Note: Dates calibrated with CALIB 4.3 (Stuiver and Reimer 1993), with a ΔR of 225 ± 35 years. For the ^{13}C/^{12}C ratios, either they were determined by the ^{14}C lab or an average of 430 years was added (Erlandson 1988a); * denotes an accelerator mass spectrometry date.

cluster encountered the poorly preserved remnants of human burials. No artifacts were found with the burials, but the remains of at least three separate individuals were identified in one cluster, suggesting that each area may have been a small village with an associated cemetery (Erlandson 1997a:98). In accordance with the wishes of Chumash representatives, these human remains were left in place and reburied.

In a summary of Middle Holocene sites along the western Santa Barbara Coast, Erlandson (1997a) identified a number of similar Milling Stone sites dating to roughly the same time period. He described these as "secondary" or small villages occupied for relatively brief periods, differentiating them from a few "primary" villages (i.e., SBA-78 at Dos Pueblos) in the area that appeared to have been occupied permanently and a number of seasonal camps or other specialized sites (shellfish-processing sites, etc.) used relatively briefly. The preponderance of secondary villages along the western Santa Barbara Coast appears to contrast with both Early and Late Holocene settlement patterns in the area, an issue we return to later in this chapter. In the meantime, understanding the structure and chronology of SBA-75 has become more complicated with further radiocarbon dating of site materials, the recognition that SBA-1326 may once have been part of SBA-75, and excavations in the lower component of SBA-72.

The initial dating of SBA-75 indicated a relatively straightforward sequential occupation of three discrete areas, for instance, but analysis of three additional ^{14}C samples indicates that the chronology of site use is more complicated (Table 5.1). Dating of an estuarine shell fragment from Area C suggests that at least the northern site area was also used as much as 8,500 years ago. This situation is reminiscent of SBA-69 at Winchester Canyon, which also appears to have been occupied during both the Early and Middle Holocene. This makes interpreting the nature of the Middle Holocene occupations of SBA-75 considerably more difficult, especially when key aspects of early Milling Stone assemblages (i.e., the abundance of manos and metates) are similar to those of later Milling Stone sites. Even the sequence of Middle Holocene occupations at SBA-75 is muddled by the new dates, however, with a second date for Area A (c. 5020 cal BP) over 500 years younger than the first (5570 cal BP) and nearly contemporaneous with a new date for Area B (c. 4970 cal BP) that is roughly 350 years younger than the first date (5310 cal BP) for this area.

Some of this variation may be related to the statistical uncertainty of ^{14}C dating, but we suspect that the new dates more accurately reflect the complexity of settlement and land use at SBA-75. There is probably some truth to the idea that three or more discrete occupations took place at the site between about 5,700 and 4,800 years ago. Rather than using essentially discrete site areas, however, these occupations probably overlapped more than previously thought. It is also possible that while one area served as the primary residential area for a group of people, they buried their dead in one of the other areas—a pattern seen in some other early sites along the Santa Barbara Coast. Further excavations and more extensive radiocarbon dating would be required to more thoroughly document the nature of past human occupations at SBA-75. Despite these uncertainties, we can still be reasonably confident that most of the archaeological materials recovered from the site date to a fairly narrow window of time, between about 5,700 and 4,800 years ago.

Artifacts and Technology

Although relatively few time-sensitive artifacts were recovered at SBA-75, they are largely consistent with this chronology. Altogether, 955 artifacts were recovered from the surface collections and excavations (Table A.2). About 93 percent of these were chipped-stone tool-making debris, mostly small and unmodified flakes and chunks produced as siliceous cobbles were worked into tools and tools were used, resharpened, or reworked. Other products of this manufacturing include 28 chipped-stone tools, seven cores, and a hammer stone. The tools include 13 expedient flake tools only marginally modified or used, 10 biface fragments, and five projectile point fragments. The points all appear to be pieces of dart tips used with an atlatl (throwing board). Only three of the point fragments retain diagnostic features, with one side-notched specimen and two contracting-stem points. Several similar points, including a large side-notched blade, were examined in a small artifact collection a local resident reported picking up on the site surface. Large side-notched points are typical of Middle Holocene assemblages, and contracting-stem points are also found in sites of the Santa Barbara Coast dated after about 5,000 years ago.

Overall, the chipped-stone artifacts from SBA-75 are made up mostly of local rock types. By weight, 47 percent of the assemblage consists of Monterey cherts local to the western Santa Barbara Coast, although some may have come from the Vandenberg region. Another 40 percent consist of Franciscan chert, which can be found locally but is more abundant in the Santa Ynez Valley. The rest of the chipped-stone assemblage is made up of other cherts (7.5 percent, of uncertain origin), local quartzites (5 percent) and siliceous shale (.4 percent), and very small amounts of fused shale and obsidian. Two small flakes of fused shale probably came from a Santa Ynez Valley source, but they could have come from more distant outcrops in Ventura County. The only artifact that indicates long-distance trade consists of a small obsidian flake from Area C, which probably came from the southeastern Sierras. Small amounts of obsidian are often found in Middle Holocene sites of the Santa Barbara Coast, but they usually consist of small pressure flakes too small to be recovered in the ¼-in screens used to process the excavated soils at SBA-75.

Attesting to the importance of plant foods to the occupants of SBA-75, 27 ground-stone tools were recovered. These include 12 metates and 11 manos, grinding tools probably used primarily to grind small seeds. Also recovered were three mortar fragments and one pestle. One of the mortars and the pestle appear to have broken during manufacture. This mix is typical of late Milling Stone sites, with the presence of some mortars and pestles also consistent with a Middle Holocene occupation.

Artifacts of shell and bone are either rare or absent in the assemblage. One spire-removed *Olivella* bead and a whole *Olivella* shell found in a test unit in Area C are the only shell artifacts identified. A few other minerals that appear to be artifacts were also recovered. These include small amounts of tar (asphaltum), which is still found on local beaches and was used by the Chumash as a glue or sealant. A few fragments of red ochre, an oxidized iron-rich rock used as a pigment or for medical purposes, were also found near a human burial in Area C. In the same area, a small fragment of a quartz crystal was found. Quartz crystals were used by the Chumash in a variety of ceremonial and healing rituals.

Faunal Remains

Shellfish. In the five test pits excavated at SBA-75, almost 5 kg (11 lbs) of marine shell were recovered, nearly all of it from Areas C and A. More than half (2.64 kg) of this shell was recovered from a single

20 cm level in Unit 1 of Area A, where a cairn of Pismo clam shells was lain over a human burial. These shells may have served as an offering of food for the dead individual. Although attesting to the symbolic significance of shellfish to the site occupants, the shell cairn may also overemphasize the economic importance of Pismo clams at the site. The exclusive use of ¼-in screens to recover archaeological materials from the test units also contributes to this effect, for the smaller or relatively fragile shells of mussels and some other shellfish (and fish bones) often fall through such screens. After processing three small (2,000 cm³) column samples excavated from the wall of Unit 2 over ¹⁄₁₆-in screens, for instance, Erlandson et al. (1988:61) showed that roughly half of the shell (primarily mussels) in the larger unit passed through ¼-in mesh.

Overall, only 12 different types of shellfish were identified at SBA-75, and just two species make up almost 98 percent of the recovered shell (Table A.3). As is the case at SBA-72, the assemblage is dominated by species found in intertidal habitats of the open coast. Pismo clam shells dominate at all three clusters, making up almost 89 percent of the site total and a minimum of 72 percent of the shell from any particular area. The California mussel is the only other shellfish that contributes more than 1 percent of the sample—making up about 9 percent of the total and at least 22.5 percent of the shell from Area C. These two open-coast species dominate the assemblage, but the remains of estuarine shellfish (*Saxidomus*, *Cerithidea*, *Chione*, etc.) were present in all three site areas. Estuarine taxa make up only about 2 percent of the overall SBA-75 shellfish assemblage, but they are more common in Area C, where they contribute nearly 5 percent of the recovered shell. These taxa make up only about .2 percent of the shell recovered from Area A and about 1.6 percent of the small assemblage from Area B. Even at Area B, most of the quiet-water assemblage consists of *Protothaca*, which can also be found in semiprotected areas along the outer coast.

With a *Saxidomus* shell from Area C dated to about 8,400 years ago, it seems likely that many of these estuarine shells are associated with an Early Holocene occupation of SBA-75. As we will see,

however, small amounts of estuarine shell were also recovered in the stratigraphically sealed lower component at SBA-72N that is firmly dated to the Middle Holocene. Thus, some of the estuarine taxa at SBA-75 may indicate the persistence of a small estuary near the mouth of Tecolote Canyon or the occasional presence of quiet-water species in semiprotected habitats of the outer coast. Alternatively, the presence of small amounts of estuarine shellfish in Middle Holocene components at SBA-75 and SBA-72 might represent occasional collecting forays to the nearby Devereaux Lagoon or Goleta Slough areas to the east or exchange with people who lived in villages around these features (Glassow 1997).

Vertebrates. Some of the same problems (screen size, stratigraphic mixing, etc.) that hinder the shellfish analysis also affect the interpretation of other animal remains recovered from SBA-75. Erlandson et al. (1988:61) noted, for instance, that approximately 90 percent of the fish bone and 75 percent of the other bone originally represented in Unit 2 (Area C) probably passed through the ¼-in screens used to recover archaeological materials from the excavated soils. The remains of smaller animals are undoubtedly underrepresented in the assemblage.

Despite these problems, at least 756 bone fragments (weighing 349 g) were recovered from the five test units (Table A.4). As is often the case in shell middens of the Santa Barbara Coast, the animal bones are heavily fragmented, and relatively few could be identified to a particular genus or species. Many of the bones could only be attributed to general categories such as large, medium, or small mammal and sea mammal, bird, or fish. Much of the bone was also coated with calcium carbonate ($CaCO_3$) derived from the chemical weathering of marine shell in the site soils. Still, the remains of at least 14 different animals were identified, including nine types of fish, three land mammals, and at least one sea mammal and one bird. Some of these bones, especially those of the pocket gopher (*Thomomys bottae*), are probably of natural origin. However, relatively high rates of burning suggest that many of the animal bones were food refuse left behind by the site occupants.

Bone fragments from large to medium-sized mammals make up almost 89 percent (by weight) of the vertebrate remains. These probably come primarily from deer (*Odocoileus hemionus*), but other land and sea mammals may also be present. About 13 percent of the bone was identified as sea mammal, including fragments found in all three site areas. Much of the sea mammal bone is probably from seals or sea lions, but sea otters and small cetaceans were also hunted by Santa Barbara Channel peoples in the Middle Holocene. Small amounts of rabbit and gopher bone were found in Areas B and C, and the remains of unidentified small mammals were found in all site areas. Relatively few of the small mammal bones are burned, suggesting that most of them are natural in origin. Although none of them was specifically identified, a few bird bones were also found in all three site areas. More than half of the bird bone is burned, suggesting a primarily cultural origin.

Finally, the remains of several marine fish were identified, including California barracuda (*Sphyraena argentea*), Pacific mackerel (*Scomber japonicus*), pile perch (*Damalichthys vacca*), giant kelpfish (*Heterostichus rostratus*), a probable surfperch (Embiotocidae) and sardine (Clupeidae), bat ray (*Myliobatis californica*), and probably soupfin shark (*Galeorhinus zyopterus*) and leopard shark (*Triakis semifasciata*). A variety of subsistence activities are represented by these remains, from hunting deer, other land and sea mammals, and birds to fishing in nearshore habitats.

Site Summary

Although SBA-75 has been known to archaeologists for 80 years, investigations at the site have been limited. Before any excavation took place, much of the southern site area was destroyed by road, highway, and perhaps railroad construction. Over the years, much of the remaining site area has been plowed, farmed, and disked. Artifacts have been collected by local workers and residents, and much of Area B was destroyed during grading for construction of a home.

Most of what we know about the site comes from the small test excavations described above. People appear to have occupied SBA-75 on multiple occasions during the Early, Middle, and Late Holocene. The early and late occupations were probably relatively ephemeral compared with the more substantial occupations dated between about 5,800 and 4,800 years ago. Early Holocene use of the site is indicated by a ^{14}C date of about 8,400 years ago on a shell from Area C, where much of the estuarine shell may date to the same time period. From what we know about sites of this age elsewhere on the Santa Barbara Coast, some of the grinding stones (manos and metates) found in this area may also be associated with use of the site by early Milling Stone peoples. Based on his surface observations, Rogers (1929) suggests that the Canaliño (Chumash) people also occupied SBA-75. We cannot be sure what led him to this conclusion, but it may be confirmed by a fragment of a flowerpot mortar—typically found in Chumash sites dating to the last 1,500 years or so—found by UCSB archaeologists in the 1980s. The lower canyon was heavily used during this time period (see chapter 6), and some activities or occupation probably took place at the site by people affiliated with the large villages of SBA-72 or SBA-73. Today, the northern portions of SBA-73 are only about 80 m from the southern edge of SBA-75, but construction of the railroad tracks, freeway, and frontage road destroyed the intervening area.

At least three discrete occupations of the site appear to have occurred between about 5,700 and 4,800 years ago, although these probably overlapped horizontally. People were buried near the center of each residential cluster, suggesting that each area may have served as a semipermanent village for a small group of people. These men, women, and children had a relatively eclectic economy, relying on a mix of resources from the land and sea. The manos, metates, mortars, and pestles suggest that gathering small seeds, acorns, and other plant foods was an important economic activity. Dart points and the bones of large and medium land mammals suggest that hunters searched nearby canyons, foothills, and coastal plains for deer and other animals. The bones of fish, sea mammals, and birds were found in smaller numbers, but the people of SBA-75 clearly hunted and fished in local waters, as well. They also harvested a variety of shellfish from the intertidal zone of nearby shorelines, especially Pismo clams dug from sand beaches and mussels collected from rock outcrops. Erlandson et al. (1988) estimated that more than 75 percent of the edible meat represented by the SBA-75 faunal remains may have come from mammals and fish, but our recent work at SBA-72 (see below) suggests that shellfish were probably more important than previously believed. The combination of protein-rich animal foods and carbohydrate-, calorie-, and vitamin-rich plants foods probably provided all the nutrients these people needed to survive.

Some of these resources may not have been inexhaustible, however. The sparse nature of the shell middens at SBA-75 (and several other Middle Holocene sites of the western Santa Barbara Coast) suggests that some villages were frequently moved, possibly because of the depletion of local shellfish beds (Erlandson 1997a:108). In most recent coastal cultures, women and older people are the primary collectors of shellfish. Because their travel is often inhibited by small children or advanced age, the proximity of productive shellfish beds is an important factor in locating a village. As the productivity of local shellfish beds declines, people must walk farther and farther to gather enough clams and mussels to meet their daily needs. Eventually, as such travel time increases, it makes more sense to move the village to a more pristine stretch of coast where shellfish beds are more productive.

If the clam and mussel beds in the Tecolote area were of limited extent, their depletion may help explain why a number of small villages sites like SBA-75 do not appear to have been occupied for sustained periods of time. In 1997, during construction of the Bacara road bridge over Tecolote Creek, we discovered a substantial shell midden buried beneath the valley floor in the northern area of SBA-72. Located just a stone's throw from SBA-75, and dating to the same general period of the Middle Holocene, this buried midden sheds further light on the activities of the people who once lived at SBA-75. It helps explain the scarcity of marine shell at SBA-75 and suggests that shellfish collecting by the site occupants was considerably more intensive than previously believed.

SBA-72N (LOWER COMPONENTS)

Located at the mouth of Tecolote Canyon, SBA-72 is situated on the low floodplain or valley floor just east of Tecolote Creek. Extending over 200 m (660 ft) north–south and 125 m (410 ft) east to west, SBA-72 was one of the key sites in Rogers's (1929) definition of his Canaliño culture. Embedded in its surface soil he found the remnants of a large Chumash village—now known to be the overlapping remains of two separate villages occupied between about 2,000 and 500 years ago (see chapter 6). As far as we know, Rogers dug no deeper than about a meter (36 in) and found no deeply buried archaeological materials. The first hint that older materials might be present in the northern SBA-72 area (SBA-72N) came in 1979, when UCSB geographers found a shell lens eroding from near the base of the Tecolote Creek bank nearly 3 m below the surface. The geographers interpreted these shells as the remnants of an ancient estuary, but the Pismo clams and California mussels in the shell lens came from sandy beaches and rocky shores rather than an estuary. The shells also appeared to be in a buried soil formed above sea level, indicating that people had carried them to the site. No substantial excavation of this buried site was possible at the time, but a ^{14}C date on Pismo clam shells was obtained, suggesting that the midden was deposited about 5,900 years ago.

In 1989, while examining a recently eroded creek bank just south of this 5,900-year-old midden, Erlandson found a second shell midden eroding from a thin soil about 2.5 m below the surface (Figure 5.4) and stratigraphically above the 5,900-year-old midden. Plans for building the Bacara Resort called for the placement of large amounts of protective fill over SBA-72 before the construction of tennis courts and other facilities east of the creek. Permit conditions required the excavation of eight test pits to document the nature of the archaeological deposits scheduled to be covered with fill. One of these test pits (Unit 89-8, 1.0 × .5 m wide) was excavated through this newly discovered shell midden. The results showed that the midden was composed almost entirely of California mussel (*Mytilus californianus*) shells. A sample of these mussel shells

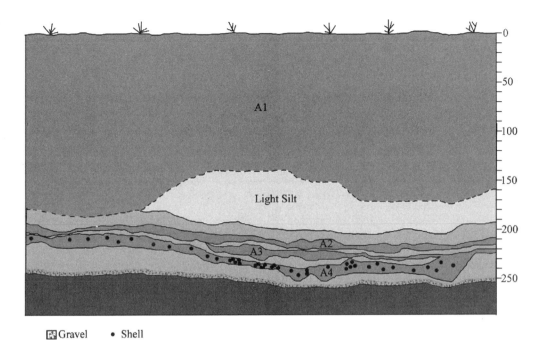

FIGURE 5.4. A 5,500-year-old mussel shell midden identified in A4 soil, 2.5 m below the surface of SBA-72N (redrawn by Melissa Reid from the original field drawing).

was later dated to about 5,500 years ago (Erlandson 1997a:103).

Eight years later, when construction of Bacara began, the first phase included building the hotel access road across the northern part of the property. After peripheral portions of SBA-72 were found to extend into this area, archaeological excavations were conducted where the large concrete bridge support was later built on the east bank of Tecolote Creek. STPs and test units were excavated to test the upper cultural deposits, but these were heavily disturbed by historical farming and oil facilities. Below this upper midden, we found massive floodplain sediments interspersed with a series of weakly developed buried soils (paleosols). About 3 m (c. 10 ft) down, however, a buried midden was encountered that contained large quantities of Pismo clam shell later dated between about 5,600 and 6,000 years old. Several test units were excavated in this lower component to sample the archaeological constituents; then mechanical excavations for the bridge abutment were carefully

monitored by archaeologists and Chumash tribal members (Vellanoweth and Erlandson 2004).

All the materials excavated from the lower components of SBA-72N were fully sorted and cataloged, but two test units (89-8 and 97-4) that were particularly productive and well preserved were selected for detailed analysis. Our interpretations of the site age, structure, and stratigraphy are derived from the cumulative investigations since 1979, but our analysis of faunal remains comes primarily from these two test units.

Site Structure, Stratigraphy, and Chronology

Where they are exposed along the bank of Tecolote Creek, the upper midden deposits at SBA-72 are built in a dark, anthropogenic (human-enriched) soil that can be more than a meter deep. This well-developed surface soil, which probably began forming at least 2,500 years ago, contains the remains of intensive occupation by Chumash people during much of the last 2,000 years. Below the surface soil, especially in the northern site area, creek

TABLE 5.2. Radiocarbon Dates from Middle Holocene Components at SBA-72N

STRATUM	LAB #	MATERIAL	PROVENIENCE	MEASURED ^{14}C DATE (RYBP)	ADJUSTED ^{13}C/^{12}C AGE (RYBP)	CALENDAR AGE RANGE (CAL BP, 1δ)
A4	Beta-28032	California mussel	Unit 89-8 (−2.5 m)	4920 ± 70	5350 ± 70	5580 (5480) 5430
A5	Beta-111649	Pismo clam	Unit 97-4: 40–50 cm	5040 ± 80	5470 ± 80	5680 (5590) 5550
A5	UCR-1116	Pismo clam	Creek Bank: −2.9 m	5270 ± 120	5700 ± 120	5980 (5870) 5720
A5	Beta-111648	Pismo clam	Unit 97-4: 20–30 cm	5400 ± 80	5810 ± 80	6090 (5940) 5890

Note: All dates were calibrated with CALIB 4.3 (Stuiver and Reimer 1993), with a ΔR of 225 ± 35 years. For the ^{13}C/^{12}C ratios, either they were determined by the radiocarbon lab or an average of 430 years was added (Erlandson 1988a).

bank profiles contain 2–3 m of stream-laid (fluvial) sediments deposited by the flooding and meandering of Tecolote Creek over the past 6,000 years. These clays, silts, sands, and gravels also contain a series of weakly developed paleosols that represent periods of floodplain stability interrupted by occasional floods, sedimentation, and channel movements within the unstable canyon bottom. Although not exposed in the creek bank, geological drilling on the valley floor identified deeply buried marsh or estuarine sediments that probably date to the Early Holocene. Thus, the sediments deposited on the floor of Tecolote Canyon tell us about both the environmental and cultural history of the Tecolote area.

Today, Tecolote Creek flows along the western edge of the buried middens at SBA-72N, where its course is fixed by a culvert that channels it under the railroad tracks and Highway 101. A backhoe trench dug to the east of Tecolote Creek exposed an ancient creek channel just east of the midden, however, a feature the midden dipped down toward. A stratum of stream gravel and small cobbles overlying the midden soil suggests that Tecolote Creek migrated westward to its current position sometime after the site was abandoned (Figure 5.5). Between 6,000 and 5,500 years ago, the buried middens at SBA-72N appear to have been deposited on a low stream terrace on the west bank of the creek, just below SBA-75. This was probably a perfect place for the people of SBA-75 to shuck and wash clams and mussels prior to carrying the meat up to their village.

In Unit 97-4, the clam-rich shell midden was up to 110 cm thick, but the density of archaeological materials was concentrated in a 20- to 30-cm-thick deposit (Figure 5.6). The upper 10 cm consisted of clayey sand mixed with marine shells, small caliche ($CaCO_3$) concretions, small amounts of animal bone, and other cultural materials. Below this, the soil was a darker brown as the density of cultural materials increased. Ancient rodent burrows (krotovina) were visible in the buried midden soil, but the extent of such mixing was limited compared with surface soils in the area. The clam midden appeared to be densest between about 20 and 50 cm below its surface, with densely packed mollusk shells in a fine, dark brown soil matrix. Below 50 cm, shell and other archaeological materials were much less dense, gradually decreasing to a depth of about 110 cm. No cultural materials were found below 110 cm, where the soil consisted of sticky, water-saturated clay. A shovel test pit excavated in the bottom of Unit 97-4 hit the water table at about 130 cm, 4.3 m below the surface of the floodplain.

To establish the age of the Pismo clam midden beneath the road bridge, we submitted two well-preserved clam shell fragments to a radiocarbon lab for dating. A shell from the 20–30 cm level in Unit 97-4 was dated to about 5940 cal BP, and one from the 40–50 cm level was dated to 5590 cal BP (Table 5.2). The stratigraphic reversal of these two dates may be related to soil mixing by gophers. At face value, these two dates suggest that the Pismo clam midden may have been deposited over a period of 300–400 years or more. Given the statistical uncertainties of ^{14}C dating, however, it is also possible

FIGURE 5.5. Test Units 97-7 and 97-9 in the lower component at SBA-72N. The shell midden, just beneath the signboard, dips to the east and is overlain by stream gravel left by Tecolote Creek as it migrated across the site after it was abandoned (photo by Bruno Texier).

FIGURE 5.6. Stratigraphic profile of Test Unit 97-4 at SBA-72N, showing a 5,800-year-old Pismo clam midden (photo by Bruno Texier).

that the midden was deposited during a much shorter interval. When averaged with the date of 5870 cal BP for clam shell collected from a similar depth in 1979, the dates from this midden stratum suggest an occupation about 5,900 to 5,700 years old (Vellanoweth and Erlandson 2004). Once this area of the site was abandoned, 30 to 40 cm of additional soil accumulated on top of this shell midden before Tecolote Creek moved westward toward its present position.

The smaller mussel shell midden located about 40 m downstream and slightly higher in the stratigraphic profile appears to have been deposited about 5,500 years ago, probably between 100 and 300 years after the Pismo clam midden. No more than about 10 cm thick and exposed for a distance of only about 8 to 10 m in the creek bank, this mussel shell midden appears to represent a single relatively brief period of occupation. Nonetheless, at one time the mussel midden appears to have contained hundreds of kilograms of marine shell.

Artifacts and Technology

Although nearly 8 m³ of archaeological sediments were hand excavated from the clam midden at SBA-72N, few artifacts were found, and none of these was temporally diagnostic. The only artifacts recovered from the test units and STPs are pieces of Monterey chert tool-making debris, an obsidian flake, and small amounts of burned rock, charcoal, asphaltum, and possible red ochre. The obsidian flake is too small for geochemical identification, but most obsidian from Tecolote Canyon sites comes from the Coso Volcanic Field in the central Sierra Nevada Mountains (see chapter 6). Two *Olivella* barrel beads and a unifacial mano fragment made of granitic rock were found when the remaining deposit in the bridge abutment area was mechanically excavated. These are generally consistent with the ¹⁴C chronology for the midden deposit.

No artifacts were recovered from Unit 89-8 in the buried mussel midden. The scarcity of artifacts in the two Middle Holocene components at SBA-72N suggests that little or no technology was needed to perform the activities conducted at the site. The dearth of burned rock, charcoal, and other cultural debris also suggests that the site was used

for a limited range of activities by people who lived elsewhere.

Faunal Remains

Several hundred kilograms of marine shell were recovered from our excavations in the Middle Holocene components at SBA-72, but only samples of this material were analyzed in detail. Animal bone was much less abundant, suggesting that the site was used largely for processing shellfish collected along the nearby coastline. As we will see, dramatic differences in the types of shell represented in the two middens suggest that the local shoreline may have undergone major changes during a few centuries of the Middle Holocene.

Pismo Clam Midden. From the Pismo clam midden, we recovered 68.6 kg (150.9 lbs) of marine shell in Unit 97-4 (Table A.5). This is a very high density of shell (62.4 kg/m³) for sites along the Santa Barbara mainland coast, but the density was considerably higher in the concentrated center of the midden. Although subject to some limited disturbances (rodent burrowing, etc.), the shell was largely unweathered and well preserved. A few shells were too fragmented, burned, or stained to identify, but over 99 percent of the shell was identifiable to species. Many of the shells appear to have been burned, with some obviously charred and blackened and others only slightly discolored. Small hairline fractures and blotchy stains on some shell surfaces suggest that they may have been steamed during cooking.

At least 20 different types of shellfish were identified in Unit 97-4, but Pismo clam dominates with almost 85 percent of the shell. Thus, stable and surf-swept sandy beaches of the outer coast appear to have been the primary habitat in which shellfish were collected. Measurements for 285 whole Pismo clam shells range from 75.1 mm to 19.2 mm long, with an average shell length of 39.9 mm. Rocky shorelines contributed most of the rest of the shellfish, including California mussels, which constitute about 14 percent of the shell assemblage. Other rocky coast shellfish are represented by small amounts of acorn and gooseneck barnacles, sea urchin, red abalone, small chitons (probably *Mopalia* and *Stenoplex* spp.), turban and top snails, platform mussels, limpets, rock scallop, and probably crab. Several species more typical of protected habitats are also represented, including Venus, Washington, and littleneck clams, as well as oyster. These species are most common in estuaries along the Santa Barbara Coast, but Washington clams, littleneck clams, and oysters can all be found occasionally in pocket beaches or other outer coast settings.

In contrast to the very high density of marine shell found in Unit 97-4, only 357 fragments (44 g) of animal bone were recovered. Several small caliche ($CaCO_3$) concretions in the midden had bone fragments inside them, so bone may have been more abundant at one time. It is also possible that occasional flooding could have removed some lighter elements such as fish bones. Of the bones recovered, medium/large mammals make up about 11 percent of the fragments and 56 percent of the weight. Two pinniped teeth were also identified, but these could not be attributed to a particular species. About 4 percent of the bone came from fish, with surfperch and bat ray the only taxa identified. The few small rodent, reptile, or amphibian bones identified are probably all of natural origin. Unfortunately, almost 78 percent of the assemblage (277 pieces) consists of tiny fragments of undifferentiated bone too small or weathered to be identified. These weigh 16.3 g or about 37 percent of the weight total.

California Mussel Midden. No animal bone was recovered in Unit 89-8, which produced 27.6 kg of marine shell. This represents a shell density of approximately 552 kg (> 1,200 lbs) per cubic meter, an extremely high value for Santa Barbara Channel shell middens. The pattern of shellfish exploitation is also dramatically different than that documented for the Pismo clam midden located upstream. California mussels contribute over 99.9 percent of the shell recovered in Unit 89-8, and not one Pismo clam shell was found. Only six other taxa were identified—acorn barnacle, platform mussel, gooseneck barnacle, littleneck clam, and undifferentiated crab and gastropod—and all were present in very small amounts. Clearly, the shellfish collecting represented in the mussel stratum at

SBA-72N took place virtually exclusively in rocky intertidal settings. We will never know how large this mussel midden originally was or how much shell it contained, but it seems likely that it once contained hundreds of kilograms of mussel shells and little else.

Site Summary

Our excavations in the lower components at SBA-72N provide important evidence about the nature of local environments and some of the more specialized human behaviors that took place in Lower Tecolote Canyon during the Middle Holocene. The dynamic nature of the Tecolote Creek channel and canyon-bottom landforms may have discouraged permanent settlement at SBA-72 during the Middle Holocene. From the evidence we have, these buried middens appear to have been shellfish-processing camps where clams, mussels, and other shellfish were shucked, cleaned, and possibly cooked or dried. These are not the ephemeral "dinner-time" camps described by Meehan (1982) for recent Australian Aborigines, however, as each component appears to contain hundreds or even thousands of kilograms of discarded shell. If the buried clam and mussel components were short-term shellfish-processing camps, they were probably associated with the village occupations of SBA-75. This is especially true of the Pismo clam component, the dates for which overlap with the residential loci at SBA-75, located on the west rim of Tecolote Canyon about 100 m northwest of SBA-72N.

Roughly 5,800 years ago, people living at SBA-75 harvested thousands of Pismo clams from a wave-swept sandy beach near the mouth of Tecolote Canyon. At the time, prior to thousands of years of coastal erosion and sea cliff retreat, Tecolote may have merged with Winchester Canyon to form a wider canyon mouth with a relatively stable sandy beach (Erlandson et al. 1988). Evidence from SBA-72N suggests that these people processed much of the shellfish they collected away from their residential village, shucking and cleaning them beside the creek below the village and leaving the shells behind. Just a few centuries later, however, the mussel midden at SBA-72N suggests that the local shoreline may have changed dramatically from a sandy beach to a predominantly rocky coast (Vellanoweth and Erlandson 2004). An abundance of Pismo clams in several later components in the area suggests that such changes may represent short-term geological phase shifts between beach types—changes governed by local or episodic fluctuations in sand supply or erosional cycles. Such short-term environmental changes might be expected at a time when coastlines and coastal streams were adjusting to major changes in sea level and shoreline dynamics.

The buried components at SBA-72N, with their limited occupations and focused activities, differ from village sites in the area that contain evidence for longer and more diversified occupation, including a wider array of artifacts and features more typical of village sites. Significantly, these small buried sites also provide higher-resolution records of local cultural and environmental changes, allowing archaeologists to isolate events and behaviors that are blurred in many larger village sites in the area where burrowing animals, plowing, and other disturbances have mixed materials from multiple occupations.

SBA-71

As discussed in chapters 4 and 6, SBA-71 was occupied on multiple occasions during the Early, Middle, and Late Holocene, although most evidence for site use comes from the period between about 2,000 and 1,500 years ago. Several lines of evidence suggest that Middle Holocene occupation of the site may have been relatively significant, but identifying the extent and nature of this is difficult because of the mixing of materials from multiple occupations and extensive historical developments within the site area. Here we summarize what can be said (or speculated) about Middle Holocene use of the site, leaving a more detailed discussion of the site structure and contents to chapter 6.

SBA-71 is one of the largest and most heavily investigated sites in the Tecolote Canyon area. Major excavations were conducted by Rogers in the 1920s and Warren and King in 1971 (DuBarton 1991; King 1980), with more limited excavations by archaeologists from UCSB in 1979–1980 (Korn-

feld et al. 1980) and Hutash Consultants in 1997. The two major excavations focused on a cemetery in the southern site area, where the heaviest concentration of artifacts and other cultural debris was also centered. Rogers (1929:185) found the remains of at least 73 human burials in this cemetery area (King 1980:40), most of which he attributed to the Canaliño and a village site now known to date between about 2,200 and 1,300 years ago. Among the human burials Rogers identified in this southern site area were three whose characteristics do not fit with the Canaliño interments. The Canaliño—or ancestral Chumash—typically buried their dead in flexed positions with knees drawn up toward the head. These three distinctive skeletons, found on the southern periphery of the Canaliño cemetery, were buried in an extended or full-length position more typical of Middle Holocene burials on the Santa Barbara Coast (Erlandson 1997a:98). One of these burials (2A-1) had no associated artifacts but was found adjacent to a large rock cairn that also had human bones in it. One of the extended burials (4G-1) was found with a mano, a "conch" shell, and a "worked egg-shaped stone" (King 1980:41). The presence of extended burials at SBA-71 suggests that the occupation of the site during the Middle Holocene was sustained enough to require several human interments—typical of village occupations in the Santa Barbara Channel area. Although only three or four of these burials were found in the southern site area, an unknown amount of this area has eroded into the sea. Rogers (1929:183) also depicted the occupation of the site by the Hunting people as being much more extensive than the others, extending well north of the Oak Grove and Canaliño components.

In his analysis of beads and ornaments recovered from SBA-71, Chester King (1980:30) identified one or two from the southern site area that are generally thought to be diagnostic of the Middle Holocene. One of these is a rectangular bead made from *Olivella* shell, a type found through much of California (and beyond) between about 6,000 and 3,500 years ago. To determine the age of the Middle Holocene use of SBA-71, we submitted a tiny fragment of this bead for accelerator mass spectrometry ^{14}C dating. The age of the bead, estimated at 3720 ± 40 RYBP and calibrated to about 3370 cal BP, suggests that the occupation dates to about 3,400 years ago. In summarizing the results of Warren and King's 1971 excavations at SBA-71, DuBarton (1991) concluded that most of the large artifact assemblage is associated with later occupation (see chapter 6). She described several artifacts that may be associated with the Middle Holocene occupation, however, including five rectangular *Olivella* shell beads and a large side-notched dart point made from obsidian. Some of the ground-stone tools (manos, mortar fragments, etc.) and contracting-stem projectile points common in the assemblage may also date to the Middle Holocene. Finally, in the northern site area a cemetery desecrated by looters in 1986 and a large stone cairn feature documented by Hutash archaeologists in 1997 may also date to the Middle Holocene.

MIDDLE HOLOCENE GEOGRAPHY OF THE TECOLOTE AREA

The geography of the Tecolote Canyon area changed dramatically during the Middle Holocene. These changes had repercussions for the people who lived in the area. Although there were undoubtedly broader changes in climate, vegetation communities, and the animals that lived in them, geographic changes are most evident in the dynamic nature of local coastlines, which can be reconstructed from the types of shellfish people harvested while living in the area.

During the Middle Holocene, local shorelines continued to adjust to sea level changes governed largely by the shift from glacial to interglacial climates. During the Early Holocene, rapidly rising sea levels flooded the canyon mouths, creating a sizable estuary in the lower reaches of Tecolote and Winchester canyons. This estuary was a low-energy environment where sediments carried by coastal streams accumulated and dropped as stream flows decelerated abruptly on entering the sluggish estuarine waters. Between 7,000 and 6,000 years ago, sea level rise slowed dramatically, changing the dynamics that created an estuary at the canyon mouth. Beginning about 7,000 years ago sedimentation probably outpaced sea level rise, causing many of the estuaries of the Santa Barbara Coast

to gradually fill in. In the Tecolote Canyon area, this process probably gradually transformed saltwater marsh habitats at the head of the estuary into freshwater marsh, then to riparian habitats, and eventually to well-drained stream terraces that supported oaks and other relatively drought-tolerant vegetation.

These processes are documented not just in the Tecolote Canyon area but along much of the western Santa Barbara Coast (see Erlandson 1994, 1997a). They are evident in the shellfish assemblages from archaeological sites and along the banks of Tecolote and Winchester creeks, where several meters of alluvial sediments (primarily sands, gravels, and silts) underlie the relatively flat stream terraces of the modern canyon floors. Soils buried in these terrace sequences testify to periods of relative stability, when sedimentation slowed dramatically or ceased. Geological evidence from SBA-72 and from terrace deposits up the length of the canyons suggest that these stream terraces and other canyon-floor habitats were relatively unstable during the Middle Holocene. This helps explain why most of the more permanent settlements in the area were located on the bluffs and canyon rims in the area.

As sea level rise slowed and coastal estuaries gradually filled in, more sediment reached the outer coast, creating more extensive sandy beach habitats. The expansion of sandy beach habitats was also fueled by coastal erosion as the sheer cliffs that mark much of the southern California Coast began to form (Graham et al. 2003; Inman 1983). The accumulation of beach sand also contributed to the formation of sandbars or spits across canyon mouths. There is also some evidence that climate patterns were generally warmer and dryer during the Middle Holocene, and reduced stream flows may have encouraged periodic blockages of coastal canyons by these sand spits. Once the tidal circulation of such estuaries was blocked, they rapidly became warmer and less saline, conditions that destroyed the diverse estuarine fauna that attracted humans and other animals to such estuaries for millennia.

By about 6,000 years ago, most of the relatively small estuaries that once existed along the western

Santa Barbara Coast had effectively disappeared (Erlandson 1997a), although the larger estuaries that indented the broader coastal plains behind Goleta and Santa Barbara continued to exist. With many of the embayments that had once indented the coastline gone, the total length of available coastline was reduced, along with the diversity of intertidal and nearshore resources available to humans. Localized events such as earthquakes or severe floods could have rejuvenated such small estuaries occasionally, but archaeological evidence suggests that this was uncommon and that those that did form were small and short-lived. In their place were broad swaths of sandy beach interspersed with stretches of rocky intertidal. Evidence from the buried midden lenses at SBA-72N suggests that local shorelines may, at times, have fluctuated between sandy and rocky states (Vellanoweth and Erlandson 2004).

During the Middle Holocene, coastal plain and riparian habitats continued to shrink, albeit more slowly than during previous millennia. The reduction of the coastal plain, already narrow in the Tecolote Canyon area, occurred gradually as sea cliff erosion progressed at rates that may have averaged 7.5–15 cm (3–6 in) per year. Riparian habitats along the length of the canyons probably gradually succumbed to progressive sedimentation along stream banks. The effects of these changes were probably less dramatic than the coastal dynamics evident in the shellfish assemblages, but over the centuries they, too, had appreciable effects on local people.

THE PEOPLE OF TECOLOTE IN THE MIDDLE HOLOCENE

Several of the eight sites in the Tecolote area known to have been occupied during the Middle Holocene appear to have been villages with small discrete cemeteries. These include SBA-75, where three loci may represent separate occupations, and possibly SBA-69, as well. Although major Middle Holocene residential bases may have existed at SBA-53 in the Goleta Slough area (Glassow 1997) and at Dos Pueblos west of Tecolote (Erlandson 1997a), village locations in the intermediate area may have shifted frequently, possibly in response to the local depletion of shellfish beds. Village sites, campsites, and specialized sites in the area may have been used by people from SBA-53 or SBA-78, perhaps by subgroups who established peripheral settlements occasionally in response to resource shortages or social stresses. Alternatively, there may have been a distinct social group that lived in the area between Dos Pueblos and the Goleta Slough area, a group that moved more frequently because its primary resource areas were less concentrated, less productive, and more susceptible to periodic depletion.

For the Middle Holocene, only the period from about 6,000 to 4,500 years ago is relatively well documented in the Tecolote area. By combining what we have learned from the Tecolote sites with what is known from sites of the broader western Santa Barbara Coast, however, we can reconstruct a reasonable picture of the nature of Middle Holocene subsistence, technology, and ecology. In our view, the picture that emerges reflects a combination of cultural continuity, culture change, and adaptive diversity.

The clearest evidence for cultural continuity comes from the persistence of a basic Milling Stone pattern from at least 9,000 years ago well into the Middle Holocene. This persistence is seen in both the Tecolote area—in the continued dominance of manos and metates at SBA-75 and SBA-1326, for instance—and also the broader Santa Barbara Coast (see Erlandson 1997a). At Tecolote, a Milling Stone pattern persisted until at least 4,500 years ago. At SBA-1900, about 12 km west of Tecolote, a similar Milling Stone assemblage appears to be well dated to about 3,000 years ago. The cultural continuity observed at these sites—technological, economic, and probably cultural—spans as much as 6,000 years. It signals the continuing economic importance of small seeds, a dietary staple for the Chumash into historic times.

Despite this fundamental continuity, evidence for cultural change is also present along the Santa Barbara Coast during the Middle Holocene. At SBA-75, SBA-1326, and possibly SBA-74, for instance, stone mortars and pestles appear to have been added to the milling technology. We cannot be certain that the few mortar and pestle fragments found at these sites are not later intrusions, but their presence in local sites by about 5,000 to 6,000 years ago is consistent with other evidence from the Santa Barbara Coast (Erlandson 1997a; Glassow 1997). The widespread use of mortars and pestles is generally believed to be related to an intensified use of acorns and other starchy plant foods. Because acorns contain toxic tannic acids that must be laboriously leached away, a shift toward acorns is generally thought to signal both an expansion of the diet and an intensification of labor.

Also added to the technological inventory in the Middle Holocene were new types of projectile points, including large side-notched and contracting-stem dart points used with atlatls. Large side-notched dart points probably first appeared in the area roughly 6,000 years ago, but they appear to have been replaced by contracting-stem points between about 5,000 and 4,500 years ago. As atlatls and darts were used in the Early Holocene, their persistence can be seen as evidence for cultural continuity, but the greater numbers of points (and animal bones) found in Middle Holocene sites suggest that the importance of hunting land and sea mammals generally increased through time. Fishing also may have increased in importance during the Middle Holocene, but plant foods and shellfish probably continued to be dietary staples for most people.

Finally, there is evidence for considerable adaptive diversity in the Santa Barbara Channel area during the Middle Holocene. While a Milling Stone pattern continued into the Middle Holocene at Tecolote, some Goleta Slough assemblages from sites just a few kilometers to the east are dominated by mortars and pestles. This diversity led William Harrison (1964) to propose that people from two distinct cultural traditions lived side by side along the Santa Barbara Coast between about 5,000 and 3,500 years ago. To us it seems more likely that such local variations in milling assemblages reflect local differences in the abundance of plant foods. Many late Milling Stone assemblages (i.e., SBA-1900) come from relatively narrow stretches of the Santa Barbara Coast, where coastal plain and lower canyon habitats with oak woodlands are limited but seed-rich chaparral communities are relatively abundant. In contrast, mortars and pestles seem to be more abundant where the coastal plain is relatively broad, where estuaries supporting starchy plant resources (cattails, etc.) persisted and larger coastal canyons supported more extensive oak groves. On the Northern Channel Islands, there is even greater evidence for Chumash adaptive diversity. Here, manos and metates are virtually absent (probably because small seeds were sparse), but fully maritime people hunted dolphins and small cetaceans, collected large red abalones, and probably fished more intensively than along the Santa Barbara Coast. Such adaptive diversity probably reflects the varied land- and seascapes of the Santa Barbara Channel area, as well as the decisions individual people or groups made about what activities to pursue in a given area.

If environmental variation within the Santa Barbara Channel area influenced the development of unique adaptations in different areas, the environmental changes that occurred in the Tecolote area over time also affected the people who lived there. Once again, we see evidence for both continuity and change. Shellfish continued to be an important resource, for instance, but the primary locations of shellfish gathering shifted from the shrinking estuaries to the sandy beaches and rocky outcrops of the outer coast. The instability of canyon-bottom landforms in the area continued to encourage permanent settlement on canyon rims, where several sites have produced evidence for settlement during both the Early and Middle Holocene. The gradual but continuing reduction in coastal plain and riparian habitats may also have affected the people of Tecolote to some extent. Along the Santa Barbara Coast, where people have always lived on a relatively narrow strip of land between the mountains and the sea, the shrinking landscape gradually reduced the total productivity of local terrestrial plant and animal resources. As terrestrial productivity declined over the millennia, people diversified the range of resources harvested, intensified the effort invested in making a living, and shifted their economic priorities in response to environmental changes. Some of these responses appear to have included changes in the types of shellfish harvested, the addition of regular acorn processing to the diet, an intensification of hunting and fishing, and a diversification and elaboration of the technologies associated with these and other activities.

Archaeologists often look to such local environmental changes to explain the cultural changes they identify in a region. It is worth noting, however, that some of the cultural changes that occurred along the Santa Barbara Coast during the Middle Holocene—including the appearance of large side-notched points, mortars and pestles, and rectangular *Olivella* beads—first appeared through much of California (and even beyond) at about this same time (Erlandson 1997b). This synchronicity suggests that some of the technological changes evident in the Santa Barbara Channel area were part of a larger process of cultural innovation, interaction, and change. The people of Tecolote did not develop in isolation; they interacted with their Chumash neighbors along the coast, on the islands, and in the interior. The Chumash, in turn, exchanged goods and ideas with neighboring tribes, who also interacted with neighbors more distant from the Chumash. This interaction sphere—one of several large information networks that connected the tribes of California and North America (see Howard and Raab 1993; Vellanoweth 2001)—facilitated the transfer of new ideas and innovative technologies. The people of Tecolote chose which ideas and technologies to adopt, a process mediated by the nature of their dynamic ecosystems, but local environmental changes may not have been the primary cause of some cultural changes along the Santa Barbara Coast. At the same time, the choices the Chumash made contributed to the development of a distinctive maritime Chumash culture. As we will see in the following chapter, the hallmarks of that unique culture are increasingly evident along the Santa Barbara Coast after about 4,000 to 3,500 years ago (Erlandson and Rick 2002) and appeared in the Tecolote area by about 2,300 years ago.

6

The Chumash at Hel'apunitse

TORBEN C. RICK AND JON M. ERLANDSON

Although numerous archaeological sites in the Tecolote Canyon area have been dated to the Early and Middle Holocene, the most intensive occupation occurred during the last 2,300 years when the Chumash and their ancestors established a series of villages clustered around the canyon mouth. Chumash vocabularies collected by linguists and anthropologists after European contact suggest that the Lower Tecolote Canyon area and possibly the villages once established there were known as Hel'apunitse, the Barbareño Chumash word for the shovelnose guitarfish (*Rhinobatos productus*). These distinctive rays, which can grow to be more than 5 ft long and weigh 40 lbs, are sometimes extremely abundant in nearshore waters such as those off the mouth of Tecolote Canyon (Eschmeyer et al. 1983:46).

At Hel'apunitse, the remains of village sites complete with houses, cemeteries, sweat lodges, dance floors, and a variety of other activity areas testify to the large Chumash population living in the canyon during the Late Holocene and the diverse array of activities conducted by these people. Compared with activity during the Early and Middle Holocene, Chumash use of the area appears to have been more intense, sustained, and diverse. The area supported a relatively large population of people who were culturally complex, with an elaborate material culture and intensive maritime activity typical of the historic Chumash who lived along the Santa Barbara Coast (Erlandson and Rick 2002). These people fished, hunted marine and land mammals, collected shellfish, gathered and processed plant foods, manufactured and maintained a variety of artifacts, interacted intensively—and sometimes violently—with their neighbors, lived and died, buried their dead, and made history in the Tecolote Canyon area. Despite heavy development of the canyon since the 1930s, much of this history remains intact, protected by Chumash descendants who still live in the Santa Barbara area today.

The Late Holocene refers to the time period between about 3,500 years ago and the present, including the later "prehistoric" periods, the early "protohistoric" phases of European contact, and the "historic" settlement and colonization of the area by Europeans and Americans. In this chapter, we cover the period from about 3,500 to 450 years ago. Tecolote Canyon has produced only scattered evidence of a Chumash occupation during the Protohistoric period (see chapter 7), and there is no clear evidence that it was occupied historically. Large historic Chumash villages existed at Dos Pueblos Canyon to the west and the Goleta Slough area to the east, however, and it seems likely that the historic Chumash made at least occasional visits to Tecolote Canyon to fish, hunt, and collect shellfish or plant foods.

A number of important events occurred during the last 3,500 years that fostered the development of Chumash complexity, a topic we return to in chapter 8. Data from Late Holocene sites in Tecolote Canyon provide important insights on the

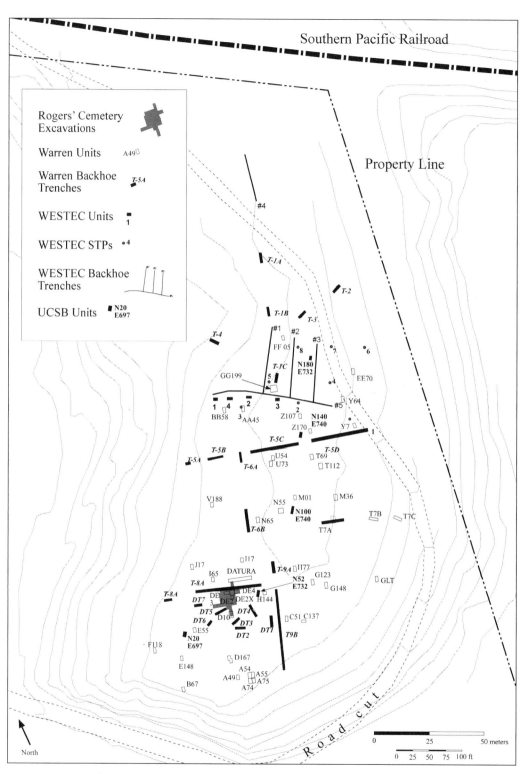

Southern Pacific Railroad

Property Line

Rogers' Cemetery Excavations

Warren Units   A49

Warren Backhoe Trenches   T-5A

WESTEC Units
1

WESTEC STPs   •4

WESTEC Backhoe Trenches

UCSB Units   N20
E697

#4

T-1A

T-2

T-1B   T-3

T-4   #1   #2   #3
FF 05   8   7   6
T-1C   N180   4   EE70
GG199   E732
5   #5   Y64
1   4   2   3   2   N140   Y7
BB58   3 AA45   Z107   E740   1
Z170   Y7
T-5C
T-5B   U54   T-5D
T-5A   U73   T69
T-6A   T112

V188   M01   M36
N55   N100   T7B   T7C
N65   E740   T7A
T-6B

J17   I17
I65   DATURA   T-9A   H77   G123
T-8A   DE4   N52   G148
T-8A   DE   DE2X   E732   GLT
DT7   3   DE2   H144
DT5   D10   DT4
DT6   DT3   C51 C137
E55   DT2   DT1
N20   T9B
F118   E697
D167
E148   A54
A49   A55
B67   A74 A75

Road cut

North

0   25   50 meters

0   25   50   75   100 ft

FIGURE 6.1. Map of field investigations at SBA-71 (drafted by Julia Knowles).

nature and scope of Chumash social organization and lifeways during this important time period. We begin this chapter by describing those sites that have produced evidence for Late Holocene occupation, focusing largely on what is known about SBA-71, SBA-72, SBA-73, and SBA-1674. We review the evidence for the age, structure, and context of each site and then describe the artifacts and faunal remains recovered, the nature of local environments, and the broader adaptations of the Chumash who lived in the area. Finally, we discuss the wider implications of the Tecolote Canyon data for understanding Late Holocene developments along the Santa Barbara Coast.

SETTLEMENT LOCATIONS

The complex of archaeological sites at the mouth of Tecolote Canyon was the scene of multiple Chumash occupations during the Late Holocene, from roughly 2,300 to 450 years ago. Three sites—known today as SBA-71, SBA-72, and SBA-73—appear to contain the remnants of several separate (but overlapping) village occupations. These three sites played key roles in D. B. Rogers's (1929) definition of the Canaliño (Chumash) archaeological culture. Archaeologists have investigated the area since the late 1800s, with additional work in the 1960s and 1970s (see Benson 1997; DuBarton 1991; Kornfeld et al. 1980), and archaeological teams directed by Erlandson and Vellanoweth have worked on the sites periodically since 1986. In addition to the three primary sites, archaeologists have identified several other smaller and less well-defined Late Holocene sites (e.g., SBA-1674) in the canyon, which are also briefly described here.

SBA-71

Situated about 30 m (~100 ft) above sea level on the narrow coastal bluff overlooking the mouths of Tecolote and Winchester canyons, this large site provided a commanding view of the surrounding landscape and access to a variety of marine and terrestrial habitats. SBA-71 was also occupied about 7,700 and 3,400 years ago (see chapters 4–5), but the most intensive use of the site was associated with a Chumash occupation beginning about 2,300

years ago. In the 1920s, the site was used to grow potatoes and probably other crops (Rogers 1929), and it later housed several buildings associated with the Ellwood Oil Field. Prior to construction of the Bacara Resort, grave robbers and relic hunters inflicted heavy damage on portions of the site. The presence of multiple occupations, the remnants of which have been mixed by both natural and cultural disturbances, complicates the interpretation of SBA-71. Nonetheless, the site is extremely significant, for its scientific research potential and its importance to Chumash descendants.

SBA-71 has been excavated by several archaeological teams, beginning with D. B. Rogers in the 1920s, who focused primarily on a cemetery he found in the southern site area. A more systematic exploration of the site took place during a field school directed by Claude Warren (University of Nevada–Las Vegas) and Thomas King (University of California–Los Angeles) in 1971, when 26 backhoe trenches and 47 test units were excavated across much of the site (Figure 6.1). This work was not reported on until Chester King's (1980) study of Tecolote collections and Anne DuBarton's (1991) master's thesis summarized Warren and King's results. During the 1979 University of California–Santa Barbara (UCSB) study, five 50-×-100-cm-wide test pits were excavated along a north–south axis in the SBA-71 area, although the two northernmost units were erroneously considered to be outside the site boundary (Kornfeld et al. 1980:158). The 1979 study produced the first radiocarbon dates and the first detailed faunal data from the site. In the 1980s and 1990s, our work at SBA-71 was limited to exploring the northern margins of the site where construction of the Bacara entrance road required a deep cut and extensive grading. Based on our findings, the site boundaries were extended northward, and the entrance road cut was redesigned twice to avoid impacts to important cultural features.

Site Structure, Stratigraphy, and Chronology
At SBA-71, the most concentrated archaeological materials are found in the southern site area, where a dense shell midden blankets the top of the

terrace to depths of over a meter. Archaeological materials are also found on the steep slope to the west that forms the eastern wall of Tecolote Canyon and a more gradual slope leading down to the mouth of Winchester Canyon to the east. Coastal erosion has removed an unknown amount of the southern site area, so the original extent of the site is not known. Rogers (1929:181), who tended to define the boundaries of sites based on their central midden areas alone, estimated the size of SBA-71 at about 120 m (~400 ft) north to south and 60 m (~200 ft) east to west. UCSB archaeologists expanded these boundaries to approximately 140 m north–south and 100 m east–west (Kornfeld et al. 1980:286). In our work related to the construction of the Bacara Resort, however, we found that low-density archaeological materials extended all the way to the Southern Pacific right-of-way, where they had been truncated by railroad construction. SBA-71 is now known to have encompassed an area at least 240 m long and 120 m wide, roughly twice the size estimated by Rogers. Test excavations and careful construction monitoring showed that the northern site area consisted primarily of a low-density scatter of chipped- and ground-stone artifacts. In the 1980s, looters badly damaged a previously unknown cemetery in the northwest site area. Two Milling Stone cairns discovered nearby during construction monitoring probably were associated with that cemetery. These mortuary features were preserved in place, but no datable materials were found with them, and their precise age remains uncertain. It seems likely, however, that these features are associated with the Early or Middle Holocene occupations of SBA-71.

Rogers focused his excavations on a cemetery in the southern site area, where he found 75 closely packed burials, including at least 69 articulated burials and four reburials (King 1980:40). These interments were attributed primarily to the Canaliño (Chumash) culture, but a few earlier (Hunting period) burials were also identified (Rogers 1929:185). One of the Canaliño burials is the famous "Swordfish Man," buried with a ceremonial headdress made from a swordfish skull and bill, with abalone inlay around the eye sockets, a cape of triangular abalone shell ornaments, and a variety of other artifacts (Davenport et al. 1993; DuBarton 1991:158–159). Ethnohistorical accounts suggest that swordfish were revered by the Chumash, who are thought to have called them "people of the sea." Along with the Swordfish Man, five nearby burials contained most of the wealth goods found in the Canaliño cemetery.

Rogers argued that the occupation of SBA-71 was separate from the villages (SBA-72 and SBA-73) located on the floor of Tecolote Canyon, with people focusing on a former estero at the mouth of Winchester Canyon. He also identified what he interpreted as evidence of a communal dance platform:

> Not far from the center of this site was unmistakable evidence that there had once been located the community dance platform. An elliptical space about one hundred feet in length, extending northeast and southwest, had been entirely cleared of stones and gravel, a thin moraine of this material completely encompassing it. Even to this day, the soil beneath this stratum is very firm, as though it had been tramped [1929:182].

After studying the available data, Chester King (1980) divided SBA-71 into central, northern, southern, northwest, and southeast areas. The central area is the most complex, containing the dance platform, burial areas, and other features. The deposits in this area were generally between about 12 and 24 in deep, but a few units extended to roughly 37 in. Shell was abundant in this area, and several rock features may have been the remains of residential structures (King 1980:37). The northern site area contained a number of rock and burned rock features but little shell. The southern site area also contained rock features, including one that may have been a cooking area. The northwest site area marked the site boundary and contained less burned rock and refuse than the other portions of this site. The deposits were only about 12 in deep in this area, but beads and projectile points were recovered (King 1980:38). Finally, the southeast site area consisted of shallow midden deposits on the slope leading down to Winchester Canyon. These

TABLE 6.1. Radiocarbon Dates for Late Holocene Components from SBA-71

LAB #	DATED MATERIAL	PROVENIENCE	MEASURED ^{14}C AGE (RYBP)	CONVENTIONAL ^{13}C/^{12}C AGE (RYBP)	CALENDAR AGE RANGE (CAL BP, 1δ)
HCRL-5	Marine shell	Burial 5: Tr. 8D-9G	1590 ± 60	2030 ± 70	1410 (1330) 1280
Beta-5320	Abalone shell	"Swordfish Man"	1610 ± 90	2040 ± 90	1470 (1340) 1270
UCR-1120	Marine shell	Unit DE1, Burial 7	1790 ± 90	2220 ± 90	1680 (1540) 1430
UCR-1119	Marine shell	Unit H144, Feat. 1	2110 ± 90	2540 ± 90	2040 (1920) 1820
OS-26446	Abalone hook	Unit E148: 15-46 cm	2230 ± 45	2640 ± 45	2120 (2040) 1970
OS-26447	Mussel hook	Unit F6: 61-76 cm	2350 ± 30	2760 ± 30	2290 (2180) 2130
Beta-140982	*Olivella* bead	Unit A55: 0-15cm	3280 ± 40	3720 ± 40	3430 (3370) 3330

Note: Dates were calibrated with CALIB 4.3 (Stuiver and Reimer 1993), using a ΔR of 225 ± 35 years. For the ^{13}C/^{12}C ratios, either they were determined by the ^{14}C labs or 430 years was added (Erlandson 1988a).

deposits may represent a downslope refuse dump (King 1980:38). King (1980:40) concludes that most of the residential activities at SBA-71 took place in the central site area, flanked by special activity areas such as the dance platform, cemetery, cooking, and refuse areas.

Based on his analysis of the artifacts recovered by Rogers, King (1980) also suggested that the southern cemetery was used by the Chumash between about 1950 and 1550 RYBP and that much of the midden in the southern site area was deposited at the same time. Pismo clam shell from near the base of the midden in this area produced an uncorrected ^{14}C date of 2110 ± 90 RYBP, and three dates are available for marine shell samples from Rogers's cemetery area, including a date of 1610 ± 90 RYBP on abalone ornaments from the Swordfish Man headdress (Table 6.1). Six ^{14}C dates for marine shell artifacts or dietary refuse now bracket the Late Holocene occupation of SBA-71 between about 350 BC and AD 650. We obtained two of these ^{14}C dates for single-piece shell fishhooks from the southern site area: an abalone hook dated to 2640 ± 45 RYBP or approximately 2040 cal BP and a mussel hook dated to 2760 ± 30 RYBP or about 2180 cal BP (Rick et al. 2002). These dates generally corroborate King's (1980) site chronology, but several small triangular concave-based arrow points (Figure 6.2) and a few *Olivella* cup beads in the 1971 collection (DuBarton 1991:63, 135; King and Serena 1980) also indicate some limited Chumash use of the site area after about AD 1300.

Artifacts and Technology

During investigations by Erlandson and Vellanoweth in the northern site area, only small samples of artifacts and faunal remains were recovered. Many of the artifacts came from disturbed contexts, limiting information about their associations or age. Among the 1,391 chipped-stone artifacts recovered, tool-making debris dominates the assemblage with 1,337 specimens (Table A.6). Formal artifacts are limited to eight bifaces, four drills, two cores, 13 retouched flakes, 18 flaked cobbles, five hammer stones, and a scraper. We also submitted two obsidian artifacts from test units at SBA-71 to Northwest Research Obsidian Studies Laboratory for geochemical analysis. Both of these were made from obsidian derived from the Coso Volcanic Field in Inyo County (Table A.7), located in the southern Sierras several hundred kilometers east of Santa Barbara, and must have been acquired through trade. Also recovered from SBA-71 were 46 ground-stone artifacts, including 15 manos, five metate fragments, 12 mortar or bowl fragments, eight pestle fragments, a charm stone, and several undifferentiated fragments of ground stone (Table A.8).

Because relatively few formal artifacts were recovered during the limited site investigations since the 1980s, we summarize the information available on the artifacts recovered by Rogers in the 1920s and Warren and King in 1971 (DuBarton 1991; King 1980). Rogers (1926) found some of the most unique artifacts from SBA-71 during

FIGURE 6.2. Chipped-stone projectile points from Late Holocene Tecolote Canyon
sites. Top: triangular concave-based arrow points; middle: leaf-shaped arrow points;
bottom: large dart points (scale in centimeters; photo by Melissa Reid).

his excavation of the southern cemetery, including abalone shells, finely made pestles, a stone vessel, a variety of personal ornaments, weapons, and ceremonial objects he attributed to his Canaliño (Chumash) culture. King (1980) also noted the presence of fish barbs, bone pins, and a variety of stone and shell beads with the burials Rogers excavated. Outside the cemetery, Rogers found a limited number of artifacts, mostly weapons and crude pestles that are more difficult to associate with a particular occupation.

A large and diverse assemblage of artifacts excavated from SBA-71 in 1971 is described by DuBarton (1991). The chipped-stone artifacts recovered include 114 whole or broken projectile points, with 20 specimens of obsidian and most diagnostic points being contracting-stem varieties. Also recovered were 119 cores, 39 large bifaces, 324 flake tools, 230 drills or perforators, and over 4,000 pieces of tool-making debris. Utilitarian ground-stone arti-

facts consist of 28 bowl or mortar fragments, 19 pestles, 42 manos, and one metate. Also recovered were 141 stone beads and three bead blanks, made predominantly from steatite or serpentine; six awl-shaped tools (abraders?); four steatite pipe fragments; and several undifferentiated ornament or tool fragments. A total of 726 shell artifacts is described by DuBarton (1991:135), including 649 made from *Olivella* shells: 620 wall disk beads, 10 cup beads, seven "whole shell" beads, five rectangular beads, one barrel bead, one bead blank, and five pieces of bead detritus. Other shell artifacts include 57 made from abalone shell (including 48 triangular specimens possibly originally associated with the Swordfish Man burial), six limpet (*Megathura crenulata*) shell rings, single beads of *Trivia* and *Dentalium* shell, and 10 fishhooks—six of mussel (*Mytilus californianus*) and four of clam (*Tivela stultorum*) shell. DuBarton (1991) also reported a small assemblage of bone tools, with nine bone awls, seven flakers of antler and bone, five bone beads, two punches, two possible atlatl (spear-thrower) spurs, a bird bone needle, a compound fishhook fragment, and a rectangular bone ornament. Finally, asphaltum, tarring pebbles, and rocks splashed with tar are also common in the assemblage (DuBarton 1991:149). Although many of these artifacts are probably associated with the Late Holocene occupation of SBA-71—including the fishhooks, steatite disk beads and pipe fragments, *Olivella* disk and cup beads, triangular abalone ornaments, and many of the projectile points— others are not temporally diagnostic, and their age and associations are uncertain.

A small assemblage of artifacts was also recovered by UCSB archaeologists in 1979. The 215 chipped-stone artifacts consist primarily of tool-making debris but include three bifaces and several flake tools (Serena 1980:234). About 83 percent of these were made from Monterey chert, 9 percent from Franciscan chert, 3 percent from quartzite, 2 percent from siltstone, and 2 percent from obsidian. Moore (1980:254) reported a single stone bowl fragment and an undifferentiated piece of ground stone. Finally, three *Olivella* saucer beads and one clam disk bead are described by King and Serena (1980:180).

Faunal Remains

No faunal remains from the limited testing conducted by UCSB, WESTEC, and Hutash archaeologists at SBA-71 were analyzed because this work was focused on the northern site margins where mostly stone artifacts were found. Small samples of shellfish and vertebrate remains from the 1979 UCSB excavations were analyzed by previous researchers, however, and are briefly summarized here. All the faunal remains were recovered from ⅛-in screen residuals, with individual specimens identified to the most specific level possible. No minimum number of individuals (MNI) values are available for these shellfish remains.

Serena (1980) analyzed about 616 g of shell from three levels of Unit N52/E732 in the central site area. He noted that the shell is poorly preserved compared with shellfish remains from other Tecolote Canyon sites but identifies roughly 25 different taxa in this small sample. The shell is dominated by California mussel (74 percent of shell weight), and rocky shore taxa make up about 76 percent of the assemblage. Clams and other bivalves from protected or semiprotected estuary or bay habitats make up at least 12.5 percent of the assemblage (Serena 1980:187), led by Venus clams (*Chione* spp., 5.4 percent), Washington clams (*Saxidomus nuttalli*, 3.5 percent), and littleneck clams (*Protothaca* spp., 3.0 percent). The only other significant contributors are the Pismo clam (*Tivela stultorum*, ~3 percent) found in surf-swept sandy beaches and undifferentiated pelecypod (7.2 percent), which is probably composed primarily of weathered clam shell fragments. DuBarton (1991:142–144) also analyzed nearly 3 kg of unmodified shell recovered during the 1971 excavations, identifying the remains of several taxa (*Cerithidea, Crepidula, Hinnites, Norrisia, Polinices,* and *Tagelus*) not present in the UCSB collection. These shells do not appear to have been systematically collected, however, and are dominated by abalone (64.6 percent), which appears to be primarily from burial areas or of technological origin. Overall, the available data suggest that people at SBA-71 gathered shellfish primarily in rocky intertidal areas, supplemented by bay/estuary and surf-swept sandy beach habitats. Much of this shell probably dates between about 2,300 and 1,300 years ago, but the small sample and the presence of some shell deposited by Early and Middle Holocene peoples limit more specific conclusions.

A small sample (2.3 g) of fish bones from two UCSB units was analyzed by John Johnson, but the limited number of identified elements hinders any conclusions that can be drawn from the assemblage. Between one and eight elements from four types of bony fishes (teleosts)—Pacific mackerel, rockfish, perch, and sardine or anchovy—and a single vertebra from a cartilaginous shark or ray (undifferentiated elasmobranch) have been identified in the sample (Johnson 1980:217). These fish were probably caught in a combination of offshore, kelp bed, rocky coast, and surf zone habitats, possibly using hook and line, nets, and other technologies. Small amounts (~75 g) of bone from other vertebrates from the two UCSB units were also analyzed. These could only be identified to general animal categories, but sea mammal, small mammal, medium mammal, and unidentified bones dominate the sample, with smaller amounts of bird and large mammal remains (Lawson et al. 1980:211). About 8 kg of animal bone from the 1971 excavations at SBA-71 were also examined by DuBarton, who noted that the assemblage was biased by the excavator's heavy reliance on ¼-in screen to process the site soils. DuBarton (1991:147) suggested that mammal bone dominates the assemblage, estimating that land and sea mammals are represented roughly equally.

Site Summary

Despite substantial excavations, the nature of the Late Holocene occupations at SBA-71 remains somewhat obscure, largely because of mixing with earlier components. Much of what we know about the site comes from the study of museum collections resulting from the work of Rogers in the 1920s and the 1971 investigations by Warren and King. The presence of a substantial Canaliño cemetery, probable residential and cooking features, and a possible dance floor suggests that SBA-71 was a Chumash village site. Radiocarbon dates indicate that this village was occupied primarily between about 2,300 and 1,300 years ago, but a small number of diagnostic artifacts also suggest some limited site use after about AD 1300. The artifacts and faunal remains recovered indicate that SBA-71 contains a variety of chipped-stone, ground-stone, shell, bone, and asphaltum-related artifacts, as well as shellfish and vertebrate remains from a variety of terrestrial and marine habitats. The presence of obsidian artifacts suggests that the Chumash occupants actively participated in long-distance trade networks, and the many *Olivella* beads and soapstone artifacts also indicate the existence of established trade relationships with Chumash groups on the islands and in the interior. The concentration of artifacts (beads, ornaments, etc.) associated with the Swordfish Man and nearby burials in the northern portion of the Chumash cemetery at SBA-71 also suggests that wealth and power were not evenly distributed among the residents of the site.

SBA-72

Another large and complex site with a long record of human occupation, SBA-72 is located just behind the beach on the low stream terrace immediately east of Tecolote Creek. Much of what we know about the general structure of the site comes from the work of D. B. Rogers, who dug extensively at the site in the 1920s. By that time, SBA-72 had been farmed intensively for many years, and it was later heavily modified by the construction of oil facilities beginning in the 1930s (see chapter 7). Rogers also noted that a local man by the name of Francisco Leyva had reportedly "dug up everything worth while on the east side of the creek" many years before (1929:191). Given all this activity, it is amazing that substantial and extremely significant portions of SBA-72 survived. Excavations by UCSB archaeologists in 1979 (Kornfeld et al. 1980), a WESTEC Services team in 1988 (Erlandson and Cooley 1988b), and a Hutash Consultants team in 1997 contributed important information on the size, structure, contents, and age of the site, as well as the daily activities of the Chumash people who lived there. Unfortunately, in recent decades this well-known village site was also heavily disturbed by looters, vandals, and grave robbers attracted by the remote location and the shelter provided by heavy brush. Such illegal activity declined after the Chumash community began regularly patrolling the area in the 1980s. Nonetheless, prior to the construction of the Bacara Resort, the site was covered with a thick layer of fill sediments to protect the burials and other cultural features from future depredations.

As described in chapter 5, SBA-72 also contains at least two Middle Holocene components, but these older deposits are buried in floodplain sediments well below the Late Holocene materials. A variety of evidence suggests that SBA-72 was used by the Chumash between about 2,000 and 500 years ago. Because these materials have been mixed by a variety of natural and cultural activities, only a relatively coarse picture of changes in Chumash culture through time is possible. As all these materials date within a roughly 1,500-year period, however, they provide an excellent view of general Chumash lifeways in the Tecolote Canyon area.

In the sections that follow, we summarize D. B. Rogers's work at SBA-72, including the results of recent studies of his collections. We then discuss the UCSB, WESTEC, and Hutash studies at the site. In 1979, UCSB archaeologists excavated seven 1-×-.5-m test units in SBA-72N and SBA-72S, as well as numerous backhoe trenches in the site vicinity. In 1988, WESTEC archaeologists excavated seven more 1-×-.5-m-wide test units in the Late Holocene deposits to mitigate the placement of protective fill over the site. In 1997, archaeologists from Hutash Consultants also excavated several test units in low-density midden deposits in the northwest corner of SBA-72N prior to the construction of the Tecolote Creek Bridge. Additional artifacts were recovered during surface collection and extensive monitoring. For the materials collected during WESTEC and Hutash excavations at SBA-72, we analyzed all formal artifacts from excavated samples, surface collections, and construction monitoring. In choosing samples of Late Holocene materials for detailed faunal and artifact analysis, however, we focused on "control" or "index" units (WESTEC Units 2 and 5 and Column Samples 1 and 5) where the deposits appeared to be relatively intact and fairly large assemblages of artifacts and faunal remains were recovered. In the sections that follow, these materials are described and compared with those recovered and analyzed by UCSB archaeologists (Kornfeld et al. 1980).

Site Structure, Stratigraphy, and Chronology

Located on the canyon floor between about 10 and 15 ft above sea level, SBA-72 is bounded by Tecolote Creek on the west, by the beach on the south, and by the canyon wall on the east. Rogers estimated that SBA-72 extended for about 180 m (~600 ft) north to south and 90 m (~300 ft) east to west. After excavating a series of test units and backhoe trenches (Figure 6.3), UCSB archaeologists extended the site boundaries slightly. During vegetation clearing associated with the construction of the Bacara access road and Tecolote Creek Bridge, low-density midden deposits were later identified in some of the UCSB team's unfilled backhoe trenches that supposedly were outside the site boundaries. As a result, the northern boundaries of SBA-72 were extended to the base of the fill slope for the Southern Pacific Railroad, roughly 700 ft from the beach.

Rogers (1929:198–199) viewed SBA-72 and SBA-73 as a single large village site with a complex organization of features that were all used more or less simultaneously. He noted that the layout of the two sites was symmetrical in many respects, suggesting some "engineering forethought" on the part of the residents. For SBA-72, Rogers described extensive residential deposits containing poorly preserved house remains and other cultural materials:

> The camp site…had evidently endured for a long period, for over the entire area, which is above the normal in extent, was strewn an enormous amount of camp litter, to an average depth of thirty-six inches. This debris is continuous from the original stony, alluvial surface up, except for the occasional intrusion of gravelly detritus in places where the creek in time of flood had, at irregular intervals, invaded the village. It included the ordinary constituents— shells, fish scales, the bones of seal, porpoise, whale and those of land mammals and birds. Few fragments of stone utensils, aside from weapons, were found at this site [1929:192].

Rogers also identified and excavated two cemeteries at SBA-72, one in the northern area and another well to the south. Between the two cemeteries, similar to the layout at SBA-71, Rogers (1929:195) described an oval ceremonial dance area surrounded by a low "moraine" of rocks. Similar features were described in early Spanish accounts of Chumash villages. Near the creek in the southern site area, Rogers also found the remnants of a semisubterranean *temescal* (sweat lodge) about 6 m (20 ft) wide, the perimeter lined with boulders and the interior containing thick deposits of charcoal and ash.

In the northern cemetery, partly disturbed by previous excavators, Rogers (1929) found 53 articulated burials and nine reburials. Among these burials, which Rogers claimed were all males, was a cluster of 17 adults who reportedly died in battle or some other violent confrontation. More recent

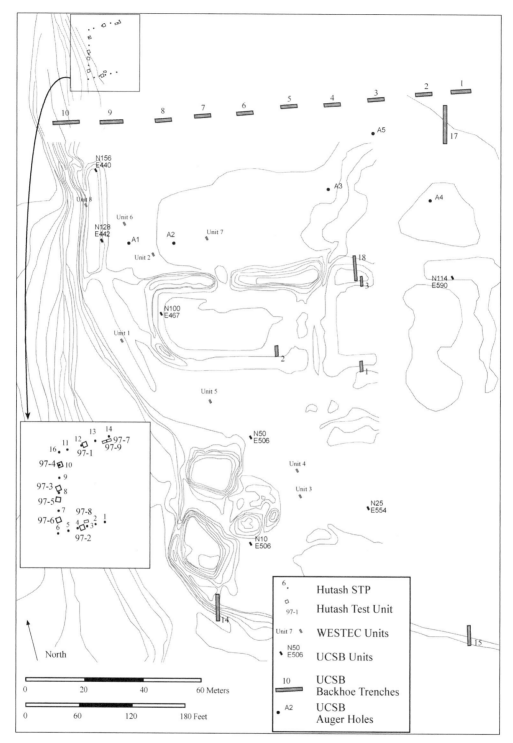

FIGURE 6.3. Map of University of California–Santa Barbara, WESTEC, and Hutash excavations at SBA-72 (drafted by Julia Knowles).

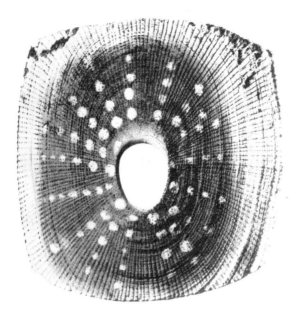

FIGURE 6.4. Painted keyhole limpet ornament from San Miguel Island, a common artifact found by D. B. Rogers in the SBA-72 cemetery (adapted from Heye 1921).

analyses have shown that this northern cemetery contained a mix of males, females, and children but confirm the high incidence of violent death (King 1980:51; Lambert 1994). Based on the abundance of *Olivella* saucer beads, *Megathura* ring ornaments, and abalone disk ornaments in this northern cemetery, King (1980; King and Serena 1980) proposed that it was used primarily between about 1550 and 1350 RYBP. A single uncorrected ^{14}C date of 1540 ± 70 RYBP for marine shell associated with one of the burials confirms this chronology, but calibration to calendar years suggests that the cemetery was used about 1,300 years ago (~AD 650). According to King (1980), wealth items in the SBA-72N cemetery appeared to be fairly evenly distributed.

In the southern cemetery, Rogers (1929) excavated 103 articulated burials and over 70 reburials. In his book, Rogers argued that this cemetery contained mostly female burials, but the burial records for the collection suggest a roughly even distribution of males and females (King 1980). Based on the presence of small *Olivella* and mussel disk beads, *Olivella* cup beads, and *Megathura* ornamented in

this southern cemetery, King (1980) estimates that it was used between about 1050 and 800 RYBP. Several ^{14}C dates obtained for marine shell samples from the cemetery indicate a somewhat wider time range, from about 1270 to 740 RYBP (Table 6.2). After calibration, these dates suggest that the southern cemetery was used for about 500 years, from roughly 1,000 to 500 years ago (AD 940–1420). Some of the most abundant artifacts found in this cemetery are ground keyhole limpet (*Megathura crenulata*) shells that appear to have been used as hair ornaments. Hundreds of these are still housed in the collections of the Santa Barbara Museum of Natural History, and, although no clear painted patterns are evident (see Figure 6.4), many appear to be stained with red pigment. According to King (1980:51), wealth items were concentrated in the southwest portion of the central cemetery area. Also present were several large and decorated whale bone grave markers. One of these, made from the shoulder blade (scapula) of a large whale, had several rows of carved pits, some still containing inlaid abalone shell ornaments (Rogers 1929: 194). Collectively, these features depict a relatively

TABLE 6.2. Radiocarbon Dates from Late Holocene Components at SBA-72

SITE AREA	LAB #	DATED MATERIAL	PROVENIENCE	MEASURED ^{14}C AGE (RYBP)	CONVENTIONAL ^{12}C/^{13}C AGE (RYBP)	CALENDAR AGE RANGE (CAL BP, 1δ)
SBA-72N	HCRL-11	Marine shell	Burial 2	1540 ± 70	1970 ± 70	1350 (1290) 1230
	UCR-1114	Marine shell	N150/E430: 90 cm	1710 ± 90	2140 ± 90	1560 (1470) 1340
	Beta-28031	Pismo clam	Unit 88-5: 140–160 cm	2060 ± 70	2490 ± 70	1950 (1870) 1790
SBA-72S	HCRL-9	Marine shell	Burial 5	740 ± 50	1160 ± 50	560 (530) 500
	UCR-1115	Marine shell	N25/E554: 60–70 cm	780 ± 80	1210 ± 80	640 (550) 510
	Beta-140983	*Olivella* bead	N25/E554: 60–70 cm	840 ± 40	1280 ± 40	660 (630) 570
	HCRL-10a	Marine shell	Burial 5	970 ± 60	1400 ± 60	780 (710) 660
	UCR-1117	Marine shell	Burial 7: Trench 4D	1060 ± 80	1490 ± 80	910 (790) 710
	HCRL-10	Marine shell	Burial 2	1080 ± 60	1510 ± 60	910 (830) 740
	HCRL-12	Marine shell	Burial 1	1200 ± 70	1600 ± 80	990 (920) 830
	UCR-1118	*Olivella* beads	Burial 1: Trench 6B	1270 ± 80	1700 ± 80	1130 (1010) 930

Note: Dates were calibrated with CALIB 4.3 (Stuiver and Reimer 1993), using a ∆R of 225 ± 35 years. For the ^{13}C/^{12}C ratios, either they were determined by the ^{14}C labs or 430 years was added (Erlandson 1988a).

complex cemetery with evidence of interpersonal violence and differences in the distribution of wealth and prestige items.

Rogers suggested that the two cemeteries at SBA-72 were used at the same time by different segments of society (men vs. women), but more recent research indicates that they were used sequentially—the northern cemetery from about AD 650 to 900 and the southern cemetery from about AD 900 to 1450. Since 1980, therefore, the northern portions of the site have generally been referred to as SBA-72N, and the southern portions, as SBA-72S. These northern and southern areas seem to represent discrete occupations from different time periods, but the areas are vaguely defined, the two occupations overlap, and archaeological materials in the central site area cannot always be separated effectively.

Eleven radiocarbon dates now bracket the Late Holocene occupation of SBA-72 between about AD 50 and 1450 (1900–500 cal BP). The radiocarbon chronology supports King's assertion that SBA-72N is generally older than SBA-72S. While this is clearly true of the two cemeteries, for which there are now seven ^{14}C dates, it also seems to hold for the midden deposits in the northern and south-

ern areas. Four ^{14}C dates are available for these residential deposits: two shell samples from SBA-72N dated to 2060 ± 70 RYBP and 1710 ± 90 RYBP and two samples from SBA-72S dated to 1210 ± 80 RYBP and 1280 ± 40 RYBP. After calibration, these dates suggest that the midden in the northern site area was deposited between about AD 50 and 550 (1900–1400 cal BP), and the midden in the southern area accumulated between about AD 1250 and 1450 (700–500 cal BP). If more dates were available from these midden deposits, these occupation ranges would probably be expanded somewhat. Still, the northern and southern site areas cannot be neatly divided into older and younger sections. The recovery of some later artifacts in the northern site area and earlier artifact types in the southern area suggests that people used and occupied much of the site area throughout the last 2,000 years.

Artifacts and Technology

Rogers, who focused most of his energy on excavating cemeteries, recovered a variety of artifacts from SBA-72, including objects made from shell, bone, stone, and other materials. Most of the artifacts were found in the southern cemetery, including bone whistles, shell beads and ornaments, bone hairpins, and quartz crystals (King 1980:52). Other unique items found in the SBA-72 cemeteries include an appliquéd crab-shell rattle, projectile points, a variety of utilitarian items (bowls etc.), paint cups, and clusters of whale bones. The SBA-72 cemeteries also contained hundreds of ornaments made from keyhole limpet (*Megathura crenulata*) shells, including whole shells, pendants, and many rings chipped or ground into square, rectangular, and oval shapes (King 1980).

Archaeological investigations at SBA-72 since the 1970s have tried to avoid cemetery areas, focusing instead on recovering representative samples of artifacts and faunal remains from residential deposits. Sizable artifact samples were recovered by both WESTEC and Hutash archaeologists, which we describe here and compare with those recovered by UCSB archaeologists.

Over 21,000 chipped-stone artifacts were recovered from excavations and surface collections at SBA-72, including roughly 299 tools and 21,267 pieces of tool-making debris (Table A.9). Many of the tools are fragmentary, but a few are relatively complete and diagnostic. These include 83 cores or chunks, 74 bifaces or projectile points, 65 expedient flake tools with retouched or utilized edges, 49 drills or boring tools, 22 flaked cobbles, and six hammer stones. The chipped-stone tools represent a variety of activities, from the hunting and processing of animals to the production and maintenance of chipped stone and other tool technologies used in various tasks.

The chipped-stone artifacts from SBA-72 are dominated by local or semilocal materials such as Monterey chert and siliceous shales, Franciscan cherts, and quartzites. Exotic materials such as fused shale and obsidian are also present. The fused shale artifacts may come from the Santa Paula area in interior Ventura County, but similar materials are now known to be available from other sources, including a Santa Ynez Valley quarry much closer to the Tecolote area. To determine the origin of the obsidian artifacts found at SBA-72, we submitted 19 specimens to the Northwest Research Obsidian Studies Laboratory for geochemical analysis. Sixteen of these artifacts were determined to come from the Coso Volcanic Field in Inyo County, and three others came from the Casa Diablo source in Mono County (Table A.7). These artifacts, obtained from volcanic glass sources roughly 275 km (Coso) and 400 km (Casa Diablo) from the Santa Barbara Coast, indicate that the Chumash residents of SBA-72 were engaged in the long-distance exchange networks that linked California Indian tribes for millennia. The results are also consistent with previous geochemical studies that suggest that the Chumash obtained most of their obsidian from the Coso area (Rick, Skinner, et al. 2001).

Ground-stone tools from SBA-72 were also relatively common, including 31 specimens from excavation units and 25 collected from the site surface (Table A.10). The 56 ground-stone artifacts recovered include 17 mortar or bowl fragments, seven pestles, four manos, two metate fragments, three girdled stones (possible net weights), and a shaft straightener or abrader. These ground-stone artifacts represent a wide range of utilitarian activities, from plant food processing to fishing, and the production of other types of artifacts. Sixty-three ornamental ground-stone beads were also recovered from SBA-72 (Figure 6.5) and are described in more detail below.

For the most part, bone tools from the excavations and surface collections are relatively fragmented and difficult to identify (Table A.11). Although 53 bone tool fragments were recovered, 44 of these are small ground or polished bone fragments that are not diagnostic. The nine identifiable bone tools include seven awl fragments, one wedge, and a possible bipoint or fish gorge fragment.

Beads made from shell, stone, and bone also were common at SBA-72. In the northern site area, 26 bone and stone beads were recovered, including a mammal bone tube bead and 25 soapstone disk, tube, cylinder, and bead fragments (Table A.12). Thirty-six soapstone disk, cylinder, and bead fragments were also found at SBA-72S. Two soapstone beads were collected from the site surface but could not be attributed to one locus or another. Also recovered were 395 beads or ornaments made from *Olivella*, mussel, clam, *Dentalium*, abalone, and other shell types recovered from the northern and southern areas of the site (Tables A.13, A.14). The

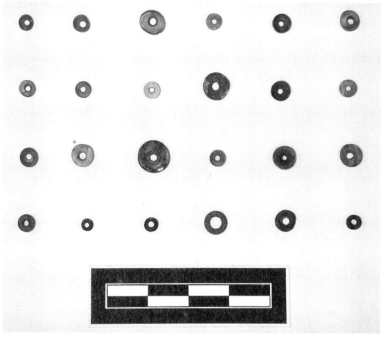

FIGURE 6.5. Shell and stone beads from Late Holocene occupations of SBA-72 and SBA-73. Top: *Olivella* cups; second row: *Olivella* wall disks; third row: *Mytilus* disks; bottom: soapstone disk beads (scale in centimeters; photo by Melissa Reid).

360 *Olivella* beads include 234 wall disks (65 percent), 109 callus cups (30 percent), nine spire-removed beads (2.5 percent), one rectangular bead (.3 percent), and eight bead fragments or beads in production (2.2 percent). Small amounts of *Olivella* bead-making debris were also recovered, with 680 fragments weighing about 114 g (Table A.15). Standardized for volume, this is only about 21 g and 126 fragments of *Olivella* detritus per cubic meter, suggesting that bead making at the site was limited and most beads were acquired through trade. This is typical of mainland Chumash sites where the densities of *Olivella* bead-making debris are much lower than those on the Channel Islands. Among the other shell beads recovered are 20 *Mytilus* disk or cylinder beads, five red abalone disk beads, three money tusk (*Dentalium neohexagonum*) beads, two clam disks, an abalone tube bead blank, a *Megathura* ring, a perforated *Trivia* shell, a punched scallop shell, and an unidentified shell bead.

Other shell artifacts recovered from SBA-72 include 76 fishhook fragments made from California mussel shell and eight fishhook fragments

of abalone shell (Table A.16; Figure 6.6). Twenty-one of the mussel fishhook fragments and five of the abalone have grooved shanks, with one plain shank mussel fragment. Forty-four of the mussel shell specimens and three of the abalone are mid-section fragments. Finally, eight fishhook blanks and two tip fragments made from mussel shell were also recovered.

Twelve small fragments of asphaltum (bitumen) with basketry impressions were identified in the SBA-72 collections. These artifacts suggest that tar was used for waterproofing baskets and boats and as a general adhesive by the people of Tecolote Canyon. Basketry rarely preserves in archaeological sites, but the Chumash were renowned for their weaving of baskets and other items. The basketry impressions preserved in asphaltum represent the proverbial "tip of the iceberg" of a diverse and sophisticated technology that is largely invisible in the archaeological record. Also recovered from the test units at SBA-72 were 24 small tarring pebbles, which were heated and swirled inside of baskets with asphaltum lumps to seal the inside of water

FIGURE 6.6. Mussel shell fishhook fragments (top center), a possible abalone fishhook blank (lower center), and stone abraders (far left and right) from Late Holocene occupations of SBA-72 and SBA-73 (scale in centimeters; photo by Melissa Reid).

bottles. Other artifacts related to the use or processing of bitumen include three asphaltum applicators (usually elongated cobbles with tar on one end) and six cobbles with splashes of tar on them (Table A.17).

For the most part, the artifacts recovered by WESTEC and Hutash archaeologists are comparable to those reported for the 1979 UCSB research. Kornfeld (1980) analyzed 1,494 chipped-stone artifacts from SBA-72, 534 from the northern locus and 960 from the southern. The assemblage consists predominantly of tool-making debris but includes 11 flake tools, three bifaces, and one core. Monterey chert constitutes 73 percent of the materials from the northern locus, followed by Franciscan chert (20 percent), obsidian (2.2 percent), siliceous shale (1.9 percent), quartzite (1.5 percent), and fused shale (.9 percent). The SBA-72S sample is similar, with Monterey chert making up almost 80 percent, followed by Franciscan chert (14 percent), obsidian (2.4 percent), siliceous shale (2.1 percent), quartzite (.9 percent), and basalt (.3 percent). Moore (1980) also noted the presence of a pestle, a bowl, undifferentiated ground stone, a tar-

ring pebble, and two steatite fishhooks at the site. Five bone artifacts were also recovered, including a ground bird bone fragment, a possible fish vertebra bead, and a mammal bone fishhook or barb (Lawson et al. 1980).

Faunal Remains

A variety of shellfish and vertebrate remains were recovered from SBA-72. Because many of the bones are heavily fragmented, burned, or weathered, identification was often difficult. Nonetheless, a relatively large assemblage of shellfish, fish, mammal, and bird remains was identified in the faunal samples from our index units.

Shellfish. Over 28 kg of shell from a minimum of 3,872 individuals and at least 41 taxa were identified from the index units at SBA-72 (Table A.18). Pismo clam shells were most abundant in the two index units, making up about 35 percent of the shell weight and 12 percent of the MNI. California mussel is next, with about 15 percent of the shell weight but 22 percent of the MNI. *Protothaca* constitutes about 9.6 percent of the shellfish assemblage.

Estuarine species are also represented, with *Chione* making up over 4 percent of the shell weight; oyster about 6 percent; and scallops about 6 percent (but 19 percent of the MNI). Most other shellfish types are minor contributors, but they show that people collected shellfish from rocky intertidal zones, sandy surf-swept beaches, and bays or estuaries. Some of the estuarine shellfish may have been obtained from the Goleta Slough area, possibly through trade with the residents of several large Chumash towns that existed in the area.

Of our four analyzed samples, two are from SBA-72N (Column Sample 1 and Unit 2), and the Unit 5 and Column Sample (CS) 5 samples are from SBA-72S. As stated earlier, the SBA-72N materials date between about 2000 and 1000 cal BP, whereas the SBA-72S materials date from about 1000 to 500 cal BP. The samples contain similar types of shellfish, with a mix of rocky intertidal, sandy beach, and estuarine taxa. In the SBA-72N samples, Pismo clam and mussel shell make up about 20–23 percent of the weight in CS 1 and about 10–16 percent in Unit 2. Estuarine species are also common, with Venus clams contributing between 10 and 20 percent of the shell weight in the two units, and oyster making up about 7–13 percent. In the SBA-72S samples, Pismo clam makes up roughly 33–40 percent of the shell weight, followed by mussels with about 14–16 percent and several estuarine taxa that make up less than 10 percent of the shell each.

Serena (1980) described a small shellfish assemblage from SBA-72 that is generally similar to our own. He noted an increase in estuarine taxa through time in the SBA-72S deposits, however, the opposite of what we found. Collectively, these data suggest variability in the types of shellfish gathered by the site occupants, with no clear changes through time.

Fish and Other Vertebrate Remains. We identified fish remains from three index units (CS 1, CS 5, and Unit 2) and other vertebrate remains from four index units (CS 1, CS 5, and Units 2 and 5). All the samples were recovered from ⅛-in screen residuals. Because many of the bones from SBA-72 are highly fragmented or burned, most of the vertebrate remains were difficult to identify beyond the level of undifferentiated fish, mammal, bird, and other bones. Only about 10 percent of the fish bones and 26 percent of the other bones were identifiable to family, genus, or species. Nonetheless, a variety of fish, mammal, bird, and other bones were identified in the collection.

Fish are the most abundant vertebrates identified in the SBA-72 samples (Table A.19). In the three index units, at least 19 teleost taxa and 10 elasmobranchs were identified. Most common among the identified fish bones are sardines or anchovies (clupeids, 47 percent), perch (16 percent), mackerel (10 percent), rockfish (9 percent), labrids (4 percent), and croakers (3 percent). Twelve barracuda, eight yellowtail, and six possible fragments of a swordfish beak were also identified, but each of these makes up about 1 percent or less of the assemblage. For elasmobranchs, 11 elements from shovelnose guitarfish, eight from bat rays, and two from soupfin sharks were identified. In each case, these contributed less than 1–2 percent of the total number of identified specimens (NISP). These fish remains are generally similar to the small samples (66.7 g) analyzed by Johnson (1980), which included perch, rockfishes, croakers, senorita, mackerel, and several sharks and rays.

The fish remains from SBA-72 suggest that people fished in a variety of habitats, including bays or estuaries, rocky shores or shallow reefs, kelp beds, and surf-swept sandy beaches. The presence of swordfish and tuna also indicates that people fished from boats (probably *tomols*) in offshore or pelagic waters. Although numerous shell fishhooks were found in the site, the fish represented suggest that people used a variety of fishing technologies. Nets were probably used to obtain the clupeids and other small fish, and spears or harpoons may have been used to obtain the large swordfish and tuna. The Chumash also used other fishing technologies—including poisons, lures, and traps—and the people of Hel'apunitse may have used these technologies, as well.

A variety of other vertebrate remains were also identified at SBA-72 (Table A.20). About 25 percent of the bones were identifiable to at least general faunal categories, including birds (3 percent of total NISP) such as cormorants, gulls, and murre; undifferentiated reptiles or amphibians (2 percent); deer (1 percent); dogs (< 1 percent); Guadalupe fur seals (< 1 percent); and other marine and land mammals. Most of the other vertebrate remains were composed of undifferentiated sea mammal bones (44 percent), followed by large and medium mammals (18 and 19 percent, respectively), and small fauna (about 8 percent). These results are comparable to vertebrate remains reported by Lawson et al. (1980), which were dominated by sea mammals followed by large, medium, and small mammal remains.

The other vertebrate remains from SBA-72 suggest that people hunted or scavenged animals in a variety of habitats. This includes hunting deer and other land mammals, as well as sea mammals, including the now locally extinct Guadalupe fur seal. The presence of dog remains suggests that the people of Hel'apunitse kept domestic dogs for a variety of purposes, including hunting, security, and companionship. Finally, although much of the sample appears to be cultural in origin, some of the bones may have been deposited naturally. Many of the rodent, small fauna, and reptile or amphibian remains are probably from natural death on the site, for instance, rather than human predation.

Dietary Reconstruction

To estimate the dietary importance of various animals (land mammal, sea mammal, bird, fish, and shellfish), we calculated dietary reconstructions for the SBA-72 samples using the weight method (Tables A.21, A.22). A dietary reconstruction for SBA-72N, based on faunal remains from CS 1, suggests that sea mammals contributed most of the meat consumed (41 percent), followed by land mammals (30 percent), fish (26 percent), shellfish (3 percent), and birds (< 1 percent). Faunal remains from CS 5 at SBA-72S suggest that fish and sea mammals each contributed about 41 percent of the edible meat represented, followed by land mammals (14 percent), shellfish (4 percent), and birds (< 1 percent). Although based on very small samples and susceptible to a variety of sources of error, these dietary reconstructions are generally consistent with the observations of Rogers, who noted an

abundance of sea mammal bone at the site, and the findings of Glassow (1980) and our previous conclusions (Erlandson and Rick 2002) that mammals dominated the meat diet at the site. They are also consistent with trends identified in a broader range of coastal Chumash sites, including an intensification of fishing through time, but also suggest a heavy reliance on sea mammals compared with many mainland and island sites (Erlandson and Rick 2002; Rick 2007).

Site Summary

SBA-72 was a substantial Chumash village occupied for roughly 1,500 years, from about AD 50 to 1500. Although heavily disturbed by farming, industrial development, and grave robbers, significant remnants of the site were encountered and sampled. Fortunately, this important site is now protected under a thick layer of construction fill. Over the years, archaeologists have provided a wealth of information on the lifeways of the Chumash occupants of the site and the nature of the surrounding landscape. Late Holocene occupation of the site seems to have begun in the northern area, later shifting primarily to the southern area—although these occupations overlap and cannot always be easily differentiated. The work of D. B. Rogers in the 1920s provided important insights into the layout of this Chumash village, including the location of living areas, two discrete cemeteries, a dance floor, and a sweat lodge. Subsequent work has helped refine Rogers's conclusions about the structure and chronology of the site, as well as providing significant information on the daily lives of its Chumash inhabitants. The occupants of SBA-72 had a rich ceremonial life, elaborate technologies, and many of the cultural traits of the historical Chumash.

The artifacts and faunal remains recovered from the site provide a small window into the complexity of Chumash culture at Hel'apunitse. Several important new technologies appeared among the coastal Chumash during this time, including the bow and arrow, *Olivella* callus cup beads used as money, and probably the frameless plank canoe or tomol. For the people of Hel'apunitse, daily life in the Tecolote Canyon area involved a diverse array of economic, social, and political activities. These included collecting and processing a variety of edible and utilitarian plants, hunting and fishing in coastal and upland habitats, manufacturing and maintaining a variety of technologies, and trading with neighboring groups for goods and materials (obsidian, shell beads, etc.) collected or manufactured elsewhere. Data from the SBA-72 cemeteries also suggest that wealth and power were not equally shared among the members of society, social interactions sometimes ended in violence, and the effects on some local resources may have been considerable. To better understand the nature of the changes and challenges faced by the Chumash at Tecolote, however, we must compare the information from SBA-72 with archaeological data derived from roughly contemporary deposits at SBA-73.

SBA-73

Just across the creek from SBA-72, SBA-73 also contains northern and southern loci. Similar to SBA-72, the site has been excavated repeatedly and extensively, beginning with the work of Stephen Bowers in 1877 (Benson 1997), Frederick Ward Putnam in 1908 (King 1980), and D. B. Rogers (1929) in the 1920s. After a hiatus of over 50 years, further studies of the site were conducted by archaeological teams from UCSB in 1979 (Kornfeld et al. 1980), 1981 (Moore et al. 1982), and 1987 (Erlandson 1987) and by WESTEC in 1988 (Erlandson and Cooley 1988c) and Hutash Consultants in the 1990s (Erlandson, Braje, et al. 2006).

By the 1970s, when the first relatively modern archaeological work was conducted at SBA-73, the site had been heavily modified by industrial development and other ground-disturbing activities. These activities damaged many site areas, including deposits near the beach where a pier once stood, much of the western margin of the site, and a section of the southern site area that appears to have been graded away during development or restoration activities. Since 1979, however, archaeological work has shown that large sections of the site escaped destruction and remain highly significant.

Similar to the case at SBA-72, early investigations by Bowers, Putnam, and Rogers focused on excavating cemeteries at SBA-73, although Rogers also trenched extensively in other site areas. Respecting the wishes of the modern Chumash community, recent excavations have tried to avoid cemetery areas, focusing instead on understanding the structure, age, contents, and environmental context of the site. In 1979, UCSB archaeologists defined the boundaries, significance, and age of the site relative to a proposed housing development. In the southern site area, five units, an auger hole, and a backhoe trench were excavated, but two of these units and the trench appear to have been in disturbed areas (Kornfeld and Erlandson 1980). Six units and two backhoe trenches were also excavated in the northern site area, which appeared to be less disturbed (Figure 6.7). The intact deposits produced diverse artifact and faunal assemblages that provide important details on the types of activities conducted at the site, complementing the larger spatial data provided by Rogers.

In 1981, UCSB archaeologists followed up their 1979 study with excavations near the northern margin of SBA-73. Prompted by the construction of an ARCO pipeline, this work involved the excavation and analysis of materials from seven 1-×-1-m-wide test units running across the site from east to west (Moore et al. 1982). The materials recovered from these peripheral site deposits consist primarily of chipped-stone artifacts (mostly tool-making debris), historical materials, and small amounts of shell and animal bone. The historical materials encountered appeared to be associated primarily with the oil and other industrial development of the lower canyon area from the 1930s to the 1950s, showing that parts of the site were disturbed by industrial and restoration activities (see chapter 7).

In 1987, UCSB archaeologists excavated 60 shovel test pits (STPs) and three 1.0-×-.5-m-wide test units along the western site margins to better define the boundaries of the site relative to the Bacara development. This work confirmed the presence of low-density shell midden deposits across a large area, including a roughly 50-×-100-m area extending up the slope and atop a knoll west of SBA-73N (Erlandson 1987). Some evidence for disturbance was found in this area, but during construction grading we determined that the midden

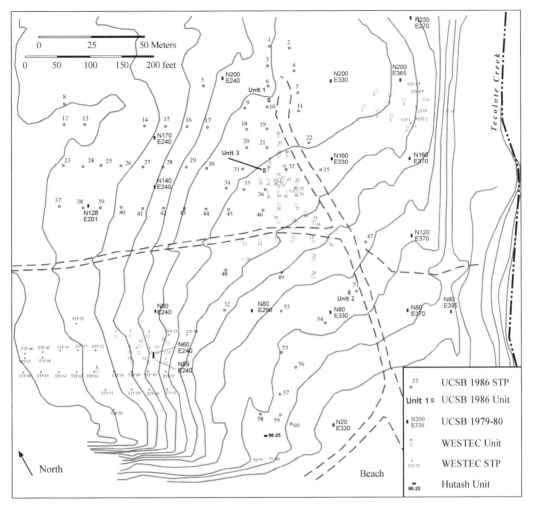

FIGURE 6.7. Map of University of California–Santa Barbara, WESTEC, and Hutash excavations at SBA-73 and SBA-1674 (drafted by Julia Knowles).

in this northwestern area was redeposited, probably during the demolition of oil facilities and restoration of the area. In 1988, archaeologists from UCSB and WESTEC excavated 11 1.0-×-1.0-m-wide test units in the northern portions of SBA-73N, where the Bacara access road and Tecolote Creek Bridge were eventually built (Erlandson and Cooley 1988c). In 1989, archaeologists from ERCE also excavated 48 test units along the western margins of SBA-73. Most of this work was focused on the northern and central site areas, but a few test units were also placed in the southern locus. During this work, several cultural features were identified, including a rock cairn burial feature at SBA-73N that required modification of development plans in the area.

Finally, in the 1990s, archaeologists from Hutash Consultants conducted limited excavations and extensive construction monitoring along the western edge of SBA-73N. This work documented and salvaged numerous cultural features, including several large burned rock concentrations that probably represented hearths, rock ovens, and other cooking facilities (Erlandson, Braje, et al. 2006). To save some of these features and avoid further damage to sensitive archaeological materials, construction plans were again altered in this area—at considerable expense to the property owner. A number of isolated artifacts were also re-covered during surface collections and monitor-ing operations along the northern and western site margins. The artifacts and faunal remains from the 1987 and later investigations are summarized in the sections that follow.

All formal artifacts recovered during excava-tions, surface collections, and construction mon-itoring at SBA-73 were analyzed. Because of the huge quantity of faunal remains and tool-making debris recovered, we focused our detailed analyses on several control or index units. The units selected for detailed analysis—based on their location, preservation, and abundance of recovered materi-als—included Unit 22 and Column Sample 11 for SBA-73N and Units 59 and 98-25 for SBA-72S.

Site Structure, Stratigraphy, and Chronology

After extensive excavations of the site in the 1920s, Rogers (1926, 1929) summarized the general or-ganization of SBA-73. He estimated that the shell midden extended over 210 m (~700 ft) north to south, from the beach to the railroad tracks, with a width of 90 m (~300 ft). Rogers believed this entire area was one large village occupied by the Chumash at the same time as SBA-72. He di-vided SBA-73 into northern and southern sec-tions, with a northern residential area confined largely to a low knoll about 90 m long by 45 m wide (~300 × 150 ft). Just south of the knoll, he exca-vated two cemeteries, one that had been excavated previously—probably by Bowers and Putnam. Rogers estimated the size of each of these ceme-teries at about 7.5 m (24 ft) wide and 11 m (36 ft) long. Because he only excavated part of each ceme-tery, however, these should be viewed as minimum values. In the northern cemetery, Rogers excavated nine articulated burials and one reburial. In the southern cemetery he found 15 articulated burials. All the burials were found in flexed positions typ-ical of the Canaliño, but Rogers reported finding few artifacts with them. After studying the ceme-tery collections housed at the Santa Barbara Mu-seum of Natural History, however, King (1980) reported a hammer stone; a digging stick weight; several projectile points; bone tube beads (some with shell bead appliqué); a bone awl, needle, and

harpoon barb; stone beads; *Olivella* disk beads; and ornaments made from abalone and *Megath-ura* shells. King believed these two cemeteries were used between about AD 300 and 900. No ^{14}C dates are available for these two cemeteries, but two dates of ~AD 800 for residential deposits in Unit 11 are consistent with this chronology.

South of the cemeteries, Rogers found rem-nants of a dance floor similar to those he described for SBA-71 and SBA-72:

> Skirting the southern group of huts on the north, was the site once utilized as a ceremo-nial dance floor, hard, compact, and clear of stones. This area was elliptical in outline, nearly one hundred feet in length by fifty feet wide, the long axis running northeast by southwest. About the borders of this place were piled great numbers of stones that had very likely been cleared from the floor [1929:197–198].

On the west bank of Tecolote Creek, just south of the dance floor, he also identified the ruins of a sweat lodge (temescal) similar to one he found di-rectly across the creek at SBA-72.

Still farther south lay some of the densest con-centrations of shell midden and domestic debris Rogers found at SBA-73. He described this south-ern site area as having two arms surrounding what he believed to be an ancient estero or marsh located west of the present creek mouth. Rogers also noted that the concentration of food refuse and ash in-creased toward the ocean, a pattern that led King to speculate that SBA-73 might contain discrete activity areas similar to those he found at a coastal Chumash village (VEN-27) in Ventura County:

> On the beach, animals were butchered, canoes repaired, and tools were made by men. Refuse from houses sitting above the beach zone was usually also discarded on the beach area. Above the beach zone, the houses had midden with a much lower refuse content although with a fair number of artifacts. Behind the houses was a zone in which outdoor cooking was done. This zone contained fewer artifacts and refuse than the other two zones [1980:64].

TABLE 6.3. Radiocarbon Dates from SBA-73

Site	Lab #	Dated Material	Provenience	Measured ^{14}C Age (RYBP)	Conventional ^{14}C Age (RYBP)	Calendar Age Range (cal bp 1δ)
SBA-73N	Beta-196354	Venus clam	Unit 11: 80–100 cm	1420 ± 40	1840 ± 40	1240 (1180) 1130
	Beta-196898	Venus clam	Unit 11: 20–40 cm	1470 ±70	1890 ± 70	1290 (1240) 1160
	Beta-8938	Marine shell	N200/E365: 40–50 cm	2090 ± 70	2520 ± 70	1990 (1900) 1820
SBA-73S	Beta-196355	*Mytilus* bead	Unit 60: 60–80 cm	670 ± 40	1020 ± 40	480 (450) 410
	Beta-140984	*Olivella* bead	N20/E330: 60–70 cm	820 ± 40	1260 ± 40	650 (620) 550
	Beta-19723	Turban shell	Test Unit 2: 0–20 cm	1000 ± 60	1430 ± 60	820 (730) 670
	Beta-144256	Littleneck clam	Trench 98-25: 65 cm	1080 ± 60	1500 ± 70	910 (820) 730
	Beta-196356	Venus clam	Unit 60: 60–80 cm	1120 ± 40	1540 ± 40	920 (890) 800
	Beta-8939	Marine shell	N20/E330: 110–120 cm	1210 ± 70	1640 ± 70	1040 (950) 900
	Beta-19724	Abalone shell	Test Unit 2: 20–40 cm	1320 ± 60	1750 ± 60	1160 (1060) 980
	Beta-144255	Venus clam	Trench 98-25: 40 cm	1610 ± 100	2040±100	1480 (1340) 1270

Note: Dates were calibrated with CALIB 4.3 (Stuiver and Reimer 1993), using a Δ*R* of 225 ± 35 years. For the ^{13}C/^{12}C ratios, either they were determined by the ^{14}C lab or 430 years was added (Erlandson 1988a).

Unfortunately, parts of southern SBA-73 were so heavily disturbed by oil-related developments in the mid-1900s that it would be difficult to test this idea today. Dense midden deposits were found in several test units (59, 60, and 98-25) excavated in relatively undisturbed residential deposits located just behind the beach, but no cemetery was found in the southern site area. The occupants of SBA-73S may have used the southern cemetery at SBA-72, which appears to overlap in time with the residential deposits at SBA-73S, or a cemetery may have been destroyed by development or lost to coastal erosion. Rogers found no artifacts indicating that the site was occupied after European contact, and King's study of artifacts from SBA-73S supports this assertion, suggesting that the southern site area was occupied between about AD 1150 and 1500. Six of the eight ^{14}C dates available from this area confirm King's chronology, with calibrated intercepts falling between about AD 1000 and 1500. Two of the dates also suggest a somewhat earlier occupation, dating between about AD 600 and 1000 (Table 6.3). As was the case at SBA-72, the southern portion of SBA-73 generally seems to be younger than the northern area, but the available dates indicate several centuries of overlap in the occupation of the two loci. Three uncorrected dates on midden shell from SBA-73N range from about 2090 ± 70 RYBP to 1420 ± 40 RYBP, with calibrated ages of about 50 BC (2000 cal BP) and AD 850 (1100 cal BP).

Artifacts and Technology

Numerous artifacts were recovered during our excavations at SBA-73. Here we summarize some of the early materials found at the site, describe the artifacts recovered since 1987, and compare the latter with those recovered by Kornfeld et al. (1980) and Moore et al. (1982). Some of the more elaborate artifacts were recovered by Rogers during his extensive investigations, including his excavation of the two cemeteries in the northern site area. Aside from burial-related artifacts described above, Rogers (1929) also noted the presence of finely made bowl and pestle fragments, a variety of chipped-stone tools, and faunal remains on the site surface and in the excavated deposits.

During excavations, surface collections, and construction monitoring directed by Erlandson and Vellanoweth, more than 69,000 chipped-stone

FIGURE 6.8. A small sandstone bowl (left) and pestle (right) from Tecolote Canyon sites (scale in centimeters; photo by Melissa Reid).

FIGURE 6.9. Bone tools from Late Holocene occupations of SBA-72 and SBA-73. Left to right—top row: antler flaker or tine, shark centrum bead, bone awl; middle row: bone barbs; bottom row: possible atlatl spur, harpoon fragment, unidentified barbed object (photo by Melissa Reid).

artifacts were recovered from SBA-73 (Table A.23). The vast majority of these consist of tool-making debris, but bifaces are relatively common with 225 specimens, including five convex-base projectile points. Also recovered were 194 flake tools, 87 drills or boring tools, 20 hammer stones, and 12 cores. Finally, 10 microdrills or microblades were collected, which may have been used for drilling shell or other bead types.

These chipped-stone artifacts were probably used for a variety of activities, including hunting and processing of animals. Concentrations of tool-making debris also indicate that people made and resharpened numerous tools at the site. The chipped-stone tools are generally comparable to the findings of Kornfeld (1980:234), who described projectile points, bifaces, and drills, along with more expedient flake tools. Chipped-stone artifacts from both the northern and southern site areas were made primarily from Monterey chert (72 and 84 percent, respectively), with lesser amounts of Franciscan chert (26 and 11 percent), and small quantities of siltstone, quartzite, obsidian, fused shale, and basalt. Most of the chipped-stone artifacts we analyzed were also made from local rock types, but obsidian and fused shale artifacts indicate the acquisition of exotic materials through trade. Geochemical analysis of 33 obsidian artifacts from SBA-73 showed that, similar to the case at other Tecolote Canyon sites, the Coso Volcanic Field dominates the obsidian artifacts ($n = 25$), with eight others coming from Casa Diablo (Table A.7).

Ground-stone artifacts are also abundant at SBA-73, with 156 specimens from the surface and excavated samples (Table A.24). These include 35 bowl or mortar fragments, 30 pestles, eight metate fragments, six manos, two abraders, and two perforated "donut stones"—the latter generally thought to be digging stick weights. Most of these ground-stone tools are made from sandstone (see Figure 6.8), which is locally abundant, but two soapstone bowl fragments found on the site surface may have been acquired through trade. Moore (1980) also reported three manos, three bowl fragments, a pestle, and a metate fragment from SBA-73.

Ninety bone tools or tool fragments were also

recovered, mostly from excavation units (Table A.25; see also Figure 6.9). Sixty-six of these are small undiagnostic fragments of ground or polished bone. Thirteen awl fragments, a barb or composite harpoon fragment, a wedge, a flaker, a bone point, a gorge, and a bird bone tube were also identified. A notched fish spine, an irregularly cut sea mammal bone, and a mammal rib with asphaltum are also among the modified bone specimens from the site. Lawson et al. (1980) reported seven bone artifacts from the 1979 UCSB excavations, noting the presence of awl or needle tips, a bead, and a possible barb. Most of the bone tools from SBA-73 are fragmented and undiagnostic, but the presence of gorges, a wedge, and a flaker suggests that Chumash people in Tecolote Canyon used bone tools in a variety of subsistence and other pursuits, including the production of basketry and other artifacts.

Beads and other ornaments were also relatively common at SBA-73, where 135 *Olivella* beads were recovered, including 124 from the southern site locus but only 11 from the northern area (Table A.13). The *Olivella* beads from SBA-72N include five wall disk beads, two cup beads, two spire-removed beads, and two beads in production or bead fragments. In the southern site area, 39 wall disk beads, 77 cup beads, a thin-lipped bead, a spire-removed bead, and six beads in production or bead fragments were identified. *Olivella* bead-making debris was relatively rare at the site, with 17.5 g/m^3 in SBA-73S and just 1.5 g/m^3 in SBA-73N (Table A.15). This suggests that most of the beads at the site were acquired through trade. Other than the *Olivella* specimens, only nine shell beads were identified: a *Dentalium neohexagonum* bead from SBA-73N and four mussel disks, a mussel cylinder, a red abalone disk bead, and a clam disk from SBA-73S (Table A.14).

Thirty-five fishhook fragments were also identified at SBA-73, 32 made from shell and three made from bone. These include 31 *Mytilus* specimens, with two grooved-shank fragments, 20 midsections, three tips, and five blanks (Table A.16). One abalone fishhook midsection and two probable bone fishhook midsections and a grooved-shank fragment were also identified. Worked fragments of *Protothaca* and abalone and a ground *Tivela* ornament are the only other shell artifacts from the 1979 and later research. Forty-four stone and bone beads were also identified: 39 of them soapstone cylinders, disks, barrels, tubes, or beads in production, with 33 from SBA-73N and just eight from SBA-73S (Table A.12). Four mammal bone tubes and a red shale disk bead were also found at SBA-73.

Finally, 62 tarring pebbles, four asphaltum basketry impressions, three asphaltum applicators, two cobbles splashed with tar, and a bone rib applicator with asphaltum were recovered at SBA-73 (Table A.17). Like the impressions recovered from SBA-72, these basketry impressions are fragments of woven water bottles or other baskets that had their interiors lined with tar to waterproof the vessel.

Faunal Remains

A large assemblage of shell and bone was recovered from SBA-73. Because of the size of the assemblage and the heavy disturbance of many site areas, we analyzed shellfish and vertebrate remains from four index units, two in the northern site area (Unit 22 and CS 11) and two in the southern area (Units 59 and 98-25). All analyzed faunal remains are from ⅛-in screen residuals.

Shellfish. Nearly 12 kg (> 26 lbs) of shell from at least 980 individual shellfish and 33 different shellfish taxa were identified in the four index units (Table A.26). Most of the shell (76 percent) was found in Unit 98-25, with the other three units contributing the other 24 percent of the shell weight. Of the identified shell, littleneck clam (*Protothaca staminea*) makes up about 34 percent of the shell weight in the index units, followed by Venus clams (*Chione* spp., 19 percent), oysters and undifferentiated clams (~8 percent each), and Pismo clam (~5 percent). California mussels, relatively common in many Santa Barbara Channel shell middens, make up only about 4 percent of the shell weight.

For the most part, the shellfish remains are similar in all four index units. Littleneck clam (*Protothaca* spp.) is the dominant shell type in CS 11, Unit 59, and Unit 98-25, for instance, where it con-

tributes 25, 27, and 36 percent of the shell weight, respectively. Venus (*Chione* spp.) clams are also relatively abundant, making up between 14 and 20 percent of the shell weight in each unit. California mussel makes up about 13 percent of the shell weight in Unit 11 but only about 3–6 percent in Units 98-25 and Unit 59, suggesting that this rocky intertidal species may have been slightly more important for the occupants of SBA-73N. Most other taxa generally make up less than about 10 percent of the shell weight. Shellfish remains in Unit 22 are relatively poorly preserved—with undifferentiated clams making up 55 percent of the shell weight—and only about eight taxa were identified. Among the identifiable shell, Venus, Pismo, and littleneck clams are all relatively abundant, each contributing about 8–9 percent of the shell weight. Collectively, these data suggest that the shellfish in the northern and southern site areas were similar, with people collecting them in rocky intertidal, estuary, and surf-swept sandy beach habitats.

The shell remains we identified are also similar to the SBA-73N and SBA-73S samples reported by Serena (1980). California mussels are more common in Serena's samples (making up ~20–26 percent of the shell weight), but such discrepancies may be related to the smaller samples he analyzed, to differential preservation in the units, or to horizontal variation in shellfish gathering, processing, and disposal patterns across the site. The available data suggest that the people of SBA-73 utilized a wide range of shellfish, possibly acquiring some of these through trade.

Fish and Other Vertebrates. Fish, mammal, bird, and reptile or amphibian bones were also relatively common in the four SBA-73 index units. As was the case at SBA-72, most of the sample is highly fragmented and burned, making identification difficult. Nonetheless, a variety of marine fish, mammals, and other taxa were identified.

Marine fish were the most abundant vertebrates at SBA-73, with 21 types of teleosts and seven elasmobranchs identified from roughly 1.4 kg and nearly 40,000 bones (Table A.27). Similar to the shellfish remains, most of the fish bones (77 percent) are from Unit 98-25. Clupeids are the most abundant fish by NISP (64 percent), but mackerel (11 percent), surfperch (8 percent), labrids (6 percent), rockfish (4 percent), and croakers (2 percent) are also relatively common. Although they generally make up less than 1 percent of NISP values, giant ocean sunfish, bonito and albacore tuna, yellowtail, and barracuda were also identified. The remains of bat ray, blue shark, salmon shark, angel shark, and soupfin shark were also identified but contribute less than 1 percent of the identified fish elements.

The fish remains are also relatively similar in each index unit, although the CS 11 and Unit 22 samples are considerably smaller than those from Unit 59 and Unit 98-25, making direct comparison of the fish remains from the southern and northern site areas problematic. Johnson's (1980:219) report of a small sample (21 g) of fish remains from SBA-73N is also similar to our samples, with roughly 24 taxa, including white croaker, mackerel, yellowtail, bonito, basking shark, bat ray, soupfin shark, and clupeids. Collectively, the samples from SBA-73 suggest that people fished in kelp forest, rocky reef, sandy beach, bay and estuary, and offshore habitats. People probably also used a variety of fishing tackle, including hook and line, harpoons, and nets.

A number of other vertebrates were also identified at SBA-73, including birds, sea mammals, and land mammals (Table A.28). Most of these (64 percent) were found in Unit 98-25 and are identifiable only to general animal categories (mammal, bird, etc.), although a few bones were identified to family, genus, or species. Sea mammal remains include eight Guadalupe fur seal bones, 56 eared seal bones, a true seal bone, and three cetacean bones, all of which make up less than 1 percent of the other vertebrate sample. Eleven deer bones, seven rabbit bones, 120 rodent bones, and numerous undifferentiated large, medium, and small mammal bones were also identified. Clearly, the Chumash people of SBA-73 captured and processed a variety of land and sea mammals.

About 179 bird bones were also recovered, including the remains of a loon, gull, grebe, and owl. Reptiles or amphibian bones are represented by 54 unidentified elements. Both bird and reptile/amphibian bones make up less than 5 percent of the assemblage. Lawson et al. (1980) also analyzed a small sample of other vertebrate remains from SBA-73N, but these are identified only to general animal categories, including large, medium, and small land mammals, sea mammals, and birds. Because of the lack of more detailed identifications and the small size of their sample, any direct comparison with our data is problematic. Similar to our study, however, their sample is dominated by the remains of sea mammals and undifferentiated large mammals.

Dietary Reconstruction

Using the weight method, we calculated dietary reconstructions for the shellfish, fish, and other vertebrate remains represented in our samples from SBA-73N and SBA-73S (Tables A.29, A.30). Dietary reconstructions for the faunal remains from CS 11 in the northern area suggest that sea mammals contributed roughly 58 percent of the edible meat represented, followed by land mammals (28 percent), shellfish (19 percent), and fish (4 percent). For SBA-73S, the faunal remains from Unit 98-25 suggest that fish contributed about 47 percent of the meat represented, followed by sea mammals (40 percent), land mammals (8 percent), shellfish (4 percent), and birds (< 1 percent). These dietary reconstructions are similar to those from SBA-72, which show an emphasis on sea mammals and fish and an apparent intensification of fishing through time.

Site Summary

Since the 1920s, archaeologists have provided a wealth of information on the structure, age, and contents of SBA-73. Its large size, complex structure, and diverse contents suggest that the site was an ancient center of Chumash life occupied for roughly 1,500 years. Similar to SBA-72, this Chumash village site contains two discrete residential areas and a wide variety of cultural features. The northern area was settled first, although the chronology of this occupation is still relatively poorly defined. Three ^{14}C dates from residential midden deposits suggest that this area was occupied between at least 50 BC and AD 800. An *Olivella* cup bead found in this area may indicate that some occupation took place after AD 1300. Two cemetery plots located on the edge of the northern locus were probably used during the earlier site occupation. In the southern site area, relatively intensive Chumash occupation appears to have taken place between about AD 450 and 1550. Between these two residential areas, Rogers identified a dance floor and temescal, although the precise age and association of these features are uncertain.

The variety of artifacts and features found at SBA-73 is consistent with findings from SBA-72 and other Late Holocene Chumash coastal villages, which generally contain a variety of artifacts associated with a diversified economy based on fishing, hunting, shellfish gathering, collecting and processing of plant foods, and a wide range of manufacturing activities, commerce, and everyday secular and ceremonial pursuits. The features documented at the site over the years range from the utilitarian (hearths and rock ovens) to the sacred (cemeteries, sweat lodges, dance floors, etc.), archaeological data that illustrate many aspects of the complexity and diversity of Chumash culture as described in early historical and ethnographic accounts.

Animal remains from the site support this diversity, showing that the people of Hel'apunitse engaged in a variety of subsistence activities. Fish from nearby kelp forests, sandy beaches, and rocky shores are fairly common, as are those from bays and estuaries and several species generally found in deeper waters. The presence of clupeids (sardines) suggests that the Chumash used nets to take these small fish en masse, while the presence of swordfish demonstrates the use of sophisticated watercraft and harpoons. A variety of sea mammals, including seals and sea lions, and land mammals (deer etc.) were also hunted, and shellfish were harvested from rocky intertidal, estuary, and surf-swept sandy beaches.

Together these data suggest that people made use of all the locally available habitats. Not surprisingly given their age, the faunal remains from SBA-73 are also generally consistent with the nature of local environments in the Tecolote Canyon area today. Although the long history of occupation at the site suggests a level of sustainability to

Chumash harvests, the enormous quantities of fish, mammal, and shellfish remains represented at the site leave little doubt that the canyon occupants also had an impact on local resources. Some of the subsistence remains may not have been procured locally, however, with estuarine shellfish possibly being obtained through trade with Goleta Slough towns to the east and seals from Chumash villages on the Channel Islands, where such resources were more abundant.

SBA-1674

Situated about 150 m west of Tecolote Creek and about 40 m from the sea cliff, SBA-1674 covered an area roughly 30 × 40 m wide. Located on the gently sloping canyon wall between SBA-73 and SBA-1673, this small shell midden was first recorded and excavated in 1979 by UCSB archaeologists. There have long been questions about whether SBA-1674 was an intact archaeological site or a cluster of materials redeposited from SBA-73. Geologist Thomas Rockwell, an expert in soils, stratigraphy, and geoarchaeology along the California Coast, examined the site to help resolve this question, but even he was not sure if the site was intact or redeposited (see below). Because it was to be completely destroyed by hotel construction, ERCE archaeologists excavated about 2 percent of the site, including 14 1-×-1-m-wide test units and 24 STPs to document its structure, age, and contents (Figure 6.7). Even these excavations provided no definitive evidence about the origin and integrity of the site. Given this ambiguity, we summarize what we learned about the site structure, contents, and age in the sections that follow. We analyzed all the artifacts recovered from the site, but our study of faunal remains was focused on materials recovered in Unit 4 and its column sample (CS 4), excavated in the denser midden deposits at the site.

Site Structure and Chronology
Excavations at SBA-1674 demonstrated that it was a small and shallow shell midden surrounded by a diffuse scatter of chipped-stone tools to the north, south, and west. This structure, typical of many shell middens in the Santa Barbara Channel

TABLE 6.4. Radiocarbon Dates from SBA-1674

Lab #	Dated Material	Provenience	Uncorrected ^{14}C Date (RYBP)	Adjusted ^{13}C/^{12}C Age (RYBP)	Calendar Age Range (cal bp, 1δ)
Beta-196359	*Olivella* cup bead	Unit 4: 20–40 cm	610 ± 40	1020 ± 40	480 (450) 410
Beta-196358	Venus clam	Unit 4: 20–40 cm	730 ± 40	1140 ± 40	540 (520) 500
Beta-196357	Venus clam	Unit 4: 0–20 cm	800 ± 40	1220 ± 40	630 (560) 540
Beta-8296	Marine shell	N60/E240: 10–20 cm	1240 ± 60	1670 ± 60	1060 (970) 920

Notes: Dates were calibrated with CALIB 4.3 (Stuiver and Reimer 1993), using a ΔR of 225 ± 35 years. For the ^{13}C/^{12}C ratios, either they were determined by the ^{14}C labs or 430 years was added (Erlandson 1988a).

area, initially suggested that the site was intact. The small size of the midden and the low density of the materials it contained indicated that it was occupied relatively briefly, probably by a family or other small group. An uncorrected ^{14}C date of 1240 ± 60 RYBP on marine shell from the 10–20 cm level in UCSB Unit N60/E240 produced a calibrated age of ~970 cal bp (AD 980), suggesting that the site was occupied about 1,000 years ago. This seemed consistent with the few time-sensitive artifacts recovered by UCSB archaeologists in 1979, including several *Olivella* wall disk beads (King and Serena 1980).

In contrast, the 1988 excavations produced two *Olivella* cup beads and one thin-lipped bead, suggesting an occupation after AD 1300. Three accelerator mass spectrometry ^{14}C dates confirmed this chronology, with two small fragments of Venus clam shell from Unit 4 producing calibrated intercepts of AD 1390 and AD 1430 and one half of an *Olivella* cup bead from the same unit producing a calibrated intercept of AD 1500 (Table 6.4). The four dates from SBA-1674 suggest at least two occupations spanning a period of about 500 years—which seems at odds with the idea that the small and low-density site formed during a brief occupation. The dates overlap with the known chronology of SBA-73S, however, suggesting that the archaeological materials at SBA-1674 were redeposited from the larger site to the east. During the controlled grading of the site, no intact cultural features (fire hearths, rock ovens, etc.) were found, but evidence of massive historical disturbances was found immediately to the west, north, and east. This includes evidence for the demolition of his-

torical industrial structures in the surrounding area and the displacement of shell midden soils to the west of SBA-73N. It now seems likely that the archaeological materials at SBA-1674 were redeposited from SBA-73S during the restoration of the area after the abandonment of oil-related facilities (see chapter 7).

Artifacts and Technology

We recovered relatively few artifacts at SBA-1674, but the shell, stone, and bone tools represent a variety of activities. The artifacts found in 1988 include the *Olivella* callus beads described above, a mussel shell fishhook fragment, single soapstone disk and tube beads, and a mammal bone tool fragment that may be part of an awl, barb, or gorge. Other than two *Olivella* wall disk beads, no bone or shell artifacts were reported for the 1979 excavations. Ten utilitarian ground-stone tools were recovered from SBA-1674: four manos, a pestle, a probable abrader, and four undifferentiated fragments (Table A.31). Also recovered were several tarring pebbles and other asphaltum applicators.

Chipped-stone artifacts were much more common at the site, with 2,382 specimens recovered and analyzed (Table A.32). Formal chipped-stone tools are limited to 12 bifaces or biface fragments, nine flake tools, six drills or boring tools, a core, a flaked cobble, and a hammer stone. Most of the chipped-stone artifacts were made of local cherts, but an artifact from the 1979 excavations and a biface and 17 pieces of debitage found in 1988 were made from obsidian. A single obsidian artifact from the site was determined to have come from the Coso Volcanic Field.

Faunal Remains

Preservation of shell and bone at SBA-1674 was relatively poor, with most specimens fragmented or burned. We analyzed the shellfish and vertebrate remains from Unit 4 (including the column sample) and found a broad range of resources and activities represented. Just 161 g and a minimum of 54 individual shellfish were recovered from ⅛-in screen residuals in Unit 4 and Column Sample 4 (Table A.33). At least 19 marine taxa were identified, but the assemblage is dominated by littleneck clams (18.9 percent by weight), undifferentiated clam (17.2 percent), Pismo clams (16.7 percent), oysters (15.4 percent), Venus clams (10.3 percent), and California mussels (9.1 percent). Most other taxa make up less than 5 percent of the shell sample and were probably either minor dietary contributors or incidental midden constituents. The general composition of the shell from the site is similar to that from SBA-72 and SBA-73, suggesting that shellfish were gathered in bay or estuary habitats, rocky intertidal areas, and surf-swept sandy beaches.

Unit/CS 4 also produced 191 fish bones (Table A.34). Among the identified specimens, mackerel (35 percent) and clupeid (30 percent) bones are most abundant, followed by California sheephead (15 percent), surfperch (10 percent), rockfish (5 percent), and bat ray (5 percent). These taxa are generally consistent with a small sample of fish remains analyzed by Johnson (1980:221), where clupeid remains are abundant ($n = 12$) but trace amounts of Pacific bonito, mackerel, kelp or sand bass, perch, and rockfish are identified. The identified taxa could have been obtained from the surf zone, rocky shore, kelp bed, bays and estuaries, and offshore waters. The fish remains from SBA-1674 are similar to those from SBA-72 and SBA-73 and might have been caught with a variety of technologies, including hook and line, nets, and spears.

Of the 918 fragments of other vertebrate remains recovered (Table A.35), large and medium mammals (deer, dog, etc.) are most abundant, with 72 and 31 bones each (41 and 18 percent of NISP, respectively). The remains of eared seals (sea lions and fur seals), undifferentiated pinnipeds, and sea mammals are also fairly abundant with 28 specimens (23 percent). Bones of rodents ($n = 7$) and small fauna ($n = 37$) are common, but most of these may be natural in origin. Only two reptile or amphibian bones were identified. These remains suggest that people hunted a variety of land and sea mammals, similar to the patterns identified at SBA-72 and SBA-73.

Site Summary

Now completely destroyed, SBA-1674 was a small site with evidence for occupation between about AD 1000 and 1550. Although the density of archaeological materials was limited, a wide range of artifacts and faunal remains was recovered. Its location on a small terrace just west of SBA-73 and similar site chronology suggest that the two sites were closely related. The site deposits were badly disturbed by historical activities and may have been redeposited from SBA-73.

OTHER POSSIBLE LATE HOLOCENE SITES

As mentioned in chapter 5, fragments of stone "flowerpot" mortars found at SBA-75 and SBA-2499 suggest some use of these sites during the past 1,000 to 1,500 years. Given the lack of other Late Holocene indicators (^{14}C dates, shell beads, arrow points, etc.) at SBA-75, it seems likely that the mortar fragment represents a limited use of this predominantly Middle Holocene site by later Chumash peoples, possibly the residents of SBA-73, which is located just 100 m or so to the south. Three sites on the east side of Winchester Canyon (SBA-69, SBA-70, and SBA-2499) have produced Late Holocene ^{14}C dates, but these are on materials with no clear relationship to the human occupation of the sites. The artifact assemblages, especially when considered along with ^{14}C dates obtained on associated marine shells, suggest that all three sites were occupied much earlier, during the Early and Middle Holocene.

Another enigmatic site that remains largely undated is SBA-1673, located on the terrace roughly 200 m west of Tecolote Creek. Most of the site is now preserved beneath a layer of fill and geotextile fabric under the Bacara parking lot. Rogers noted a few ground-stone tools scattered in this area, but the site was only recorded in 1979 when UCSB

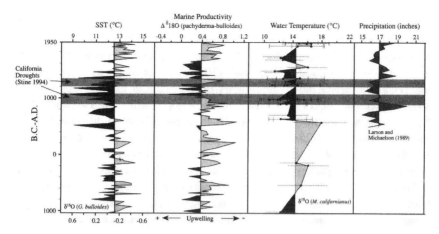

FIGURE 6.10. Some Late Holocene environmental changes in the Santa Barbara Channel area (adapted from Kennett and Kennett 2000).

archaeologists surveyed the area. The site is a low-density lithic scatter, with small amounts of shell and bone. Some of the marine shell at the site was almost certainly of historical origin, however, especially a sparse scatter of *Olivella* and other shells near the sea cliff that seems to have been imported in beach sands and gravels. Other shell at the site is probably archaeological (and Native American) in origin, but it is clustered around two historic houses associated with twentieth-century oil facilities (see chapter 7). This heavily weathered shell may have been brought in with soil from SBA-72 or SBA-73, possibly to enrich garden areas around the homes. Although a number of artifacts have been recovered from SBA-1673 (Cooley and Erlandson 1989), the few diagnostic specimens seem to be associated primarily with Early and Middle Holocene site use. Given its proximity to SBA-73 and SBA-72, however, SBA-1673 was probably used occasionally by the people of Hel'apunitse.

LATE HOLOCENE GEOGRAPHY

Other than a rectangular shell bead from SBA-71 dated to about 3,400 years ago, we have no record of human settlement in the Tecolote area between about 4,400 and 2,100 years ago and no ecofacts from archaeological sites to help reconstruct local environments. Regional environmental records can help fill this gap, but they tell us little about the specific nature of Tecolote Canyon habitats. Pol-

len records from the Santa Barbara Channel area suggest that Late Holocene vegetation communities were similar to those found in early historic times, for instance, with a mix of coastal sage scrub, grassland, riparian, oak woodland, and other habitats. Global and regional records also tell us that sea level rise had slowed dramatically by this time, during which local coastal habitats gradually developed an essentially modern character. After a relatively warm and dry period in the Middle Holocene, southern California's coastal climate during the Late Holocene was probably more similar to modern conditions.

There is considerable evidence for environmental change during the past 3,000 years (Figure 6.10), including extended droughts and warm El Niño–like ocean temperatures. Archaeologists have long suggested that changes in climate and oceanic conditions affected marine and terrestrial productivity in the Santa Barbara Channel area, contributing to important changes in Chumash culture. Arnold (1987, 1992a, 1997), for instance, used long records of sea surface temperature from Santa Barbara Basin sediments (Pisias 1978) to propose that an extended period of warm ocean temperatures significantly reduced marine productivity from about AD 1150 to 1300, contributing to a major reorganization of Chumash society. Pisias has proposed that some of his warm intervals in local waters were of a magnitude (c. 21–25°C) that almost certainly would have devastated the rich kelp forests of the Santa Barbara Channel and could have decimated Chumash fisheries. More recent research (Kennett 1998, 2005; Kennett and Kennett 2000) suggests, however, that the magnitude of some Holocene changes in the temperature of channel waters was much less than that estimated by Pisias, that the supposed warm water interval between AD 1150 and 1300 was actually relatively cool, and that local fisheries were relatively productive. More attention is now focused on the possible effects of two major droughts that may have reduced the availability of freshwater and terrestrial resources during what is often referred to as the Medieval Climatic Anomaly (Jones et al. 1999; Raab and Larson 1997). These droughts, visible in drowned forests in some Sierra lakes, are believed to have afflicted the southern California area between AD 892 and 1112 and from AD 1210 to 1350 (Stine 1994). Erlandson et al. (2001) have identified a sharp decline in the number of Island Chumash village sites dated to the Medieval Climatic Anomaly, which may have been caused by these droughts (see also Yatsko 2000). There is no evidence for an abandonment or decline of Chumash settlement in the Tecolote Canyon area, however, where several ^{14}C dates from SBA-72 and SBA-73 fall within each of these proposed drought episodes.

Late Holocene changes in local landforms appear to have affected Chumash settlement in the Tecolote Canyon area. Archaeological and environmental data from SBA-75 and the buried components at SBA-72N suggest that near the end of the Middle Holocene productive estuarine habitats had essentially disappeared from the Tecolote area, the canyon mouth was relatively unstable and prone to periodic flooding, and local shorelines were dominated by a mix of surf-swept sandy beaches and rocky intertidal habitats. The establishment of villages at SBA-72N and SBA-73N about 2,000 years ago suggests that some stream terraces and other landforms in the canyon bottom had stabilized by this time, but low-lying landforms near the beach may have remained highly dynamic and restricted settlement in the southern site areas. Rogers (1929) noted that some of these low areas were periodically flooded during their occupation,

for instance, which may also have altered the freshwater marshes at the mouths of both Tecolote and Winchester canyons. Even today, with the creeks stabilized by the concrete tunnels under the highway and railroad tracks, these marshes are changed dramatically by floods. Chumash occupation at SBA-72 and SBA-73 shows a progressive southward shift over the centuries, however, suggesting that the villages expanded toward the modern coast as the margins of the Tecolote marsh gradually stabilized over time. The Chumash themselves may have contributed to this stabilization by depositing masses of midden material—tons of marine shell, burned rock, animal bones, and other debris—along the margins of the marsh.

Faunal data from Tecolote Canyon sites spanning much of the last two millennia provide little evidence for changes in local environments. Thousands of animal bones from SBA-72 and SBA-73 suggest that local mammal and fish fauna were highly productive and similar to those typical of the area prior to the historical eradication of sea otters, Guadalupe fur seals, and other native species. One possible exception is found in the shellfish remains from SBA-72 and SBA-73, where estuarine species (Venus and Washington clams, scallops, etc.) reappear during the Late Holocene, contributing about 10 to 20 percent of the shell in the samples we analyzed. As Serena (1980) suggested, this may indicate that a productive estuary existed at the mouth of Tecolote or Winchester Canyon during the Late Holocene. No estuary exists here today, however, and no geological evidence for the existence of such an estuary was found during extensive coring and trenching around the mouth of Tecolote Canyon. Likewise, other canyons along the western Santa Barbara Coast have provided no evidence for the persistence of substantial estuaries into the Late Holocene (Erlandson and Rick 2002). It seems more likely that the remains of estuarine shellfish at SBA-72 and SBA-73 came primarily from more distant habitats such as the Goleta Slough area, either through direct foraging or through trade with neighboring villagers.

Finally, it should be noted that we found no clear faunal evidence for extended periods of warm ocean temperatures, major reductions in marine productivity, or a collapse of local kelp forests in any of the Late Holocene sites at the mouth of Tecolote Canyon. This does not necessarily mean that they did not occur in the Santa Barbara Channel area, but they certainly left no clear faunal signature at SBA-72 or SBA-73. This could be related to stratigraphic mixing in the Tecolote sites, which limits the resolution of our cultural and environmental reconstructions, but Erlandson and Gerber (1993) also found no evidence for such environmental perturbations in a long and well-stratified Late Holocene sequence at SBA-1731 about 10 km to the west.

The Chumash at Hel'apunitse

Although Late Holocene archaeological records from the Tecolote area are limited to the period from about 2,300 to 500 years ago, the intensive occupations during this 1,800-year period provide a wealth of information about the development of Chumash society. In fact, D. B. Rogers's excavations at SBA-71, SBA-72, and SBA-73 in the 1920s played an important role in the definition of an archaeological signature for the Canaliño or coastal Chumash culture. They also provided important details on the structure of coastal Chumash villages, including descriptions of residential areas, dance floors, cemeteries, and sweat lodges. Later researchers have used Rogers's data, supplemented with radiocarbon dates and other types of information not available in the 1920s, to illustrate the rich social, spiritual, and political lives of the Chumash and their ancestors, as well as some of the trials and tribulations they encountered.

Settlement Dynamics

In the Tecolote Canyon area, we have identified only three sites clearly occupied during the Late Holocene: SBA-71, SBA-72, and SBA-73. To this list we might add SBA-1674, which was probably redeposited, and SBA-75 and SBA-2499, which produced single flowerpot mortar fragments diagnostic of Late Holocene site use. These compare to at least five sites occupied during the Early Holocene and eight sites occupied in the Middle Holocene. The relatively small number of Late Holocene

sites is somewhat misleading, however, for SBA-72 and SBA-73 both have two discrete loci and SBA-71 was occupied on two or three separate occasions during the past 3,400 years. The Late Holocene occupations at all three sites also appear to have been relatively intensive and sustained.

Compared with Early and Middle Holocene occupations in the area, which were widely dispersed in both the Tecolote and Winchester drainages, settlement by Late Holocene peoples was strongly focused at the mouth of Tecolote Canyon. The dispersed nature of earlier settlements may have been the result of human responses to the reorganization of Early and Middle Holocene coastal habitats—the formation and silting in of estuaries and changes in the location of freshwater sources. By the Late Holocene, in contrast, the geography of Tecolote Canyon was broadly similar to that of today, and Chumash occupation was focused near the freshwater sources and the productive marine habitats near the canyon mouth. The relatively large cemeteries associated with these villages also suggest that the semisedentary settlement proposed for the Middle Holocene (see chapter 5) had given way to the relatively permanent residential sedentism of the coastal Chumash.

In fact, ^{14}C dates from SBA-71, SBA-72, and SBA-73 suggest that the Lower Tecolote Canyon area was more or less continuously occupied between about 2,200 and 450 years ago (c. 250 BC to AD 1500). Working before the development of such dating methods, Rogers argued that SBA-72 and SBA-73 were parts of one large village complex. He suggested that both sites began with northern and southern residential clusters, which grew into larger and essentially contiguous deposits through time. Rogers (1929) noted similarities in the layout of residential areas, cemeteries, dance floors, and sweat lodges on either side of Tecolote Creek, suggesting that these represented advanced planning in the organization of activity areas by the Chumash occupants. He even suggested that discrete cemeteries at SBA-72 were used to bury women vs. men, an idea now known to be incorrect. Nonetheless, Rogers believed that SBA-72 and SBA-73 were components of a single village occupied contemporaneously.

After studying museum collections from the Tecolote Canyon sites, King (1980) suggested that the chronology of Chumash settlement in the area was more complex than Rogers recognized. King believed that the cemeteries and residential areas dated to different time periods during the last 2,000 years and various areas were used sequentially. He proposed that SBA-71 was occupied first, followed by SBA-72N, SBA-73N, SBA-72S, and SBA-73S. Following King's settlement scheme, supported by a handful of ^{14}C dates, later archaeologists generally have divided SBA-72 and SBA-73 into discrete northern and southern loci and analyzed the materials found in these areas as separate temporal entities (Erlandson 1986, 2002; Glassow 1980; Kornfeld et al. 1980; Moore et al. 1982).

With additional research, and many more ^{14}C dates, it now appears that the changes in Late Holocene settlement and land use in the Tecolote Canyon area were more complicated than either Rogers or King originally envisioned. The general chronological framework proposed by King has been shown to be largely correct, with ^{14}C dates from the major areas of SBA-71, SBA-72, and SBA-73 supporting his cemetery and settlement chronology. His assertion that the northern portions of SBA-72 and SBA-73 were occupied earlier than the southern areas also appears to be generally true. The available ^{14}C dates suggest that there is considerable overlap in the age of the occupations in various areas, however, with 1-sigma calibrated age ranges of about 250 BC to AD 600 for SBA-71, AD 1 to AD 720 for SBA-72N, 50 BC to AD 820 for SBA-73N, AD 820 to AD 1450 for SBA-72S, and AD 470 to AD 1550 for SBA-73S. Some of this overlap may be related to the statistical uncertainties inherent in radiocarbon dating, but the distribution of temporally diagnostic artifacts supports even greater overlap in the ages of various site areas, and it seems unlikely that the available ^{14}C dates fully represent the age range of occupation in each area. Some confusion may also be related to the use of cemeteries located outside of their associated residential areas—including the apparent use of the Canaliño cemetery at SBA-71 by the occupants of SBA-72 and SBA-73—but the residential debris in many of these site areas also seems to overlap in age. Thus, the chronology of Late Holocene settlement in Tecolote Canyon also confirms aspects of Rogers's settlement model. It now appears that SBA-72N and SBA-73N were occupied simultaneously from at least about AD 1 to 1130, for instance, and SBA-72S and SBA-73S also appear to have been occupied simultaneously later in time. At times then, residential areas on either side of Tecolote Creek do appear to have operated as a single village, although the cemeteries used by the Chumash residents may have been more discrete. In our view, the complexity of settlement dynamics at Hel'apunitse offers a more realistic view of human behavior, with the Chumash residents of the area spreading their homes and activities across a variety of available landforms around the mouth of Tecolote Canyon.

Technology, Subsistence, and Ceremonialism

The artifacts and faunal remains from these Late Holocene sites also provide a wealth of information about the elaboration of Chumash technologies, coastal subsistence, social and economic interaction, and the ceremonial activities conducted in Tecolote Canyon. Cemetery excavations by Rogers produced some spectacular finds: the headdress of the "Swordfish Man" buried at SBA-71 about 1,400 years ago; large whale bone (scapulae) grave markers inlaid with shell ornaments from SBA-73S; beautiful bone whistles, daggers, and pins; a wide variety of shell, stone, and bone beads; and hundreds of keyhole limpet ornaments emblematic of the Late Holocene at Tecolote. A much wider range of formal and expedient artifacts made from stone, bone, shell, asphaltum, and other materials also testifies to the more mundane subsistence activities and everyday lives of the site occupants. The abundance of mortars, pestles, manos, and metates testifies to the importance of plant foods to the coastal Chumash. A variety of projectile points, barbs, scrapers, and knives—as well as thousands of burned and broken mammal bones—clearly illustrate the importance of hunting on land and at sea. Sea mammals, including the now locally extinct Guadalupe fur seal and California sea otter, were important resources, and deer, rabbits, and raccoons were also hunted. Numerous fishhooks, including two shell specimens from SBA-71 that are among the earliest known from the Santa Barbara Channel area (Rick et al. 2002), indicate that fishing was also a major activity. The analysis of thousands of fish bones indicates that other technologies (nets, harpoons, boats, etc.) were used to capture fish in a variety of nearshore and pelagic waters. Our dietary reconstructions also suggest that the importance of fishing expanded through time, an intensification consistent with broader patterns in the Santa Barbara Channel area. Although shellfish densities in the Late Holocene components remain relatively high, and shellfish were clearly harvested or obtained from a variety of different habitats, dietary reconstructions indicate that the economic significance of shellfish had declined significantly from earlier times. Clearly, the people of Tecolote Canyon made use of all available habitats and had a rich local knowledge of the plants and animals available in the area. Overall, Late Holocene subsistence strategies appear to have been more diverse and complex than those earlier in time, a pattern well documented for the coastal Chumash in general (Erlandson and Rick 2002).

Beads and ornaments were also relatively abundant in the Late Holocene components, and the variety of ornaments was much greater than that found in Early and Middle Holocene sites in the area. Evidence for the local manufacture of such artifacts is limited, however, and most of them were probably obtained through trade with other Chumash groups on the Channel Islands, on the mainland coast, or in the interior. Artifacts of soapstone (steatite and serpentine) may have been obtained through exchange with Chumash neighbors in the interior, as well as Tongva people from Santa Catalina Island. Artifacts made from fused shale, high-quality Monterey and Franciscan cherts, and other materials were probably also obtained through trade within the Chumash world. Analysis of obsidian artifacts from the Tecolote Canyon sites demonstrates that the people of Hel'apunitse were engaged (directly or indirectly) in larger trade and interaction networks that encompassed much of southern and central California, as well as the Sierra Nevada, the Western Great Basin, and the American Southwest.

Ultimately, the intensive settlement of the Tecolote area during the last 2,200 years reflects regional trends toward higher population densities and increased territoriality among the Chumash in the Late Holocene. Archaeological evidence suggests that the western Santa Barbara Coast was densely settled during the past two millennia. Growth in the number and size of villages in the area probably constrained the ability of people to move and reduced the size of hunting, fishing, and foraging territories among the coastal Chumash. This encouraged the intensification of resource harvests within smaller territories, creating an increasingly anthropogenic landscape more heavily influenced by human hunting, prescribed burning, and other activities. At Tecolote, such changes in the social and natural landscape encouraged the diversification and intensification of marine fishing, with a wider range of species captured from a greater variety of habitats, including more fishing for large species (swordfish, tuna, etc.) in pelagic habitats. The people of Hel'apunitse may also have intensified their harvest of acorns and other plant foods, which were probably abundant in the upper reaches of the canyon, storing food surpluses for trade with their Island Chumash neighbors. Through such intensification, increased commerce, and village specialization—facilitated by the development of shell bead currencies and large oceangoing tomols—the Chumash developed a set of cooperative responses to try to overcome the social and environmental stresses brought on by population growth and periodic resource shortages, a topic discussed at greater length in chapter 8.

With larger populations and fewer resources, however, the effects of occasional ecological disruptions (droughts, El Niño events, overhunting, etc.) became increasingly serious in the Late Holocene. That competition, social conflict, and territorial aggression sometimes trumped the cooperative responses of the Chumash is evident at Tecolote, where a number of individuals who died violently were buried at SBA-72N about 1,300 years ago. This conflict was part of a regional increase in the incidence of illness and violence in the Santa Barbara Channel area about this time, a pattern that may be related to a combination of growing environmental and social stresses, along with the destabilizing effects of the introduction of the bow and arrow (Lambert 1994). Although the Chumash world had become considerably more crowded and interdependent, rates of violence later declined, and the Chumash appear to have been thriving again by the time Europeans first explored the region in the mid-1500s.

After nearly a century of systematic archaeological explorations in the area, no evidence has been found for contact between the people of Hel'apunitse and these early European explorers. Whether the Chumash settlement at Tecolote was abandoned before the first of these contacts, which occurred in AD 1542, is uncertain. It is intriguing, however, that the Chumash sites at the mouth of Tecolote Canyon appear to have been occupied intensively and continuously from at least 2,200 to about 500 years ago, only to be abandoned about the time Europeans first arrived in the area. This topic is explored in more detail in the following chapter, along with a summary of the history of the canyon over the past 500 years.

7

History and Historical Archaeology

Jon M. Erlandson

In the preceding chapters, we defined "history" very broadly, emphasizing that the history of the Tecolote Canyon area is written in the rocks and landforms of the canyon, as well as in the shells and artifacts left behind by Native people for more than 10 millennia. Traditionally, Western science has taken a much narrower view of history, one limited to those natural and cultural events that have been written down. In that sense of the word, human history is limited to the last 5,000 years or so, beginning in Mesopotamia (in modern Iraq) with cuneiform writing. In the Tecolote Canyon area, this narrow view of history would limit us to less than 500 years, beginning with the first known contact between the Chumash and Europeans in AD 1542, when three Spanish ships commanded by Juan Rodriguez Cabrillo explored the North Pacific Coast and the Santa Barbara Channel area.

In this chapter, I summarize the history and archaeology of the Tecolote Canyon area and the coastal Chumash from Cabrillo's time to the present. I begin with the poorly documented "Protohistoric" period from AD 1542 until about AD 1769, when the Spanish initiated their systematic colonization of Alta California. I then describe the general history of land use in the Tecolote Canyon area during the Spanish and Mexican periods, for which we currently have no direct archaeological evidence, followed by detailed descriptions of land use and archaeological materials from the American period, from about AD 1850 to the present.

THE PROTOHISTORIC PERIOD: PARADISE OR APOCALYPSE?

In chapter 3, I summarized a number of early accounts of Chumash society recorded by Spanish chroniclers of the late 1700s. Along with archaeological data, these accounts and ethnographic data collected from Chumash descendants in the early 1900s make up the bulk of what we know about "traditional" Chumash society prior to sustained contact with Europeans. Historians and anthropologists have relied heavily on these ethnohistorical and ethnographic accounts to understand the nature of Chumash culture before Europeans arrived in the Santa Barbara Channel area. However, Europeans entered the area 227 years before the first detailed accounts of Chumash life were written down. These early contacts, like the later colonization of California by European colonial powers, were part of a global process of empire building and economic competition created by the expansion of Europeans around the world.

Shortly after Columbus "discovered" America in AD 1492, Spanish conquistadors moved into much of the Western Hemisphere and took effective control of most of the Pacific Ocean. After Hernán Cortés engineered the Spanish conquest of the Aztecs and Mexico in 1519, a period of colonial consolidation, exploration, and expansion began under a policy of subjugation via "the sword and the cross." As part of this process, a flotilla of three ships commanded by Cabrillo sailed north from the port of Navidad in New Spain (now Mexico), entrusted by Cortés and the Spanish crown to explore the west coast of North America. His ship's log, which survived only in summary form, tells of his passage along the Santa Barbara Coast in October and his contacts with the Chumash as he sailed westward from what was probably Rincon Point:

> Always there were many canoes because all the coast is heavily inhabited, and there came many Indians to the ships, and pointed to the towns and told the names which were Xuco, Vis, Sopono, Alloc, Xabaagua, Azcotoc, Potultuc, Nacbul, Quelqueme, Mininagua, Miseropamo, Elquis, Coloc, Mugu, Xagua, Aracbuc, Partocac, Suniquei, Quanmugua, Asimui, Aguen, Casalic, Tucumu.... Up to this point they were on very good land, with good plains and many groves and savannas.... The following Tuesday, the 17th, they traveled three leagues with calm weather, and from dawn there were many canoes traveling with the ships. The captain gave them many gifts, and all the coast along which they passed was inhabited by many people. The Indians brought in their canoes fresh and very good sardines, and said that in the interior were many towns and much food. These Indians... dressed in skins and wore their hair very long and tangled, with very long cords intricately woven into their hair, and between these cords and the hair were many daggers of stone and of bone and wood. The earth appeared to be excellent [Paez 1968:10–11].

During this passage, Cabrillo and his ships probably passed the mouth of Tecolote Canyon—which may or may not have been inhabited at the time. As far as we can tell, the area was abandoned as a permanent settlement between about AD 1450 and 1550, when most of the Chumash occupants may have moved to one of the larger villages around the Goleta Slough or to Dos Pueblos to the west. With evidence for what appears to be continuous and relatively intensive settlement of the canyon from about 250 BC to at least AD 1500, the abandonment of the Tecolote area about the time of

Cabrillo's voyage suggests the possibility that the two events may have been linked, a topic I return to below.

Between Cabrillo's voyage and AD 1769, when the Spanish first began to settle Alta California, contacts between the coastal Chumash and Europeans were sporadic, limited to occasional commerce between the Chumash and the crews of Manila galleons that crossed the North Pacific annually between AD 1564 and 1815 while sailing from the Philippines to New Spain. Contacts with Manila galleons were rarely recorded, however, because this trade was carried out in great secrecy. The galleons carried the wealth of an empire and were preyed on by pirates and privateers such as Sir Francis Drake and Miles Cavendish. After Cabrillo's exploratory voyage, the only documented Protohistoric contacts between European voyagers and the Chumash were with members of Spanish expeditions led by Unamuno in AD 1587, Cermeno in AD 1595–1596, and Vizcaino in AD 1602–1603 (see Erlandson and Bartoy 1995; Wagner 1929).

There has never been any doubt about the devastating effects of European contact on California Indians, especially those caused by the introduction of Old World diseases such as smallpox, cholera, and influenza that Native Americans had never been exposed to and carried no immunities for. Through Native North America, these and other diseases rolled like a wave of death, killing millions of people and contributing to the European conquest and occupation of the continent. This apocalypse is well documented historically, beginning within decades of sustained contact between Europeans and indigenous peoples throughout the Americas, Australia, and the Pacific Islands (see Jackson 1994; Stannard 1989; Thornton 1987).

Although scholars have long agreed about the tragic effects of historical contacts between Europeans and California Indians, most have suggested that such impacts began after AD 1769. The potential for the introduction of earlier Protohistoric disease epidemics is sometimes mentioned, but most scholars have concluded that no significant cultural changes occurred among the Chumash and their neighbors as a result of Protohistoric contacts with Europeans:

Seemingly all the changes were minor: a few European words in the languages, a few children of mixed blood, a few iron knives and pieces of cloth, perhaps a few ideas about the Christian religion. Otherwise, there is little or nothing to indicate an important European influence among the Indians of California prior to the eighteenth century [Kelsey 1985:502].

The destruction of the Indians of California occurred in a series of steps…. The first of these stages accompanied the settlement of the coastal strip from San Diego to San Francisco, and was associated distinctly with the development of the Catholic missions. This phase may be considered as beginning with the expedition of Gaspar de Portola and Junipero Serra in 1769 [Cook 1978:91].

Recently, as part of a broader debate about the effects of early European contacts and diseases on Native Americans, some scholars have argued that occasional Protohistoric contacts with Europeans may have had a major impact on California Indian tribes (see Preston 1996). For the Chumash, Erlandson and Bartoy (1995) have suggested that Cabrillo's men—who wintered on San Miguel Island in AD 1542–1543—may have transmitted deadly Old World diseases that could have decimated the coastal Chumash 240 years before Mission Santa Barbara was established. The large coastal populations with their intensive social and economic interaction would have made the Chumash unusually susceptible to the spread of epidemic diseases. Cabrillo's men were a rough lot, and one can imagine their behavior when let loose among Native women of the Channel Islands after months at sea:

Cabrillo's and Vizcaino's crews were exclusively male, mostly sailors or soldiers armed with sixteenth century attitudes about women and indigenous peoples. These men were isolated from contact with women for long periods of time. During extended stays of days, weeks, or months among the Native peoples of the California coast, with crew members possessing exotic items prized by the natives, numerous forced or consensual sexual encounters almost certainly occurred. Such encounters would have been likely sources for the spread of disease from crew members to native Californians. Diseases like syphilis and influenza are relatively benign and easily cured today, but they had a rapid and devastating impact on many indigenous peoples first exposed to them in the sixteenth, seventeenth, and eighteenth centuries [Erlandson and Bartoy 1995:165].

Because of the sporadic nature of Protohistoric European contacts with the Chumash, and the fact that such diseases rarely leave traces on the human skeleton, evidence for sixteenth-century epidemics cannot be documented by traditional methods of history or paleoepidemiology. Instead, archaeological data must be used to identify changes in demography, social organization, or burial practices that might have resulted from diseases or other cultural impacts. Because historians, anthropologists, and other scholars had generally dismissed the idea that Old World diseases affected California Indians prior to the establishment of the missions, archaeologists have only just begun to examine such evidence.

In search of evidence that Protohistoric diseases may have had an impact on the Chumash, Bartoy and I cited King's (1980) chronology for Chumash settlement of Tecolote Canyon, suggesting that the area was "abandoned at roughly the time of Cabrillo's voyage, after virtually continuous occupation spanning at least the past 1,500 years" (Erlandson and Bartoy 1995:167). Radiocarbon dates on archaeological materials from Tecolote Canyon sites now confirm that the villages at the canyon mouth were abandoned by the Chumash in approximately AD 1500, give or take 50 years. These dates are suggestive, but radiocarbon dating is not sensitive enough to be certain that Tecolote Canyon was still occupied when Cabrillo sailed along the Santa Barbara Coast.

In search of more definitive evidence, my colleagues and I (Erlandson et al. 1997) analyzed the distribution of hundreds of calibrated ^{14}C dates from Chumash sites along the Santa Barbara Coast,

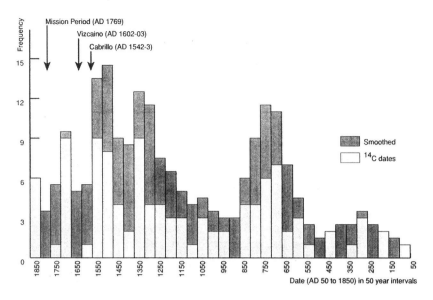

FIGURE 7.1. Plot of ^{14}C dates from the Northern Channel Islands, possible evidence for Protohistoric population collapse among the Island Chumash (from Erlandson et al. 2001).

looking for evidence of significant demographic changes during the Protohistoric period. We identified a steep decline in the number of dated sites roughly corresponding with Cabrillo's voyage, a decline that might result from population losses caused by Old World diseases. More recently, we (Erlandson et al. 2001) analyzed more than 200 Late Holocene ^{14}C dates from the Northern Channel Islands—the "ground zero" where the effects of diseases transmitted by Cabrillo's crews should have been most devastating—and found a similar pattern (see Figure 7.1). Although more research needs to be done, these patterns suggest that the coastal Chumash may have been devastated by Old World disease epidemics associated with Cabrillo's voyage along the California Coast. Whether the people of Hel'apunitse were decimated by such epidemics remains uncertain, but a variety of data suggests that Chumash populations recovered later in the Protohistoric period and the Chumash were thriving once again when the Spanish first settled the Santa Barbara area in the late 1700s.

Whatever caused its abandonment, we currently have no evidence for Chumash settlement of the Tecolote area between about AD 1550 and recent times. Several sites in the area have yet to be investigated, but what we know of them suggests that they are unlikely to date to the Protohistoric or early Historic periods. Chumash people undoubtedly hunted, fished, and gathered in the area during these times, but they may have done so primarily from villages located around the Goleta Slough or at Dos Pueblos. If the Tecolote Canyon area was occupied during the Protohistoric period, it was probably used seasonally rather than as a permanent village site. At the time, it must have been a quiet place, with a relatively pristine mosaic of oak woodland, grassland, chaparral, and riparian vegetation supporting a rich array of wildlife. Even this landscape was actively managed by the Chumash, however, who periodically burned the area to maintain a relatively open and productive character. People regularly fished the rich kelp beds offshore, walked the beaches, and swam in the surf. And just as today, people retreated here to avoid the stresses of everyday life or to laugh on the beach with the ones they loved.

HISTORICAL OVERVIEW OF THE TECOLOTE CANYON AREA

After the Spanish settlement of the Santa Barbara area, more information is available on the nature of human use of the Tecolote Canyon area. A combination of historical accounts and archaeological data can be used to summarize the history of the Tecolote Canyon area since about AD 1769. In that fateful year, European settlement of the Santa Barbara area began with the overland Portola Expedition's exploration in preparation for the establishment of a Spanish colony in Alta California anchored by a series of missions and forts (presidios). The building of this colonial network was a response to perceived threats from Russian, English, and American expansion or commercial activity in the area. Although Spanish missions opened in Chumash territory at San Luis Obispo as early as 1772, the Santa Barbara Presidio was not founded until 1782, followed by Mission Santa Barbara in 1786. As various missions were built, a transportation corridor linking them was also developed. Known as El Camino Real (the King's Road), this early trail or road traversed the western Santa Barbara Coast and ran through the Tecolote Canyon area. It was probably during the Spanish era that Tecolote ("Owl" in Spanish) Canyon received its modern name. During the early years, what we call Bell, Winchester, and Ellwood canyons together were known as Los Armitos or Las Armas (the Weapons) Canyon (Tompkins 1966).

With the founding of Mission Santa Barbara, the Tecolote area became a part of the mission lands administered by the padres and supposedly held in trust for the Chumash people. The missions relied on a pastoral economy based on the production of cattle and other livestock. Cattle raised primarily for the marketing of hide and tallow products (not meat) were the main economic focus of the missions, but sheep and other livestock were raised as well. By the end of the eighteenth century, the rapid growth of mission and private livestock herds in the Santa Barbara area was altering the natural balance of native plant communities, making it more and more difficult for the Chumash to maintain their traditional economy and lifeways. Inexorably, more and more Chumash people were drawn to the missions or took jobs in local pueblos and ranches whose growth was spurred by the emergence of increasingly global markets.

Records of land-use practices in the Tecolote area are scarce for the Mission period, but the canyon clearly played a role in the ranching activities

of Santa Barbara Mission. The earliest known reference to the use of the area for ranching dates to 1803 but suggests an earlier use as well: "During this same year, according to Fr. O'Keefe, a new corral was constructed at Tecolote. The report for this year tells us that on July 28, 29, and 30, 1,084 head of sheep were branded at Mission San Buenaventura and exchanged for another herd of the same number which was then sent to stock Tecolote" (Engelhardt 1923, cited in Fuller and King 1980:101). D. B. Rogers also noted the possibility of a limited Chumash occupation of Tecolote Canyon during the Mission period, noting that "among the old settlers of the vicinity, there linger memories of the last survivor of this village, who, as an old man, had told of the duties imposed upon him as a youth; these were to turn back the herds belonging to the Mission when they strayed up the coast" (1929: 201). Use of the Tecolote Canyon area primarily as pasture lands and logistical facilities associated with ranching persisted for a century or more and spanned the Spanish, Mexican, and American eras, from the 1780s into the early 1900s.

After Spanish rule gave way to the Republic of Mexico in AD 1822, the mission ranchos appear to have continued as before until Mexico officially secularized the Catholic missions in 1834. The Mexican government deemed secularization to be in the "best interests of the Indians...that they be allowed full liberty and given land on which to support themselves." Although large tracts of mission lands—along with half of their livestock, grain, and tools—were supposed to be divided among local Indian people, the policy was an "utter failure," with few Indians receiving any land and those who did "so harassed by whites that their lot became unendurable" (Hawley 1987:107). In Santa Barbara County, vast tracts of the mission lands held in trust for the Chumash were transferred to Spanish, Mexican, and other European colonists, including the Tecolote area, which was granted to Nicolas Den in AD 1842. Den incorporated the Tecolote area into his Rancho Los Dos Pueblos, named after the two Chumash towns of Mikiw and Kuyamu located at Dos Pueblos Canyon west of Tecolote. The part of Den's land grant lying east of Winchester Canyon was temporarily returned to

Mission Santa Barbara in a court case presided over by the Mexican governor, Manuel Micheltorena, but the disputed land was restored to Den on appeal (Tompkins 1966:35).

In AD 1846, the relative quiet and peace of most Santa Barbarians were broken by the outbreak of war between Mexico and the United States of America. As part of a larger conflict over lands stretching from Texas to Oregon, American settlers in northern California instigated the Bear Flag Revolt, declaring California an independent republic. In July, 250 U.S. soldiers occupied Monterey, the seat of Mexico's government in Alta California, and declared the area an American territory (Holliday 1981:31). As described by Tompkins (1966) in *Goleta the Good Land*, the ebb and flow of the Mexican–American War partly played out in the Santa Barbara area, which briefly became the Mexican capital of Alta California after the abandonment of Monterey. In August 1846, a small force of American marines landed at Santa Barbara and raised the American flag at the presidio (Tompkins 1966:41). Mexican patriots retook Santa Barbara for a day in September before Captain John Fremont secured the Santa Barbara garrison the following day. The conflict was not resolved until 1848, with the signing of the Treaty of Guadalupe Hidalgo, which ceded vast amounts of Mexican territory to the United States and fulfilled the dream of manifest destiny, with an America stretching from sea to shining sea.

With the discovery of gold in the Sierras early in 1848, the great gold rush began, and a flood of American immigrants descended on California. The gold rush created both problems and opportunities for the people of Santa Barbara County. Many residents left for the gold fields—Robinson (1948:134) estimated that 80 percent of all able-bodied men in California were working the gold fields by the end of 1848—but the inflated markets created for meat and other goods by the influx of thousands of miners provided a huge boost to the California economy and fortunes for some of those who stayed behind. According to Tompkins, Nicolas Den and several other Santa Barbara ranchers became wealthy "by driving cattle up to the Mother Lode country to furnish beef-hungry

miners with steaks for which they gladly paid as much as an ounce of gold dust—$19—for a ten ounce serving!"(1975:38).

The population boom created by the gold rush also fueled statehood for California, which entered the union as the thirty-fourth of the United States of America in AD 1850. By 1853, California's population had mushroomed to over 300,000 people, and over $260,000,000 worth of gold had been wrested from the state (Robinson 1948:135). With the adoption of an American style of government, an early concern of the California legislature was the improvement of the transportation network that linked the growing communities of the new state. A law passed in AD 1859 provided funds for the construction of a coastal wagon and stagecoach road through Santa Barbara County. Along the western Santa Barbara Coast, the proposed County Road generally followed El Camino Real, not far from Highway 101 today. This wagon and stagecoach road opened in AD 1861 and passed through Goleta Valley, where at "Ellwood Canyon it turned north at right angles for one mile, and thence wound over the steep hill at Tecolote Canyon" (Tompkins 1966:61). A detailed 1868 map of the area (Figure 7.2), the first of its kind, shows this stagecoach route. Another road runs from Ellwood to the mouth of Bell Canyon, where it followed the beach to the west side of Tecolote Creek and then cut diagonally across what is now the Bacara property to meet the main road at the north edge of the coastal plain.

When Nicolas Den died in AD 1862, his will divided Rancho Los Dos Pueblos between his wife, Rosa Hill, and his 10 children. His daughter Katherine had first choice among the children and reportedly selected property in what is now known as the Bell Canyon area (Tompkins 1976:172). Rancho Los Dos Pueblos continued to be managed by Den's heirs and a series of executors. After severe flooding in the winter of 1861–1862, an epic drought afflicted southern California from 1862 to 1864, severely disrupting the local and regional economy. In the Santa Barbara area, the drought was accompanied by large wildfires and heavy erosion, with up to 14 ft of silt deposited in the nearby Goleta Slough. The combination of flooding and

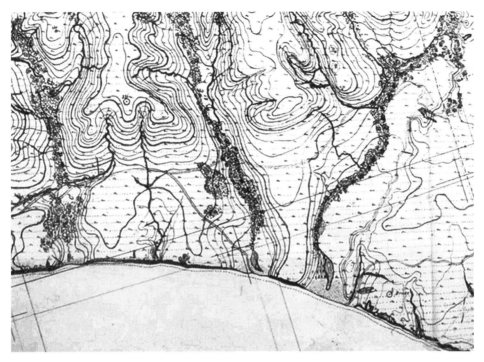

FIGURE 7.2. An 1868 map of the Lower Tecolote and Winchester Canyon area (courtesy of the University of California–Santa Barbara Maps and Imagery Library; photo by Jon Erlandson).

drought devastated the once vast livestock herds of Santa Barbara County. According to Tompkins (1960:183), cattle sold by Rancho Los Dos Pueblos for $50 a head during the gold rush were now worth barely $3.00 a head.

A few years later, the first detailed maps of the Tecolote Canyon area and the Santa Barbara Coast were made by surveyors employed by the U.S. Coastal and Geographical Survey. The 1868 map of the area shows the Lower Tecolote and Winchester Canyon areas, including the adjacent coastal plain, as completely undeveloped except for the two wagon roads and grazing lands. Small marshes are depicted at the mouth of each canyon, where the flow of their creeks was impounded by sand dunes.

According to Tompkins (1976:132), in AD 1869 Ellwood Cooper purchased 2,000 acres of the Dos Pueblos Ranch in the Winchester Canyon area for about $22 an acre. A renowned horticulturalist who reportedly introduced eucalyptus trees and ladybugs to California, Cooper planted about 7,000 olive trees and built an olive mill in the upper reaches of Winchester Canyon in AD 1872. Although Cooper also maintained 12,500 walnut trees, he was known for a time as the "Olive King of North America."

Also in AD 1872, the Tecolote area was sold to Thomas and Daniel Hayes, property that later became known as Tecolote Ranch (Fuller and King 1980:102). The sale of the land, unauthorized by the Den heirs or probate court, was contested by the Den Estate. At the end of 1875, however, Tecolote Ranch was sold to Shelton Sturges, a Civil War veteran and distant relation of William Hollister (Tompkins 1966:91). Sturges sold the land for $20,000 in gold two years later to his sons, one of whom (William) became the sole owner in 1883. The Sturges family maintained a ranch house in the canyon about 2 mi from the ocean and developed Tecolote into a diversified ranch. According to Fuller and King,

Sturges maintained a herd of about two hundred cattle…a small number compared to some other area ranches…. No longer was the hide and tallow trade the main impulse for cattle raising. Under Harold Sturges beef sales were the central ranch concern…. One of Sturges' ranch hands, Smiley Olvieda, "used to drive the cattle down from the upper part of the ranch across the highway to the lower part near the beach every morning and then would drive them back again near the ranch house every night" [1980:103].

Under Sturges management, if not before, the lower canyon area near the beach was also used to grow barley and corn, which could be grown without irrigation. The farming of the lower canyon, which continued for several decades, undoubtedly affected the remnants of the Chumash villages at SBA-72 and SBA-73. Sturges also raised hogs on the ranch, which were allowed to forage in the grain fields after they were harvested. According to the 1933 testimony of William Main and A. K. Langlo, "swine were allowed on the beach" to forage during dry years when grain production was poor (Fuller and King 1980:104). Sturges also built the first pier at Tecolote Canyon in the early 1880s, apparently using it primarily to ship lumber. The Sturges family also used the beach, fenced off to prevent public access, for fishing, picnics, clambakes, and barbeques, According to Fuller and King (1980), Sturges fished for trout and hunted ducks in the small marsh at the mouth of Tecolote Creek.

The Sturges's ownership of Tecolote Ranch was legally contested by representatives of the Den Estate, who claimed it was sold by Charles Huse without proper authorization. According to historian Walker Tompkins, this dispute was settled when

the court ruled the Den Estate was entitled to recover all Dos Pueblos trust property illegally sold by Huse, and that defendants were not entitled to compensation for what they had spent in improvements over the years, the court holding that they had received enough income off the ranches during that time to offset this amount. Harold Sturges, who had been sole owner of Tecolote Ranch since his two brothers left California in 1883, bowed to the inevitable and vacated the Tecolote Ranch [1966:169].

For legal services and loans made to the Den Estate during litigation, Thomas Bishop took over Tecolote Ranch in AD 1887. Incorporation papers for Bishop's Tecolote Land Company described the purpose of the business as the breeding of "horses, sheep, hogs, and other livestock" and "farming and cultivating agricultural and horticultural products" (Fuller and King 1980:105). Bishop and others also formed a Tecolote Water Company authorized to manage, store, and distribute water in the area. Construction of dams in the upper canyon and a water tank on "Tecolote Hill" allowed for irrigation that broadened the range of crops that could be grown on the ranch. In AD 1891, the upper road through Tecolote Canyon was the scene of a tragic accident, when W. E. Nichols from Dos Pueblos was killed as his wagon rolled over him on a sharp curve near the base of the steep canyon wall (Tompkins 1966:61). Although the area was still sparsely populated, a Tecolote School District was created in AD 1893 and granted a half acre of land on a hilltop above the County Road. A one-room schoolhouse was built at the north end of the coastal plain on the east rim of Tecolote Canyon and stood until 1949 (see Figure 7.3), when it was demolished (Fuller and King 1980:105).

Tecolote Canyon continued to be used for a variety of purposes—grazing, farming, recreation, and more—throughout the 1880s and 1890s. The lower canyon was transformed in the late 1890s, however, after the Southern Pacific Railroad acquired a 100-ft right-of-way through the area. A railroad line from Los Angeles to Santa Barbara and Goleta was completed in AD 1887, but the tracks stopped at Ellwood. This was the end of the line for 14 years, with the gap between Goleta and Santa Margarita negotiated primarily by stagecoach (Tompkins 1976:186). A railroad link bridging the gap was completed in AD 1901, crossing Winchester and Tecolote canyons with a combination of cut and fill features still visible in the area today. To ensure access between the upper and lower portions of the canyons for ranch residents and operations, tunnels with beautiful sandstone culverts were built for both creeks by a local stonemason named Tom Pollard (Fuller and King 1980; see Figure 7.4).

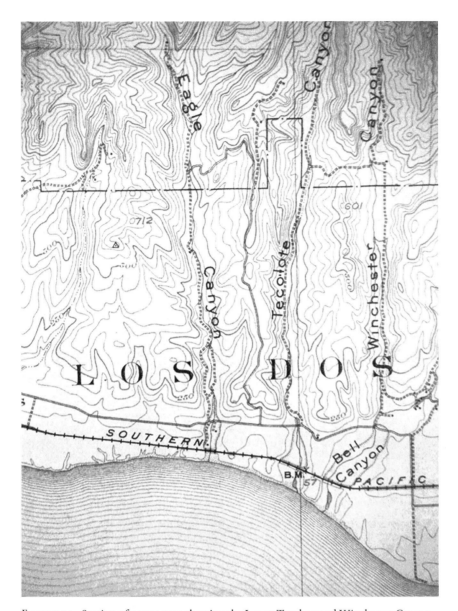

FIGURE 7.3. Section of a 1903 map showing the Lower Tecolote and Winchester Canyon area. Note the schoolhouse next to the coast road at the north edge of the coastal plain, just east of Tecolote Canyon (courtesy of the University of California–Santa Barbara Maps and Imagery Library; photo by Jon Erlandson).

In AD 1908, at the invitation of Mrs. Thomas Bishop, the first professional archaeological excavations took place in Tecolote Canyon when University of California Professor Frederick Ward Putnam excavated two Chumash burials from a badly disturbed cemetery at SBA-73. The disturbance noted by Putnam was probably the work of Stephen Bowers, the incorrigible antiquarian whose notes indicate that he spent two days plundering "a great number of skeletons" on the west side of "Haye's Canyon" in August 1877 (Benson 1997:104). Putnam's work also shows that the owners of Tecolote Ranch were aware of and interested in the archaeological sites on their property at a very early date. It also documents that the deplorable looting of Chumash cemeteries in the area—

FIGURE 7.4. Southern entrance to the sandstone tunnel channeling Tecolote Creek under the Southern Pacific Railroad, built c. 1900 (photo by Jon Erlandson).

which continued into the 1990s—goes back well over a hundred years.

With agricultural potential enhanced by irrigation, the area south of the railroad tracks continued to be cultivated and grazed. At one time or another, hay, oats, corn, barley, potatoes, and lima beans were all grown there. After windbreaks of cypress trees were planted "somewhere between 1908 and 1912"—remnants of which can still be seen along the east bank of Tecolote Creek—a 9-acre lemon orchard was planted in the western area. A "salt breeze" killed the lemon trees, however, and they were later removed (Fuller and King 1980:108).

A new and improved County Road from Goleta to Gaviota was completed in 1912, crossing Tecolote and Winchester canyons immediately north of the railroad right-of-way and involving extensive cut and fill operations (Figure 7.5). In 1918, Bishop leased a portion of the beach property for a short-lived kelp-harvesting factory, which tried to produce potash, iodine, and other chemicals for the World War I effort. According to Fuller and King (1980), "200 loads of rock were hauled from nearby hills" to build a road for the kelp factory, and two burners, four bunkhouses, and a cookhouse

were all built on the property. Between 1922 and 1924, the beach area at Tecolote Canyon was also leased to a local fisherman named John Traves, who "built a shack near the estero" that was removed after the Bishops sold the ranch in AD 1926. Also in 1926, David Banks Rogers conducted his extensive excavations at the Tecolote Canyon archaeological sites of SBA-71, SBA-72, and SBA-73.

During the Prohibition years after World War I, the remoteness of the beaches in the Tecolote area attracted rumrunners and other illicit activity. At least one employee of Tecolote Ranch was deputized by the local sheriff to patrol the beach and make arrests where necessary. According to Tompkins, bootleggers in the Ellwood area once used a fake Richfield Oil truck, which Jack Ross reportedly followed to the mouth of Bell Canyon one night. "There by moonlight, Ross saw a boat anchored beyond the breakers and a small boat loaded with kegs pulled up on the beach" (Tompkins 1976:286), with men emptying kegs of booze into the tanker truck. During Prohibition, some Goleta area residents reportedly were offered as much as $100,000 to hide liquor shipments destined for Los Angeles (Tompkins 1976).

FIGURE 7.5. Horse-drawn graders building the county road cut through Tecolote Canyon in 1912 (adapted from Tompkins 1966:260).

In AD 1926, the Bishops sold the 1,320-acre Tecolote Ranch to Silsby Spalding, a prominent "Beverly Hills real estate and oil tycoon" who was also a "keen conservationist" deeply protective of the natural beauty of Tecolote Canyon (Fuller and King 1980:110). Spalding built a large Spanish-style home that "for sheer opulence outshone the Victorian manor-houses and mansions" in the area (Tompkins 1966:276). He also developed Tecolote into "one of the most attractive and successful ranches in Santa Barbara County" (O'Neill 1939:91), converting much of the cattle ranch into lemon, orange, and avocado orchards while also raising cattle and thoroughbred horses.

On the beachfront property, they continued to grow hay on the western terrace and beans on the valley floor. In 1926, the Spaldings also built a beach house at the southeast corner of the valley floor that became a social hub for picnics, horseback riding, luncheons, and swimming parties for several years. A concrete foundation was visible for many years in this location, and the remnants of an associated cobblestone retaining wall could be seen near the base of the bluff along the edge of the beach access road in this area (Figure 7.6). An improved gravel road connecting the upper ranch with the beach parcel was constructed in AD 1927, passing through the Tecolote Creek tunnel that runs under the railroad tracks. A concrete slab exposed in the creek bank just north of the Tecolote Creek Bridge may be part of a "Texas Crossing"

that provided access from this creek-bottom road onto the adjacent terrace (Figure 7.7). A new steel and barbed wire cyclone fence was also built along the eastern and western margins of the property to keep cattle in and the public out.

Whatever conservationist inclinations the Spaldings may have had for their Tecolote beach property could not withstand the discovery of oil in the late 1920s. Oil products had been important to people of the Santa Barbara Coast for thousands of years, with tar (asphaltum) from natural oil seeps used by the Chumash to caulk boats, seal baskets, and glue or repair a variety of objects. Commercial exploitation of asphaltum began in the 1850s with the establishment of a small distilling plant near the Carpinteria oil seeps, but major oil development did not begin in the Santa Barbara area until the discovery of a large oil field near Summerland in the 1880s (Fuller and King 1980:113). About the same time, a major seep at Coal Oil Point east of Tecolote was promoted by many "responsible medical men" as a place where oil vapors could be inhaled to treat a variety of pulmonary ailments (Tompkins 1976:266). Commercial mining of massive asphaltum deposits on what is now the University of California–Santa Barbara (UCSB) campus also began in the 1880s, and by 1890 over 32,000 tons of pulverized asphaltum had been shipped from Goleta—some of it used to surface some of the first paved streets in San Francisco (Tompkins 1966:132). As early as AD 1897,

FIGURE 7.6. A historical cobble wall (Feature PW-8) located in the southeast corner of SBA-72, looking southeast toward the beach (photo by William Glover, 1997).

FIGURE 7.7. Concrete slabs of Feature PW-14, possible remnants of a "Texas crossing" exposed in the east bank of Tecolote Creek adjacent to SBA-72N (photo by Robert Sheets, 1997).

geologist A. C. Cooper suspected that oil existed beneath the Tecolote area. A test well drilled to a depth of 1,000 ft near Bell Canyon produced no oil, however, and exploration lapsed for the next 30 years (Tompkins 1966:233). In AD 1927, deeper wells drilled in Tecolote Canyon produced limited amounts of oil and gas and then seawater. In 1928, however, a well drilled through over 3,150 ft of bedrock in Lower Bell Canyon encountered a major oil and natural gas deposit in porous 30-million-year-old Vaqueros sands (Tompkins 1966:279).

The discovery of this Ellwood Oil Field set off a wild scramble to empty this vast reservoir of high-quality oil. Virtually overnight, oil and gas leases were snapped up for surrounding parcels, and development of the field by several oil companies proceeded at a frenetic pace. Almost immediately, the Spaldings applied for state permits to explore for oil on the tidelands off the mouth of Tecolote Canyon. After receiving a permit and commissioning engineering and geological studies, Silsby Spalding leased the eastern portion of the beach property to Pacific Western Oil Company of Delaware. Spalding deeded the western part of the property to his wife, Caroline, who was granted a separate exploration permit and spent $372,000 drilling wells, building a pier, and developing the property (Fuller and King 1980:116). After her "Blue Goose No. 2" well began producing in November 1929, Caroline Spalding leased the property and facilities to Pacific Western for a substantial cash payment and a percentage of future profits.

Although the Spaldings took some steps to ensure the protection and restoration of the beach property, the transformation of Lower Tecolote Canyon was dramatic. The relatively serene and natural beauty of the beachfront property gave way to numerous oil piers, storage tanks, warehouses, administrative buildings, pipelines, roads, oil wells, mud sumps, staging areas, and the constant cacophony of industrial activity (Figures 7.8, 7.9). Fuller and King quote a contemporary account from a 1929 *Oil Bulletin* that illustrates a transformation only an oil executive could love: "Trucks, tractors, pile drivers, steam shovels, concrete mixers, carpenters with hammers and saws, and offshore, lumber boats and barges—all play a part in creating a

picturesque scene, the like of which has never been seen before" (1980:117).

Most of this transformation took place from AD 1928 to 1931, with oil production peaking in 1931 at about 7.5 million barrels. As early as 1928, however, windfall tax revenues of over $1.5 million from the Ellwood Oil Field paid for the construction of the world-famous and architecturally unique Santa Barbara County Courthouse, completed in 1929. By AD 1933, a map of the Ellwood Oil Field shows 15 piers, numerous oil wells, storage tanks, and other production facilities (see Figures 7.8 and 7.10). Two long piers once extended seaward from the mouth of Tecolote Canyon (remnants of one of these were identified during archaeological excavations in 1980) and another three from the mouth of Winchester (Bell) Canyon. What appear to have been large oil-storage tanks were located near the entrance to Bacara where the Sandpiper Golf Course now stands, in the location of the current Venoco plant on the floor of Bell Canyon, and on the valley floor east of Tecolote Creek. The basic industrial configuration of Lower Tecolote and Bell canyons remained largely unchanged for the next 25 years.

During World War II, Tecolote played a role in the coastal defenses of the United States, housing an air raid siren and an aircraft-spotting tower. Less than three months after Pearl Harbor, these facilities were involved in a bizarre incident that still represents the only wartime naval attack on the continental United States by a foreign power since 1812. As told by Walker Tompkins in his 1966 book, *Goleta the Good Land*, the incident occurred about twilight on January 23, 1942, when a 348-ft-long submarine from the Japanese Imperial Navy appeared about a mile off the Ellwood Coast for about 40 minutes. The submarine fired about 25 5.5-in cannon shells at the oil-storage tanks around the mouth of Winchester and Tecolote canyons. According to Tompkins (1966:305), the events were witnessed by two volunteers manning the spotting tower at Tecolote. Most of the shells reportedly did not explode, and only minor damage was done before the submarine disappeared offshore. In a strange twist, it was later learned that the commander of the Japanese sub, Kozo Nishino, had sailed oil tankers to Ellwood before the war,

FIGURE 7.8. The Ellwood Oil Field in 1930. Coal Oil Point is at the top center, and the Bacara property is at the lower left (photo courtesy of the Atlantic Richfield Company and the University of California–Santa Barbara Department of Anthropology).

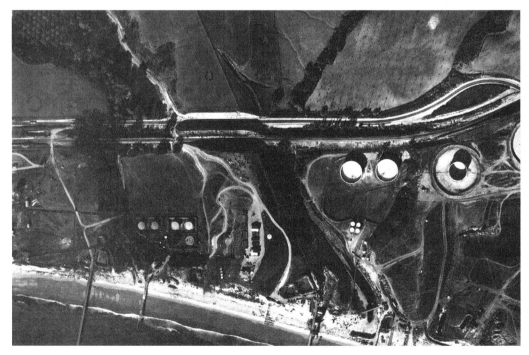

FIGURE 7.9. The Lower Tecolote Canyon area during the oil boom era. SBA-71 is in the center, with Tecolote to the left and Winchester to the right (photo courtesy of the University of California–Santa Barbara Department of Anthropology).

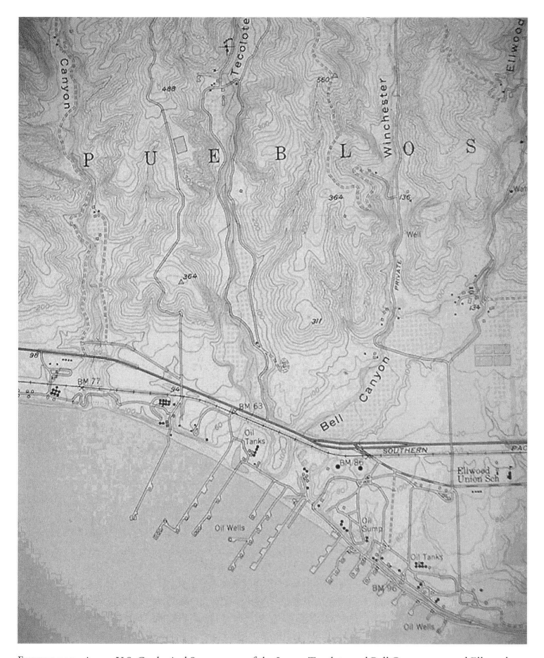

FIGURE 7.10. A 1951 U.S. Geological Survey map of the Lower Tecolote and Bell Canyon area and Ellwood Oil Field (courtesy of the University of California–Santa Barbara Maps and Imagery Library; photo by Jon Erlandson).

where he was once humiliated by American laughter after he fell into a thicket of prickly pear cactus on the shore (Tompkins 1975:305). After the barrage, one of the unexploded cannon shells was reportedly found in Tecolote Canyon and turned over to the military, but during a 1955 wildfire sev-

eral large explosions in the area were attributed to shells that had lain hidden in the brush for 14 years (Tompkins 1966).

After World War II, oil production continued to be the primary activity in the lower portions of Tecolote and Winchester canyons, with agricultural activity in the upper. U.S. Geological Survey maps from AD 1943 and 1951 clearly show these oil piers, tanks, and other facilities clustered around the mouths of Tecolote and Winchester canyons. The 1951 map (Figure 7.10) also shows two structures on the western terrace (under the Bacara parking lot) that reportedly were houses occupied by employees of Pacific Western Oil. By the 1960s, however, oil production from the Ellwood Oil Field was rapidly waning. The field had produced over 100 million barrels of high-quality crude oil and enormous quantities of natural gas. By 1966, oil production that peaked in 1931 at 7.5 million barrels had declined to 220,000 barrels (Tompkins 1966:282), and the economic viability of the Ellwood Oil Field had become marginal. Because oil companies were required to remove their facilities as production ceased, most of the piers and other structures associated with the great oil boom of the mid–twentieth century have been dismantled. Although not well documented historically, the demolition of oil facilities and partial restoration of the beachfront property probably continued through the late 1950s and early 1960s. Conditions of the lease required that all above-ground facilities be removed from the property or buried at least 5 ft deep.

In *Goleta the Good Land*, Walker Tompkins implicates the Tecolote Ranch in what he describes as "the most notorious Goleta land scandal" in history (1966:334). The scandal began in AD 1959, when Deborah Spalding Pelissero sold the ranch for nearly a million dollars to Los Angeles entrepreneurs H. R. Steele and I. H. Harris. Steele and Harris developed promotional brochures that promised an elaborate development, including a yacht marina (or embarcadero) built at the mouth of Tecolote Canyon. With help from their influential Winchester Canyon neighbor, state senator Jack Hollister, they formed the Embarcadero Municipal Improvement District (EMID), sold 628 trust deeds for lots never legally recorded, and sold over $1.2 million in bonds for sewer, water, and other improvements. Harris and Steele organized another vote authorizing the sale of $5 million in additional bonds to construct a marina, but these were unsold when the venture collapsed into bank-

ruptcy. In AD 1962, according to Tompkins, Steele and Harris were found guilty of 32 felony counts of mishandling EMID funds, with their investors left "holding the bag." In 1965, their convictions were thrown out on a technicality, but in 1966 Harris and Steele pled guilty to charges of grand larceny and falsifying records. Thankfully for the Chumash village sites located near the mouth of the canyon, the marina at Tecolote was never built.

With the collapse of Harris and Steele's grandiose scheme, the bankrupt "Rancho Embarcadero" was placed under federal receivership, while the legal subdivision of a housing tract north of the highway was completed and the sale of houses and lots was used to recover assets lost to the bankruptcy. The remaining assets, including the beachfront property, were sold in 1966 to financier Maxwell L. Rubin, who sold the property to the Wallover Corporation in 1968. Since the 1960s, the upper canyon area has been intensively farmed as an avocado ranch, a use that continues to this day.

From the 1960s to the mid-1990s, the lower canyon remained largely undeveloped. Known by locals as Haskell's Beach, it was the haunt of surfers, sun worshipers, joggers, relic hunters, and others looking for a secluded place to participate in activities both legal and illegal. A study of the thickly vegetated property by UCSB archaeologists in AD 1979 documented a variety of these behaviors (Haley 1980), discussed in greater detail later in this chapter. Since the late 1970s, with the support of the landowner, representatives of the local Chumash Indian community have regularly patrolled the beachfront property to help combat grave robbing and artifact collecting. In one infamous case, we documented the location and size of dozens of large craters dug by grave robbers at SBA-72 and SBA-73 and collected several human bones shattered by looters. Weeks later, local sheriffs and federal agents arrested a local man who confessed to grave robbing at the sites after a human jaw fragment found in his home was matched with a jaw fragment found around a looter's pit. In another case, a homeless man living in a tent in thick brush near Tecolote Creek was found to be digging in and around an ancient Chumash cemetery. In response, angry Chumash tribal members collapsed his tent while he slept, rolled him up in it and threw him in the back of a pickup truck, confiscated his equipment, and deposited the bewildered man none too gently on the edge of the highway 20 mi out of town. Cases like these have taught most collectors in the Santa Barbara area that the looting or vandalizing of Chumash sites is not a legal or rewarding hobby.

HISTORICAL ARCHAEOLOGY IN THE TECOLOTE CANYON AREA

Since 1979, archaeological studies in the Tecolote Canyon area have collected a variety of information on the historical archaeology of the area, ranging from railroad features built around AD 1900, to extensive oil-related facilities dating between about 1929 and the 1950s, to surfer shacks and illegal campsites dating to the late 1970s. Although the area has been integrated into the activities of successive Spanish, Mexican, and American communities since the late 1700s, historical sources and the archaeological record of such activities are dominated by evidence dating to the twentieth century. Such historical materials were largely ignored by early archaeologists, but more recent work has led to the detailed documentation of historical land-use activities, including a variety of features, structures, and artifacts that help illustrate the development of the historical landscape of the Tecolote area. In the lower canyon, development since the 1950s has erased or obscured much of the physical evidence of this history, but historical buildings and other features are better represented in the upper canyon, where they are still protected within the Tecolote Ranch and Preserve. The historical resources of the upper canyon are largely unstudied, however, and cannot yet contribute much to our knowledge of the historical archaeology of the Tecolote area.

During the construction of the Bacara Resort, Hutash archaeologists recorded 23 historical features located around the mouths of Tecolote and Winchester canyons (Table 7.1). Most of these appear to be related to the Pacific Western Oil facilities and the related industrial and residential activities that rapidly transformed the area after the 1928 discovery of the Ellwood Oil Field. In the lower canyon, however, the traces of even earlier historical developments are also some of the most enduring—those related to the construction of the Southern Pacific Railroad.

Southern Pacific Railroad

Completed over a century ago in AD 1901, the Southern Pacific Railroad still operates in its original right-of-way. Four historical features that appear to be related to the railroad were encountered on the Bacara property, one of them (SPRR-4) the beautiful quarried sandstone façade at the south end of the tunnel carrying Tecolote Creek under the railroad and Highway 101 fill (Figure 7.4). Another feature, SPRR-1, is a rock wall just south of the railroad fill on the west bank of Winchester (Bell) Creek, now located below the Bacara access road bridge that passes over the creek (Figure 7.11). This wall, with at least four courses of rectangular quarried sandstone blocks set in concrete mortar, was visible for at least 12.2 m (40 ft) along the creek bank, with the northern half angled into the bank to deflect water flow. The materials and construction methods used to build this wall are so similar to those used for the Tecolote Creek tunnel that the two are almost certainly related and probably the work of the same fine stonemason(s).

Two other stone wall features, designated SPRR-2 and SPRR-3, were found on the west bank of Winchester Creek across from SPRR-1. Both of these were oriented perpendicular to the creek bank and were more makeshift structures. SPRR-2 was built of stream or beach cobbles piled in a bank over 1.8 m (6 ft) high and up to 1.2 m (4 ft) wide (Figure 7.12). It extended roughly east–west for a distance of at least 4.6 m (15 ft) and appears to have been built as a veneer or retaining wall laid against an existing creek or cut bank. On average, the cobbles are between 30 and 46 cm (12–18 in) in diameter, with a few boulders up to 76 cm (30 in) long near the base of the wall. Near the bottom of the wall on its north face were several pieces of milled lumber, including one upright 2-×-4-in post, and a bent and heavily corroded ½-in bolt about 36 cm (14 in) long.

A few meters to the northwest and closer to the creek, part of another stone wall (SPRR-3)

TABLE 7.1. Historic Features Identified in the Tecolote Canyon Area

FEATURE NUMBER	SITE	FEATURE LOCATION AND DESCRIPTION
PW-1	SBA-73N	Rock berm or embankment located on the west rim of Tecolote Creek and the east edge of SBA-73N; composed of boulders, cobbles, and historic debris, feature is about 48 m long, up to 9 m wide, and 1 m thick and may have buttressed an old roadbed
PW-2	SBA-72S	Concrete platform on the valley floor east of Tecolote Creek, on the southwest side of the soil berms for the tank farm; poorly defined or preserved portions of a concrete platform with 61-cm-wide (2 ft) octagonal base of concrete piling
PW-3	SBA-72S	Portion of a concrete slab, approximately 7.5 m long and 4 m wide, located between PW-2 and PW-4 on the valley floor east of Tecolote Creek; long axis runs east–west
PW-4	SBA-72S	Remnants of a rectangular concrete slab foundation located south of the berms on the valley floor east of Tecolote Creek; c. 3.9 m wide and 9.4 m long; long axis runs east–west
PW-5	SBA-72S	Remnants of a small concrete slab just east of PW-4 on the valley floor east of Tecolote Creek; 82 cm wide and at least 2 m long; long axis runs east–west
PW-6	SBA-72S	Large and complex concrete foundation of oil-related pump house and workshop (see text) located just behind the beach near the southeast corner of the valley floor east of Tecolote Creek; includes rectangular oiled surface just north of the foundation
PW-7	SBA-72S	Square concrete slab located just east of PW-6, in the southeast corner of the valley floor east of Tecolote Creek; approximately 12.2 m (40 ft) wide
PW-8	SBA-72S	Remnants of low retaining walls of cobbles set in mortar, located east of PW-6 and PW-7 in the southeast corner of the valley floor; mapped for 25–30 m north–south along the edge of the old road
PW-9	SBA-1673	Rectangular brick feature associated with the southern residence on the western terrace; 1-×-2-m-wide feature contains four courses of fired bricks set in mortar, with metal pipe associated; identified by former resident as the remains of a domestic incinerator
PW-10	SBA-1673	Two parallel strips of concrete pavers, a total of about 35 m long, for a driveway for the southern residence on the western terrace; includes three pavers for a walkway to house
PW-11	SBA-1673	Driveway similar to PW-10, with 4-×-5.8-m concrete garage foundation at the west end and remnants of a sidewalk leading to the northern residence on the western terrace
PW-12	SBA-1673	Standing flagpole located near the sea cliff on the western terrace
PW-13	SBA-1673	17-cm-wide (6.75 in) pipe protruding from a 1-m-wide (3.3 ft) concrete encasement located on the western terrace; possible remains of a capped wellhead?
PW-14	SBA-72N	Remnants of concrete slabs eroding from the east bank of Tecolote Creek in the northeast corner of SBA-72N; possibly the remains of a "Texas" creek crossing
PW-15	SBA-72S	Large pipe with asphalt located east of Tecolote Creek near the east edge of the valley floor, possibly with concrete box with crude oil
PW-16	SBA-73N	Concrete foundations and debris associated with a demolished industrial facility located west of Tecolote Creek on the western edge of SBA-73N
PW-17	SBA-1674	Poorly preserved remnants of a brick wall nearly 20 m long found in a disturbed debris field west of SBA-1674; associated with fired slag
PW-18	SBA-1673	Steel pipes used as posts located near houses on western terrace, near PW-10
PW-19	SBA-72	Remnants of high earthen containment berms that once surrounded portions of the tank farm on the valley floor east of Tecolote Creek
SPRR-1	None	Dressed sandstone wall on the west side of Winchester (Bell) Creek; wall of rectangular blocks set in mortar is at least four courses high and 12 m long
SPRR-2	None	Uncemented cobble wall on the east side of Winchester (Bell) Creek; may connect with SPRR-3, probably associated with railroad construction
SPRR-3	None	Short segment of stone wall exposed on the east bank of Winchester Creek near SPRR-2; mix of loose cobbles and quarried sandstone blocks suggests that the feature is related to railroad construction
SPRR-4	None	Dressed sandstone culvert in Tecolote Creek, south side of tunnel carrying creek under the Southern Pacific Railroad and Highway 101 fill

Note: PW features are probably related to the Pacific Western Oil facility; SPRR features are probably related to the Southern Pacific Railroad.

FIGURE 7.11. Dressed sandstone-block wall (Feature SPRR-1) built on the west bank of Lower Winchester Creek (photo by Bruno Texier, 1997).

FIGURE 7.12. Stone wall (Feature SPRR-2) on the east bank of Winchester Creek (photo by Robert Sheets).

was found during construction of the Winchester Creek bridge. Partially submerged below the water table in a construction trench, a roughly 1.5-m (5 ft) stretch of this wall was uncovered. The long axis of this wall, which was about 1.1 m (3.5 ft) wide and at least .9 m (3 ft) high, did not appear to line up with SPRR-2. The two wall sections were also built differently, with the north face of SPRR-3 consisting of cut sandstone blocks set in mortar and the south side consisting of rounded cobbles set in concrete. The presence of dressed sandstone blocks in SPRR-3 strongly suggests that it is also related to the construction of the Southern Pacific Railroad. All three walls in Winchester Canyon may have been built to help divert or control Winchester Creek or possibly to support a temporary road and bridge over the creek.

Pacific Western Oil Facilities

During the construction of Bacara, we identified a number of archaeological features related to the larger Ellwood Oil Field development. A complex of oil-related buildings once existed on the eastern terrace at SBA-71, on the ridge between Tecolote and Winchester canyons. These buildings were probably demolished as part of the restoration of the property after the oil facilities were abandoned, and little or no trace of them exists today. Because most of this area remains undeveloped, we did little work in the vicinity of these buildings, but we also observed no concrete slabs, foundations, or other construction materials on the surface south of the Bacara access road. This area appears to have been thoroughly restored after the abandonment of the oil-related facilities. Roads dating to the Ellwood Oil Field era are still used to access this eastern terrace, however, and are visible on the canyon walls on either side of SBA-71 and the base of the sea cliff just behind the beach.

On the valley floor east of Tecolote Creek, in contrast, we found numerous features related to the Ellwood Oil Field. One of the most dramatic features associated with this era—for some reason never leveled during restoration efforts—was a complex of high rectangular earthen berms located roughly where the Bacara tennis courts are today. These berms once surrounded at least eight oil-

storage tanks visible in Figure 7.8, two large tanks to the north and six smaller ones to the south. The berms were built with archaeological soils excavated from the Chumash village (SBA-72) that lay beneath the tank farm. Because they contained sensitive archaeological materials, the berms were covered with a geotextile fabric to protect them and then buried beneath up to 20 ft of fill. Located south of these berms, we found the remnants of several concrete slabs or other structures (PW-2, -3, -4, -5, -6, and -7) associated with oil production. These include the concrete foundations of a relatively large and complex building that reportedly served as a pump house and workshop complex (Feature PW-6) for the Pacific Western Oil Company facility (Figure 7.13). Located just behind the beach near the snack bar east of Tecolote Creek, this building complex was a maximum of about 25.6 m (84 ft) long and 12.5 m (41 ft) wide, with 6-in-wide footings around the exterior and between rooms. It included two main rooms, a small bathroom added to the southwest corner sometime after the initial construction, and a square concrete slab about 4.9 m (16 ft) wide outside the southeast wall. The larger eastern room was rectangular, encompassing an area about 12.5 m (41 ft) long and 11.3 m (37 ft) wide, had a simple concrete slab floor, and probably served as the workshop. The smaller, L-shaped western room was much more complex and probably served as the pump house. It contained several elevated concrete footings, the tops of which were studded with 1-in-wide threaded bolts cemented into 3-in iron pipe. Two 6-in iron pipes entered the room from the north in one of two concrete-lined pipe trenches (with steel-plate trench covers) leading to two large (12 × 2.5 ft) concrete footings. Another concrete-lined pipe trench paralleled the north and west walls of the building, carrying two 3-in pipes and a 1-in water pipe, and a 4-in-wide pipe also entered the room under the west wall. All of these features appear to be related to the pumping of crude oil, probably from wells on nearby oil piers to the storage tanks that once stood to the north. The rectangular bathroom, added outside the southeast corner of the western room, had a cozy interior just 76 cm (2.5 ft) wide and 168 cm (5.5 ft) long. On the north side of the

FIGURE 7.13. A workshop and pump house foundation (Feature PW-6) located at SBA-72, looking west, with the western terrace in the distance (photo by Bruno Texier, 1997).

larger building was a rectangular area of oiled and heavily compacted soil that may have been a parking area or storage yard.

A square concrete slab (PW-7) approximately 12.2 m (41 ft) wide was also found just east of PW-6. A short distance farther east we found the remnants of a low stone wall (PW-8) of cobbles set in mortar that extended for at least 25–30 m north to south (Figure 7.6). This may have been a retaining wall supporting an oil field road leading around the base of the bluff at SBA-71. It is also possible, however, that the low cobblestone wall and the nearby concrete slab (PW-8) were built prior to the oil era, possibly as part of the beach house the Spaldings had constructed here in 1926.

Also documented on the east side of Tecolote Creek were portions of large concrete slabs eroding from the east creek bank in the northeast corner of SBA-72 (Figure 7.7). The sloping slabs of concrete still embedded in the stream bank just above the creek level suggest that this feature (PW-14) may be the remains of a "Texas Crossing" by which ve-

hicles could cross the creek. This ramp-like feature may have been built prior to the oil boom era, allowing vehicles to cross the creek after the railroad inhibited access to the beachfront property. In Figure 7.9, however, a dirt road can be seen leading to this area, suggesting that it was used—and may have been built—sometime during the development of the oil field facilities.

Walking across the pedestrian bridge that links Bacara with the facilities east of Tecolote Creek, a concrete foundation for an old road bridge dating to the oil era is visible in the eastern creek bank. The western end of the pedestrian bridge is anchored in fill related to this older bridge. On the west side of Tecolote Creek, restoration efforts associated with the demolition of the oil facilities appear to have been relatively thorough. Here, too, we found evidence of extensive industrial and residential activity, some of it deeply buried.

On the west rim of Tecolote Creek, where the Bacara road bridge now spans Tecolote Creek, we found a linear embankment of large sandstone

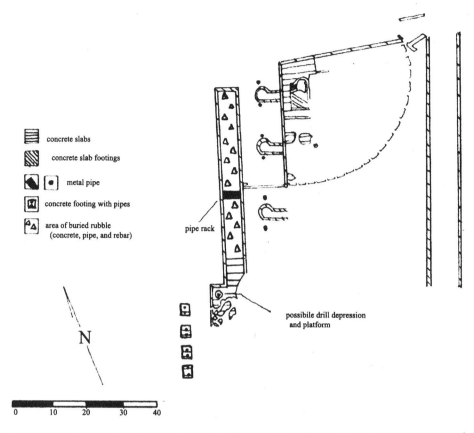

concrete slabs

concrete slab footings

metal pipe

concrete footing with pipes

area of buried rubble
(concrete, pipe, and rebar)

pipe rack

possibile drill depression
and platform

N

0   10   20   30   40

FIGURE 7.14. Ruins of an oil-processing facility (Feature PW-16) located on the western margin of SBA-73N (drawing by Deana Dartt from an original field map by Dustin Kay).

cobbles and boulders mixed with imported soil and historical debris. This feature (PW-1) was about 48 m (160 ft) long, a maximum of about 8.4 m (29 ft) wide, and up to 1.1 m (3.5 ft) thick. After a preliminary reconnaissance, Haley (1980) suggested that the large stones might have been piled on the eastern edge of SBA-73N during the clearing of farm fields. Because portions of this feature were to be affected by construction of the Tecolote Creek Bridge, however, we conducted more detailed investigations, including the hand excavation of a trench through it to examine a stratigraphic section. The results suggest that Feature PW-1 contained a mix of large sandstone cobbles and boulders, chunks of concrete and asphaltum, a few fragments of ancient ground-stone tools, and large quantities of historical trash dating to the 1930s and 1940s. The trash contained both industrial materials (pipe fittings, cable and chain, machinery parts, electrical insulators) and residential

debris such as fragments of porcelain and whiteware ceramics, liquor bottles, and condiment jars (Imwalle 1997). This large stone embankment may have buttressed a roadbed related to the development of the oil fields from the 1930s to the 1950s. Given the contents of the feature, it may have been constructed near the end of the oil field era, possibly during demolition and removal operations in the 1950s.

On the top of a low knoll just west of SBA-73N, where a scatter of shell midden soil was thought to mark an ancient Chumash presence, we found the buried remnants of more industrial debris, including huge concrete blocks, twisted and bent metal pipes, and other materials. Near the base of the knoll, buried beneath as much as 6 ft of soil were the partially intact foundations of an oil-related structure, including a concrete floor, possible pipe rack supports, metal pipes, and other debris (Figure 7.14). Moore et al. (1982) also note the presence

FIGURE 7.15. Concrete driveway and garage foundation (Feature PW-11) associated with one of two houses at SBA-1673 (photo by Bruno Texier, 1997).

of debris-laden fill soil on portions of SBA-73N between PW-1 and PW-16, which suggests that these features may be part of a larger debris field related to the twilight of the oil-production era at Tecolote, when contractual obligations required the lessees to demolish any remaining industrial facilities or bury them beneath at least 5 ft of soil. During construction of the Bacara Resort, after thick brush had been removed from the SBA-73S area, we also found evidence for massive grading in much of this area, possibly to generate soil for these restoration efforts. Given the scale of development and land modification associated with the Ellwood Oil Field, it is amazing that portions of the Chumash villages in the area survived relatively intact.

Another complex of features associated with the oil field era was found on the western terrace, beneath what is now the Bacara parking lot. Aerial photos and oral histories suggest that two houses existed here and were used by employees of the oil-production facilities. A sparse scatter of glass, tile, and linoleum fragments—probably dating mostly from the 1940s and 1950s—was found in this area during initial grading for the Bacara Resort. Also

found were several features (PW-9, -10, -11, and -12) associated with these homes. One of these, PW-11, was the well-preserved remains of a concrete driveway associated with the northern residence, with two parallel rows of concrete pavers leading to a concrete garage floor (Figure 7.15) and a 3-m-long (9 ft) section of walkway leading to the house. A similar driveway feature (PW-10) about 35 m (115 ft) long was associated with the southern residence on the western terrace but lacked any evidence of a garage foundation. In the yard of this southern home, we also documented the base of a concrete and brick feature (PW-9) identified by a former resident (Paul Bush) as a domestic garbage incinerator (Figure 7.16). This feature was approximately 1-×-2-m wide, with portions of four courses of fired bricks set in mortar still intact and a metal pipe leading to its west end, probably for natural gas.

Recreation on the Fringe
As the Ellwood Oil Field was gradually exhausted, the economics of oil production in Tecolote Canyon no longer made sense. Most of the oil piers,

FIGURE 7.16. Brick and mortar foundation (Feature PW-9) for a domestic incinerator associated with a historic house at SBA-1673 (photo by Bruno Texier, 1997).

wells, storage tanks, processing facilities, and other buildings associated with oil production were dismantled or demolished. Following the contractual obligations of the oil leases, most of the property was restored to a seminatural state. Located on the margins of the growing urban and residential centers of Goleta and Santa Barbara, much of the property quickly became overgrown with thick brush. Although the property was fenced in an attempt to keep the public out, without regular patrols by local police or the property owners the fence was ineffective. As more than one landowner has learned, it takes a lot more than a chain-link fence to keep surfers from a good shore break.

From the 1960s on, "Haskell's Beach" was a popular destination used primarily by surfers, sunbathers, and other local residents seeking to escape the more crowded beaches of Santa Barbara and Goleta. During the 1979 survey of the property by UCSB archaeologists, physical evidence for a variety of legal and illegal activities was noted. On or near the beach, Haley (1980) noted the presence of hearths, huts built of driftwood and cane, and a stashed surfboard as evidence of beach-oriented recreation. Other common visitors were local residents who came to Tecolote to walk their dogs. Archaeologists found conclusive evidence that some of these people and their canine companions became deeply attached to the Tecolote Canyon area, when test excavations inadvertently uncovered the remains of two historical dog burials—including one wearing rhinestone and plastic collars (Figure 7.17). A local resident described burying another dog on the property because of "spiritual vibrations" of the land, providing ethnographic confirmation that the area was widely used as a pet cemetery (Haley 1980).

Most of the people who used the area undoubtedly respected the beauty and serenity of the property, but others left a debris field of thousands of beverage cans and bottles scattered through the brush, most of which was not cleaned up until the Bacara Resort was being built. Unfortunately, the secluded and unsupervised nature of the property attracted people intent on a variety of other illicit activities. These included serious grave robbers and small-time arrowhead hunters, people illegally dumping garbage, gun enthusiasts, young

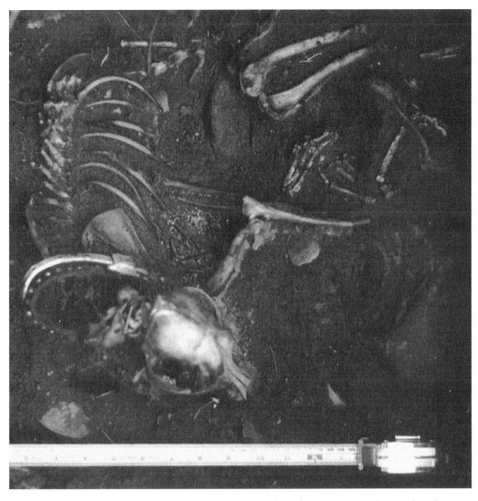

FIGURE 7.17. A historic dog burial found by University of California–Santa Barbara archaeologists in 1980 at SBA-73 (photo courtesy of the University of California–Santa Barbara Museum of Anthropology).

males on dirt bikes, homeless squatters, members of a religious cult, and many others. Some came to Tecolote to commune with nature; others to attain altered states of a chemical origin; still others, in search of a latrine area. Hidden in the brush, especially on the more remote east side of the creek, we documented (or directly observed) a plethora of evidence for alcohol and drug abuse, as well as the illicit cultivation of marijuana. Often associated with the remnants of controlled substances were a variety of materials related to outdoor recreational sex. Caches of pornographic materials, condom clusters, discarded underwear and other clothes, and couples in the act were all observed at one

time or another. Numerous campsites were found in the area over the years, from ephemeral scatters of old blankets or sleeping bags to relatively elaborate camps with architectural features, furniture, and discrete activity areas. The most astounding of these was an elaborate tent camp with kitchen facilities, a latrine pit, and a battery-operated television set. Another elaborate campsite is described by Haley, who noted that a

> sophisticated camp or habitation site was found on the west slope of the east terrace and consisted of a roofed wooden structure concealed by bush and trees, a platform in a tree, cleared

areas, and a midden. The structure contained several pieces of furniture suitable for sleeping and an ice chest for storage. Surfing pictures on the walls suggested a function of this site as a camp for surfers. One informant stated that he lived in the structure for several months [1980: 262].

Unfortunately, much of the illegal camping on the property was done by individuals actively engaged in the looting of Chumash sites in the area. Others inadvertently damaged or defaced the sites through a variety of vandalism, garbage dumping, or activities that caused subsurface disturbances.

In September 1979 a fierce wildfire swept through the Tecolote Canyon area, incinerating the exotic eucalyptus trees and other dense vegetation that had obscured much of the property. Virtually all flammable surface evidence of recent historical activities was also obliterated, leaving scorched cans, bottles, and other inflammable debris with which to reconstruct them. Signs of this wildfire can still be seen on a few burned tree trunks on the property, but the eucalyptus and other vegetation quickly grew back, sheltering another generation of legal and illicit activities. By the 1980s, however, members and friends of the Chumash Indian community actively patrolled the property with the consent of the owner, to minimize further damage to the archaeological sites of their ancestors. When the landowners proposed to build a five-star resort at the mouth of Tecolote Canyon, pledging to avoid sensitive archaeological and biological resources, to clean up and restore the property, and to protect the Chumash archaeological sites for future generations, the Coastal Band of the Chumash Nation agreed to cooperate in the planning and construction of the Bacara Resort. This volume, documenting the amazing history of the area, is just one result of that cooperative endeavor.

Summary and Conclusions

In reviewing the past 500 years of human history in the Tecolote Canyon area, we stand at the recent end of a cultural continuum that spans the millennia. Occupied continuously by the Chumash for at least 1,600 years, the canyon was abandoned between about AD 1500 to 1550, within a few years or decades of the arrival of the first Europeans in the Santa Barbara Channel area. Whether these two events are related is not known, but within just 250 years or so, once the Spanish colonial presence in the Santa Barbara area was firmly established, a canyon that had been home to the Chumash and their ancestors for at least 9,000 years was taken from them without recourse or compensation.

Prior to the establishment of the Spanish missions and pueblos in the area, Tecolote Canyon was also a relatively pristine anthropogenic ecosystem intensively managed and harvested by the Chumash. From AD 1782 to 1928, the canyon was transformed into a pastoral and agricultural landscape increasingly modified by Europeans or Euro-Americans. Nonetheless, through the Spanish, Mexican, and early American periods, the canyon retained much of its rural character. Completion of the Southern Pacific Railroad in AD 1901, with its creek channelization and massive cuts and fills, accelerated the taming and transformation of the lower canyon and signaled major changes in the lives of local residents. Even today, the sounds of occasional freight or passenger trains passing can invoke memories of early American history, when building the railroads that link our nation was a national enterprise and the ability to travel by train from Santa Barbara to San Francisco spelled the end of an era of stagecoaches and steamboats. Still, the farming, ranching, smuggling, kelp harvesting, fishing, and other economic activities that took place in the area during the early 1900s were relatively benign compared with the jarring transition brought about by the 1928 discovery of the Ellwood Oil Field. Almost overnight, the beaches, marshes, and canyon mouths of the area were recast from relatively serene and peaceful places to a noisy industrial landscape teeming with machinery and human activity.

Compared with any other event in the human history of the area, development of the Ellwood Oil Field did far more to destroy or damage the history and power of Tecolote Canyon. To some, that wild and destructive stampede to tap the oil-soaked sands locked deep below the earth may symbolize the dark side of corporate and capitalist

America, where greed overpowered any conservationist leanings the already wealthy Spaldings had for their beloved canyon. It now seems miraculous that, with no laws to protect them, even fragments of the original history and ecology of Tecolote survived that fevered rush. With the exhaustion and abandonment of the Ellwood Oil Field, however, time and extensive restoration efforts have helped to heal the landscape. Fortunately, Tecolote has recaptured a semblance of the beauty and serenity that characterized it for millions of years. In its history and its rejuvenation, there is a message of hope for the Santa Barbara Coast, for California, and for other places of beauty and serenity around the world.

8

Power, Place, and History—
Tecolote Canyon through Time

Jon M. Erlandson and Torben C. Rick

Places have power, a power that grows from the majesty of the landscape and the history of the people who inhabited it. In this volume we explored the long history of the Tecolote Canyon area and the Santa Barbara Coast. Despite the dramatic changes Tecolote Canyon has seen over the millennia, its power remains embedded in its beauty, its history, and its mystery. For Chumash descendants, Tecolote has a power and importance that stem from their deep connection to the landscape of the canyon, the Santa Barbara Channel area, and the California Coast. Tecolote is a place where their ancestors lived for millennia, where they fished, danced, prayed, died, and were buried. For the Chumash, it is also a place where tribal members, other Native Americans, and non-Indian friends came together to preserve their past, protect their heritage, and learn from one another. After reading this book, we hope that you, too, have gained a better understanding of the long history of this remarkable place and that its power has grown on you.

A geological perspective can help place the actions of humans in perspective. The rocks, fossils, and landscape of the Tecolote area have indelibly recorded the power of the earth and the sea in California's coastal landscape. From the sea cliffs to the summits of the Santa Ynez Mountains, the rocks are mostly marine in origin—from the Miocene mudstones of the Rincon Formation, to the Coldwater sandstones and Cozy Dell shales. Ecosystems millions of years old are preserved here: in

the billions of tiny skeletons of zooplankton that sank to the bottom of Miocene seas and now make up our sea cliffs; in oysters and scallops turned to stone that erode from sandstone boulders far up Tecolote Creek; in the paper-thin bones of fishes pressed between the pages of a shale book thousands of meters thick; and in the lithified vertebrae of ancient whales weathered onto the beach, where they were collected and used by the Chumash to make tools.

Through immense geological forces, these rocks and fossils were tilted and raised above the sea to form the mountains that add drama to Santa Barbara's coastal landscape. The sea, rising and falling many times over the past two million years, flooded and truncated the rocks and foothills taken from it. Walking on the beach at Tecolote, the evidence for this power can be seen in the sea cliffs, in the contact between cream-colored shales and the overlying terrestrial sediments, an ancient beach that cut its way inexorably landward through solid rock. Sitting by the pool at Bacara you can see it in the relatively level bluff that marks the canyon rim east of Tecolote Creek, a marine terrace cut by a Pleistocene shoreline more than 125,000 years ago, long before humans walked California landscapes. Behind the beach at the base of the cliffs, the sea repeats itself—as it will long after we are gone—slowly eroding the coastal plain and gradually erasing the long history of the area. We may slow it for a time, but only another ice age can stop it, an increasingly unlikely scenario given the global warming that the growing power of humans has unleashed on our planet.

Even the seemingly solid ground beneath us has shifted dramatically. Where the Chumash once lived, where oil tanks once stood, and where tennis players now volley on the valley floor, a deeply carved canyon existed 18,000 years ago. Wooly mammoths, camels, and saber-toothed cats walked the land, only to disappear as a new and very different mammal arrived on the scene. As the world warmed, America's first human immigrants brought dogs and diseases with them, they burned the landscape to enhance its human potential, and they hunted with an intelligence and sophisticated technologies never before seen in this hemisphere. At about the same time, most of the large Pleistocene mammals disappeared from the Santa Barbara Coast—as they did from North America as a whole—leaving only their bones to testify to their presence long ago. Were they driven to extinction by climatic warming and landscape changes, by new diseases that came with new mammals moving into the Americas from Asia, by the hunting pressures of their energetic two-legged relatives, or by other causes? This is a question for the ages, strenuously debated by scholars for decades, and no one knows the answer for sure. Even as they disappeared, however, the sea was rapidly rising, the coastal plain was flooding, and the deeply carved canyon was transformed into a bay and then an estuary, where the boats of the first Californians left wakes that reflected late Pleistocene sunsets more than 10,000 years ago.

The human history and historical ecology of Tecolote Canyon over the past 10,000 years have been our main focus in this book. Although our knowledge is unevenly distributed across the millennia, a wealth of information has been presented in previous chapters. What remains to be accomplished is a summary of that history and ecology, one that looks at the power and place of Tecolote in relation to some broader issues of regional, national, and even global significance. We begin with a summary of the cultural history of the western Santa Barbara Coast—a synthesis based on data collected from archaeological sites in the Tecolote

area and the western Santa Barbara Coast during 25 years of archaeological research in the area.

A Culture History for the Santa Barbara Coast

Our dating of Chumash and earlier Native American archaeological sites in the Tecolote and Winchester Canyon areas shows evidence for a nearly continuous occupation that spanned almost 9,000 years (Table 8.1). There are some substantial gaps in this occupational sequence, including the Protohistoric and early Historic periods (post–AD 1500) and the periods from about 2,300 to 3,300 years ago and 3,450 to 4,860 years ago, and smaller gaps between about 7950 and 8360 BP and 8540 and 8780 BP. Several sites in the area (SBA-106, SBA-1326, SBA-1673, etc.) remain undated, however, others (SBA-68, SBA-69, SBA-74, etc.) have relatively few dates, and some substantial site areas have been destroyed by construction. Further dating of ^{14}C samples and sites would almost certainly fill or narrow some of these gaps, suggesting that our study area was occupied more or less continuously from at least 9,000 years ago until European contact. At present we have no direct evidence for a Chumash occupation of the Tecolote Canyon area during the Protohistoric or Historic periods, but Chumash people surely used the area for hunting, fishing, gathering, and other activities.

Historical accounts indicate that the area was also used for grazing and ranch-related purposes during the Mission period, but no archaeological evidence has surfaced to corroborate these sources. There is extensive evidence for historical land use beginning in the mid-1850s, however, and the archaeological record contains substantial evidence for use of the area during virtually all phases of the twentieth century.

One of our goals in this volume was to summarize what is currently known about the archaeology, history, and paleoecology of the western Santa Barbara Coast, as viewed through the lens of an ancient canyon system. With archaeological sites and other documentary sources from the Tecolote Canyon area spanning most of the past 9,000 years, the previous chapters provided a broad foundation for examining and explaining some of the general

TABLE 8.1. Radiocarbon Dates from Tecolote Canyon Area Archaeological Sites

Site	Lab #	Dated Material	Provenience	Uncor-rected ^{14}C Date (RYBP)	Adjusted ^{13}C/^{12}C (RYBP)	Calendar Age Range (cal BP, 1δ)
SBA-73S	Beta-196355	*Mytilus* bead	Unit 60: 60–80 cm	670 ± 40	1020 ± 40	480 (450) 410
SBA-1674	Beta-196359	*Olivella* cup	Unit 4: 20–40 cm	610 ± 40	1020 ± 40	480 (450) 410
SBA-1674	Beta-196358	*Chione* shell	Unit 4: 20–40 cm	730 ± 40	1140 ± 40	540 (520) 500
SBA-72S	HCRL-9	Marine shell	Burial 5	740 ± 50	1160 ± 50	560 (530) 500
SBA-72S	UCR-1115	Marine shell	N25/E554: 60–70cm	780 ± 80	1210 ± 80	640 (550) 510
SBA-1674	Beta-196357	*Chione* shell	Unit 4: 0–20 cm	800 ± 40	1220 ± 40	630 (560) 540
SBA-73S	Beta-140984	*Olivella* bead	N20/E330: 60–70 cm	820 ± 40	1260 ± 40	650 (620) 550
SBA-72S	Beta-140983	*Olivella* bead	N25/E554: 60–70 cm	840 ± 40	1280 ± 40	660 (630) 570
SBA-72S	HCRL-10a	Marine shell	Burial 5	970 ± 60	1400 ± 60	780 (710) 660
SBA-73S	Beta-19723	Turban shell	Test Unit 2: 0–20 cm	1000 ± 60	1430 ± 60	820 (730) 670
SBA-72S	UCR-1117	Marine shell	Burial 7: Trench 4D	1060 ± 80	1490 ± 80	910 (790) 710
SBA-73S	Beta-144256	*Protothaca* shell	Trench 98-25: 65 cm	1080 ± 60	1500 ± 70	910 (820) 730
SBA-72S	HCRL-10	Marine shell	Trench 6B: Burial 2	1080 ± 60	1510 ± 60	910 (830) 740
SBA-73S	Beta-196356	*Chione* shell	Unit 60: 60–80 cm	1120 ± 40	1540 ± 40	920 (890) 800
SBA-72S	HCRL-12	Marine shell	Burial 1	1200 ± 70	1600 ± 80	990 (920) 830
SBA-73S	Beta-8939	Marine shell	N20/E330: 110–120 cm	1210 ± 70	1640 ± 70	1040 (950) 900
SBA-1674	Beta-8296	Marine shell	N60/E240: 10–20 cm	1240 ± 60	1670 ± 60	1060 (970) 920
SBA-72S	UCR-1118	*Olivella* beads	Burial 1: Trench 6B	1270 ± 80	1700 ± 80	1130 (1010) 930
SBA-73S	Beta-19724	Abalone shell	Test Unit 2: 20–40 cm	1320 ± 60	1750 ± 60	1160 (1060) 980
SBA-73N	Beta-196354	*Chione* shell	Unit 11: 80–100 cm	1420 ± 40	1840 ± 40	1240 (1180) 1130
SBA-73N	Beta-196898	*Chione* shell	Unit 11: 20–40 cm	1470 ±70	1890 ± 70	1290 (1240) 1160
SBA-72N	HCRL-11	Marine shell	Trench 6A: Burial 2	1540 ± 70	1970 ± 70	1350 (1290) 1230
SBA-71	HCRL-5	Marine shell	Burial 5: Tr. 8D–9G	1590 ± 60	2030 ± 70	1410 (1330) 1280
SBA-71	Beta-5320	Abalone shell	"Swordfish Man"	1610 ± 90	2040 ± 90	1470 (1340) 1270
SBA-73S	Beta-144255	Venus clam	Trench 98-25: 40 cm	1610 ± 100	2040 ±100	1480 (1340) 1270
SBA-72N	UCR-1114	Marine shell	N150/E430: 90 cm	1710 ± 90	2140 ± 90	1560 (1470) 1340
SBA-71	UCR-1120	Marine shell	Unit DE1, Burial 7	1790 ± 90	2220 ± 90	1680 (1540) 1430
SBA-72N	Beta-28031	Pismo clam	Unit 89-5: 140–160 cm	2060 ± 70	2490 ± 70	1950 (1870) 1790
SBA-73N	Beta-8938	Marine shell	N200/E365: 40–50 cm	2090 ± 70	2520 ± 70	1990 (1900) 1820
SBA-71	UCR-1119	Marine shell	Unit H144, Feature 1	2110 ± 90	2540 ± 90	2040 (1920) 1820
SBA-71	OS-26446	Abalone hook	Unit E148: 15–46 cm	2230 ± 45	2640 ± 45	2120 (2040) 1970
SBA-71	OS-26447	Mussel hook	Unit F6: 61–76 cm	2350 ± 30	2760 ± 30	2290 (2180) 2130
SBA-71	Beta-140982	*Olivella* bead	Unit A55: 0–15cm	3280 ± 40	3720 ± 40	3430 (3370) 3330
SBA-75B	Beta-137616	*Protothaca* shell	Unit 5: 0–20 cm	4550 ± 60	4970 ± 60	5060 (4970) 4860

TABLE 8.1. (cont'd) Radiocarbon Dates from Tecolote Canyon Area Archaeological Sites

SITE	LAB #	DATED MATERIAL	PROVENIENCE	UNCOR-RECTED ^{14}C DATE (RYBP)	ADJUSTED ^{13}C/^{12}C (RYBP)	CALENDAR AGE RANGE (CAL BP, 1δ)
SBA-75A	Beta-137615	*Protothaca* shell	Unit 3: 20–40 cm	4560 ± 60	5000 ± 60	5200 (5020) 4910
SBA-75B	Beta-8299	Pismo clam	Unit 5: 40–60 cm	4780 ± 90	5210 ± 90	5450 (5310) 5250
SBA-72N	Beta-28032	California mussel	Creek bank: 2.5 m	4920 ± 70	5350 ± 70	5580 (5480) 5430
SBA-75A	Beta-8297	Pismo clam	Unit 1: 40–60 cm	4990 ± 80	5420 ± 80	5630 (5570) 5470
SBA-72N	Beta-111649	Pismo clam	Unit 97-4: 40–50 cm	5040 ± 80	5470 ± 80	5680 (5590) 5550
SBA-75C	Beta-8298	Pismo clam	Unit 4: 40–60 cm	5080 ± 80	5510 ± 80	5730 (5630) 5570
SBA-72N	UCR-1116	Pismo clam	290 cm	5270 ± 120	5700 ± 120	5979 (5870) 5710
SBA-72N	Beta-111648	Pismo clam	Unit 97-4: 20–30 cm	5400 ± 80	5810 ± 80	6090 (5940) 5890
SBA-74	Beta-111647	Pismo clam	Surface: Highway cut	5560 ± 80	6020 ± 80	6290 (6200) 6120
SBA-69	Beta-144417	Pismo clam	Surface: Central Area	5840 ± 60	6280 ± 60	6550 (6470) 6400
SBA-68	Beta-193486	Chione shell	Surface	5940 ± 50	6340 ± 50	6630 (6540) 6470
SBA-70	OS-44641	California mussel	Surface	—	6730 ± 45	7085 (7000) 6920
SBA-70	OS-31799	Chione shell	Surface	—	6820 ± 45	7200 (7150) 7020
SBA-70	OS-31682	Estuarine shell	Surface	—	6890 ± 45	7250 (7210) 7150
SBA-70	OS-44642	California mussel	Surface	—	7010 ± 40	7360 (7310) 7260
SBA-70	OS-31681	Marine shell	Surface	—	7070 ± 50	7420 (7370) 7300
SBA-71	Beta-36075	Abalone shell	Rock Feature	7080 ± 120	7510 ± 120	7860 (7730) 7620
SBA-2499	Beta-78947	California mussel	Unit 1: 80–90 cm	7200 ± 80	7630 ± 80	7940 (7850) 7760
SBA-75C	Beta-137617	*Saxidomus* shell	Unit 2: 20–40 cm	7780 ± 80	8210 ± 80	8540 (8410) 8360
SBA-69	Beta-144418	*Saxidomus* shell	Surface: Central Area	8210 ± 110	8610 ± 120	8980 (8900) 8780

Note: Soil carbon dates from SBA-69 and -70 and modern charcoal dates from SBA-2499, with no known relationship to archaeological materials, are omitted. Dates were calibrated with CALIB 4.3 (Stuiver and Reimer 1993), using a ΔR of 225 ± 35 years. For the ^{13}C/^{12}C ratios, either they were determined by the ^{14}C labs or 430 years was added (Erlandson 1988a).

patterns of cultural and environmental changes that have occurred in the area through time. These include reconstructing environmental and ecological changes that occurred in the area since the last glacial, exploring the origins and early development of Native American societies in the area, examining the technological and demographic changes associated with the evolution of cultural complexity among the Chumash and their ances-tors, and discussing the cultural and environmental impacts associated with the colonization of the area by Europeans.

MARITIME ORIGINS

As we noted in earlier chapters, determining when humans first arrived in the Americas and on the Santa Barbara Coast is a topic steeped in controversy and uncertainty. The first relatively clear evidence for humans along the central or southern California Coast is found in a few isolated stone points made with a distinctive fluting technology that thinned the base of the points to facilitate hafting. Technologically, these fluted points strongly resemble those made by Clovis and Folsom peoples elsewhere in North America between about 13,000 and 11,000 years ago. Although none of the fluted points from the California Coast is well dated, it seems likely that they are Paleoindian in origin and date (at least roughly) to Clovis or Folsom times. Whether these early people reached the Americas by land or by sea remains uncertain, but we know they used boats to settle the Channel Islands at least 13,000 years ago (Johnson et al. 2002). The earliest occupation of Daisy Cave on San Miguel Island, dated between about 11,700 and 11,000 years ago, has produced a small assemblage of shellfish remains and chipped-stone artifacts (Erlandson et al. 1996). These early islanders may have spent part of the year on the Santa Barbara Coast. The fact that Paleocoastal groups spent part of their time on the islands—where terrestrial resources were very limited—using boats and gathering marine shellfish suggests that they were maritime peoples well adapted to life by the sea. Because the shorelines they lived along are largely submerged or destroyed, we can currently say very little about these terminal Pleistocene peoples.

We know much more about the maritime peoples who lived in the Santa Barbara Channel area between about 10,000 and 9,000 years ago. Sites on San Miguel and Santa Rosa islands, as well as the Vandenberg area, show that these early groups were collecting shellfish, fishing, and hunting in a variety of coastal habitats (Erlandson 1994; Erlandson et al. 1999; Glassow 1996; Rick, Erlandson, et al. 2005). Along the Santa Barbara Coast, evidence from both the Tecolote Canyon area and other sites shows a strong estuarine focus in early settlement and subsistence. Sites dating between about 9,000 and 7,000 years ago clustered around ancient bays and estuaries that provided access to a variety of resources: freshwater and stable canyon-rim landforms; terrestrial plants and animals used for food and technological purposes; and marine shellfish, fish, and mammals, as well as the sheltered

waters in which to pursue them (Erlandson 1994). At Winchester, Tecolote, and many canyons to the west, these estuaries have completely disappeared, and only small brackish or freshwater marshes exist today. The estuaries may be gone, but the estuarine shells found in many early sites testify to the existence of these geological features. Gathering shellfish and small seeds seems to have been the most important subsistence activity for early peoples along the Santa Barbara Coast, supplemented by fishing and hunting in a variety of habitats. Along with the relatively low density of fish and mammal bones, small numbers of fishing or hunting tools confirm the economic importance of shellfish, just as the abundance of manos (Figure 8.1) and metates tells us that the gathering and processing of plant foods were a crucial pillar of early economies. This basic subsistence pattern, with a focus on milling tools and mollusks, is characteristic of the coastal Milling Stone Horizon.

During the Early Holocene, Milling Stone populations were probably relatively small, although they must have grown somewhat through time. They also appear to have been relatively sedentary, spending much of the year in a primary village (Erlandson 1994:116; Glassow et al. 1988). The semi-subterranean house pits described by D. B. Rogers for SBA-70—which may be as much as 7,500 to 7,000 years old—seem to confirm the sedentary nature of Milling Stone peoples along the Santa Barbara Coast. Nonetheless, with comparatively low population densities, settlements were probably widely scattered and made up of relatively small groups of people. Larger settlements may have been located in areas that offered the most productive and diverse array of resources, but people were free to roam fairly widely and establish smaller villages or seasonal camps in a variety of locations. Although some localized depletion of shellfish beds or other resources may have been caused by these early coastal peoples, particularly where such resources were limited in size, human impacts on local resources were probably limited. When they occurred, such problems were easily solved by relocating to unoccupied areas nearby, where key resources had not been heavily exploited, or by switching to alternative foods.

FIGURE 8.1. Bifacial mano typical of Early Holocene sites of the western Santa Barbara Coast (slightly smaller than actual size; drawing by Deana Dartt).

Along the Santa Barbara Coast, there is considerable continuity in the estuarine and seed-based adaptations of early Milling Stone peoples and only limited evidence for technological or cultural change for roughly 3,000 years. This might suggest that Early Holocene peoples in the area were relatively conservative and static, with only rudimentary maritime skills. Within the larger Santa Barbara Channel region, however, there is considerable evidence for economic and adaptive diversity among early coastal peoples. Along the west-facing coast north of Point Conception, for instance, where no productive estuaries appear to have existed during the Holocene, early Milling Stone peoples relied heavily on California mussels and other shellfish gathered from rocky intertidal zones (Glassow 1996). Because the higher wave energy limited the use of boats, fishing and marine hunting may have been less important north of Point Conception than along the Santa Barbara Coast.

Except for a single estuary identified on the southeast coast of Santa Rosa Island (Rick, Kennett, and Erlandson 2005), early peoples on the Northern Channel Islands also relied primarily on shellfish harvested from rocky coastlines (Erlandson et al. 1999). Between 10,000 and 8,500 years ago at Daisy Cave on San Miguel Island, however, people were fishing intensively with the oldest fishhooks (small bone gorges or bipoints) in the Americas and making twisted cordage and twined basketry that is the oldest from the Pacific Coast of North America (Connolly et al. 1995; Erlandson et al. 1996; Rick, Erlandson, and Vellanoweth 2001). On the islands, moreover, the Milling Stone assemblages so emblematic of early mainland peoples are completely lacking, probably because of the absence or low productivity of mainland chaparral plants that produced large annual harvests of small seeds rich in carbohydrates, fats, and calories. Although these early islanders clearly had seaworthy boats and early sites are relatively abundant, there is little evidence that they lived permanently on the islands prior to 8,000 years ago. It is conceivable, therefore, that the Milling Stone people of the Tecolote area were one and the same as the early mariners who left a very different archaeological record on the Northern Channel Islands. This variation in Early Holocene sites of the Santa Barbara Channel area suggests that a more dynamic, flexible, and maritime foundation existed in the area for later peoples to build on.

For several thousand years, these coastal peoples may have enjoyed relatively idyllic conditions. With low population densities, abundant resources, flexible settlement and subsistence strategies, and wide open spaces, Early Holocene peoples of the Santa Barbara Coast probably lived in relative harmony with their natural environment and their neighbors. When the social friction that seems to be nearly inevitable in human societies occurred, aggrieved groups could move away from conflict if they desired. Thus the unoccupied areas along the coast, on the islands, or in interior valleys provided a pressure-release valve that kept cultural interaction, resource depletion, territoriality, and social conflict at relatively low levels. Such conditions limited the need for elaborate rules to govern human behavior, social hierarchies to enforce such rules, and the elaborate markers of social identity found among later cultures in the area. The result was a society that appears to have been relatively egalitarian in nature, where status was earned rather than inherited, with little evidence for strict divisions of labor or economic specialization, and only limited investments in the costly signaling of wealth or ritual items (beads, ornaments, etc.) that often accompany more complex social relationships. Low population densities and abundant resources, along with limited violence and warfare, also may have fostered relatively healthy communities, longer life spans, and the gradual growth of coastal populations.

Cultural Continuity and Change in the Middle Holocene

Over the millennia, especially when combined with reductions in land area caused by sea level rise and coastal erosion, such population growth increased pressures on Santa Barbara's coastal peoples and their landscape. Between about 7,000 and 3,500 years ago, there is evidence for both cultural continuity and change in the Santa Barbara Channel area. Continuity is found in the persistence of basic Milling Stone technologies and adaptations at some sites dated throughout the Middle Holocene, but evidence for change is also found at nu-

merous sites along the Santa Barbara Coast. Major changes in coastal geography also occurred during the Middle Holocene, and these had significant consequences for the occupants of the area.

Along the western Santa Barbara Coast, most of the small estuaries that attracted Early Holocene peoples seem to have disappeared or declined dramatically by about 6,000 years ago (Erlandson 1997a:104). The declining productivity of area estuaries was caused by a dramatic slowing of postglacial sea level rise about 7,000 years ago, the formation of sand spits across the mouths of many coastal canyons, and the gradual filling of these coastal basins with stream-borne sediments. Lower rainfall and stream flows associated with the warmer and dryer Altithermal period may also have contributed, as substantial stream flows are required to keep many estuaries open to marine circulation. These changes probably contributed to an overall reduction in the productivity of shellfish along the western Santa Barbara Coast, although an increase in Pismo clams in expanded sandy beach habitats may have compensated for some of this decline. The proximity of the vast Goleta Slough estuary, which remained a productive source of shellfish into historical times, may have buffered the effects of these changes on the occupants of the Tecolote area, but Middle Holocene shellfish assemblages from Tecolote and Winchester Canyon sites are dominated by Pismo clams and California mussels from wave-swept outer coast habitats. This is consistent with broader patterns of shellfish exploitation by Middle Holocene peoples along the western Santa Barbara Coast and may suggest that cultural connections to Middle Holocene village sites in the Goleta Slough area were not particularly strong.

At the same time that productive estuaries were disappearing along the western Santa Barbara Coast, sea level rise and sea cliff retreat continued to reduce coastal plain habitats and the overall land area that could be occupied and regularly harvested by local peoples. The Santa Barbara Coast is what archaeologists describe as a "circumscribed" environment, where cultural territories are limited by an encroaching coastline and the steep flanks of the Santa Ynez Mountains. Over the centuries, marine erosion gradually reduced the extent of viable land area and increased population densities even if overall population levels remained the same. It appears, however, that Middle Holocene population levels did not stay the same along the western Santa Barbara Coast. Erlandson (1997a) analyzed all the radiocarbon dated sites in the area, for instance, and found that 16 date to the Early Holocene and 36 date to the Middle Holocene, an increase of more than 100 percent. These and other measures suggest that local population levels expanded significantly between about 7,000 and 3,500 years ago.

The combination of increasing population densities and declining estuarine productivity appears to have had several repercussions on the occupants of the Tecolote area and the broader Santa Barbara Coast. One of these was a logistical shift toward shellfish gathering along the outer coast, with a focus primarily on California mussels found along rocky shores and Pismo clams found in sandy beaches. This may seem like a minor adjustment, but Pismo clams and California mussels are more widely dispersed along the relatively linear western Santa Barbara Coast. Because they are generally limited to a narrower band of intertidal shoreline than in the mudflats of estuaries, they may also be less productive overall and more susceptible to overexploitation by humans.

These changes appear to have had multiple effects on the people of Tecolote and the western Santa Barbara Coast. One was a shift in settlement, with villages being moved more frequently. Another was a gradual reduction in the dietary importance of shellfish, a protein loss that had to be made up elsewhere in the local environment. This was probably accomplished primarily by increasing the intensity of fishing and hunting of large land and sea mammals, a shift visible in larger numbers of projectile points and large mammal bones found in local archaeological sites. This pattern was first noted by D. B. Rogers (1929) in the 1920s, who referred to these Middle Holocene groups as the Hunting People. The types of projectile points found were also new (Figure 8.2): large side-notched dart points that seem to appear in the area about 6,000 years ago and large contracting-stem varieties a millennium or two later (Erland-

son 1997a). Another technological hallmark of the Middle Holocene is marked by the introduction and increasing numbers of mortars and pestles found in local sites. Generally thought to be related to the intensive harvest and processing of acorns and other relatively starchy plant foods (Glassow 1997), the introduction of mortars and pestles represents a significant broadening of the diet and further evidence for the intensification of Middle Holocene economies.

Other technological changes that may first appear during the Middle Holocene include the first well-documented appearance of tarring pebbles and notched stone net sinkers. The appearance of tarring pebbles, heated and swirled with asphaltum inside baskets to make watertight bottles, may be related to the increasing aridity of the Altithermal and a greater need to transport and store freshwater (Braje et al. 2005). The use of notched stone sinkers may reflect an expansion of fishing technologies, possibly including a variety of nets. Although associated hunting technologies are relatively poorly documented, the presence of dolphin, porpoise, and other large and complex marine fauna in Middle Holocene sites on the mainland and Channel Islands also indicates increasingly sophisticated maritime subsistence technologies during this time period. Viewed together with the introduction of mortars and pestles and a broader intensification of hunting and fishing, such technological changes provide evidence for human ingenuity, a broadening of the economy, and adaptive responses to environmental change and human population growth. By extension, such changes imply that growing Middle Holocene populations were extracting more resources from local environments and that their effects on local ecosystems were also increasing.

Another significant change in Middle Holocene technologies in the Santa Barbara Channel area may be seen in an expansion in the variety of bead and ornament types used by Native peoples. During the Early Holocene, *Olivella* shells with their spires removed were the primary bead type used in the area. During the Middle Holocene several new bead types probably first appeared, including *Olivella* barrel beads, rectangular or square

FIGURE 8.2. Large bifacial points or knives from Tecolote Canyon sites (courtesy of Hutash Consultants; photo by Melissa Reid).

Olivella wall beads, tube beads made from *Dentalium pretiosum* shells, and soapstone beads and pendants. Two *Olivella* barrel beads were recovered from the 5,500-year-old buried component at SBA-72N, and others have been found in Middle Holocene sites on San Miguel Island, including a 6,600-year-old stratum at Daisy Cave. King (1990: 285) noted that a few rectangular *Olivella* beads had been found in two early Santa Barbara Channel sites, one near the Goleta Slough (SBA-142) and another on Santa Rosa Island (SRI-3). Middle Holocene components have since been identified at both sites, however, and they seem to date primarily between about 6,000 and 3,000 years. In the Tecolote area, a rectangular *Olivella* bead from SBA-71 was directly dated to about 3,400 years ago, the very end of the Middle Holocene.

A distinctive type of rectangular shell bead, the *Olivella* grooved rectangle (OGR), dated be-

tween about 5,500 and 4,500 years, is significant in this regard. OGR beads have been found primarily on the Southern Channel Islands, adjacent mainland areas of Los Angeles and Orange counties, and interior areas now occupied by Shoshonean or Uto-Aztecan peoples of the Western and Northern Great Basin (Howard and Raab 1993; King 1990; Vellanoweth 2001). The distribution of these beads, found as far north as central Oregon (Jenkins and Erlandson 1996), has been used to suggest that Uto-Aztecan peoples, including the ancestors of the Tongva (Gabrielino) peoples who occupied the Los Angeles Basin and Southern Channel Islands historically, may have migrated to the southern California Coast much earlier than generally believed. Very few OGR beads have been found in coastal Chumash territory, including two at a site near Rincon Point and another found recently in the Vandenberg region, suggesting that separate "cultural interaction spheres" may also have existed in the Chumash and Tongva regions during the Middle Holocene. If OGR beads mark an early coastward expansion of Uto-Aztecan peoples and the development of separate cultural interaction spheres, such events may have pushed Chumash-speaking peoples northward and increased population densities, resource stress, and social conflict in the Santa Barbara Channel area during the Middle Holocene.

The greater variety of bead types found in Middle Holocene sites of the Santa Barbara Channel area suggests a growing complexity in the social relationships of the ancestral Chumash, with an increased importance of symbols related to cultural identity and social status. Other social changes may also have roots in the Middle Holocene. Although their origins and antiquity are obscure, there are hints that some of the divisions of labor, territoriality, and more frequent interaction and warfare characteristic of the Chumash may have begun to emerge in the Middle Holocene. Such changes might be expected to occur as Santa Barbara Channel landscapes filled with people, more effort was expended to harvest a more diverse array of resources, and competition between social groups became more intense.

Catalysts to Complexity: The Coastal Chumash in the Late Holocene

Late Holocene population growth in the Santa Barbara Channel area is indicated by a general increase in the number of sites, as well as the larger size of many village sites and cemeteries dating to the past 3,500 years, and by the greater density of archaeological materials found at such sites. These traits also suggest that Late Holocene peoples were generally more sedentary, moving the location of their villages less frequently than Middle Holocene peoples did. Under such circumstances, environmental changes that posed relatively limited challenges to Early and Middle Holocene peoples may have had more serious consequences for more densely packed Late Holocene populations. As a landscape fills with people, especially bounded landscapes like the Santa Barbara Coast, the bal-

ance between people and resources can become increasingly precarious. Larger populations require more space, food, and resources of all kinds to survive. In the process, they generate more waste and generally have a greater impact on local environments, creating greater opportunities for social conflict.

In 1970, anthropologist Robert Carneiro defined a process he called territorial circumscription, a kind of social saturation of the landscape, which may have been important in the development of cultural complexity among the Chumash. Chumash territories became socially circumscribed when villages and towns throughout the Santa Barbara Channel area were so closely spaced that their resource territories overlapped. Territorial circumscription is difficult to measure archaeologically, but there is little question that Chumash territories were circumscribed at the time of European contact. Examining a variety of evidence, we have argued that the coastal Chumash approached territorial circumscription between about 3,000 and 4,000 years ago (see Erlandson and Rick 2002). Under such circumstances, groups of people could no longer move into unoccupied or underused areas in response to social or economic stress. This required more intensive use of local environments, including the harvesting of a wider range of resources, and may have increased territorial disputes as well as cooperative trade relationships with neighboring groups (Kennett and Kennett 2000). Ample evidence for both cooperation and conflict was found at Tecolote, where a variety of trade goods (obsidian, fused shale, steatite, shell beads, etc.) testify to regular trade between Chumash groups, but several individuals also died violently as a result of interpersonal conflict or intermittent warfare.

In the last decade or so, some archaeologists have argued that key aspects of Chumash social complexity—the emergence of a formal social hierarchy governed by chiefs and other specialists, the appearance of specialized craft guilds, and the development of large seagoing watercraft—all evolved relatively recently and rapidly (c. AD 1150–1300) in response to environmental problems (see Arnold 1992a, 2001). Initially, the most likely "trigger" for these cultural changes was believed to be an extended period of warm-water conditions identified by Pisias (1978) in Santa Barbara Basin sediments, an event thought to have caused an El Niño–like reduction in marine productivity. Recent archaeological and paleoecological data have raised doubts about this scenario, however, suggesting that coastal waters were highly productive during the period in question (Kennett 2005). More recent models have focused on severe droughts associated with what is often called the Medieval Climatic Anomaly, between about AD 800 and 1350 (Jones et al. 1999). These droughts may have reduced terrestrial productivity and limited the availability of freshwater, forcing the Chumash to aggregate in larger groups around a smaller number of permanent water sources.

There is evidence for either an aggregation or decline in Chumash populations on the Channel Islands during the Medieval Climatic Anomaly (see Erlandson et al. 2001; Kennett 2005), and such changes could well have contributed to some re-organization of Chumash society at this time. We have argued that the Chumash successfully adapted to numerous droughts, El Niños, and other environmental perturbations over the millennia, however, and evidence from both the islands and the mainland coast suggests that significant changes in Chumash society began considerably earlier than the Medieval Climatic Anomaly (Erlandson and Rick 2002; Rick 2004, 2007).

Aspects of a cultural elaboration reminiscent of the classic Chumash or Canaliño pattern are evident as much as 3,500 years ago at Rincon Point and at Canada Verde on Santa Rosa Island, for instance, where cemeteries containing elaborated grave goods were found by Harrison (1964) and Orr (1968). At SBA-81, near the mouth of Las Llagas Canyon west of Tecolote, D. B. Rogers (1929) found evidence for 12–16 semisubterranean Chumash-style houses roughly 9 m (30 ft) in diameter, a large cemetery containing the remains of at least 364 individuals, and a ceremonial *temescal* (sweat house). On the floor of the temescal, Rogers (1929:388) reported finding two clusters of cigar-shaped charm stones arranged in radiating starburst patterns. In the cemetery, the differential distribu-

tion of grave goods—including thousands of shell beads and ornaments, as well as charm stones, stone effigies and pipes, and bone pins—led King (1990: 99) to conclude that wealth and power were not equally divided among the village occupants. Two ^{14}C dates obtained for shell artifacts from SBA-81 suggest that the Chumash occupied the site from about 2,750 to 2,350 years ago (Erlandson and Rick 2002). By this time, fundamental aspects of Chumash sedentism, architecture, village organization, elaborated material culture, and possibly formal social hierarchy all seem to have been present along the western Santa Barbara Coast. Because the dates for SBA-81 fall within a gap in the known occupation of the Tecolote Canyon area, it is conceivable that the descendants of the people who lived and died at Las Llagas later moved to SBA-71, where evidence for elaborate Chumash ritual continued with the famous "Swordfish Man" (Davenport et al. 1993; Rogers 1929:410).

If key aspects of Chumash culture evolved prior to 2,500 years ago, major developments also took place after this time (Figures 8.3, 8.4). Not apparent at early Canaliño sites at Rincon, Canada Verde, or Las Llagas, for instance, is evidence for intensive marine fishing (Erlandson and Rick 2002). Single-piece circular and j-shaped fishhooks first appear among the Chumash about 2,500 years ago (Rick et al. 2002), for instance, and the density of fish bones increases significantly in many coastal sites after that time. Toggling harpoons that may have increased the effectiveness of sea mammal hunting are also thought to have appeared during the last 3,000 to 2,500 years. Another important Late Holocene technological innovation is found in the introduction of the bow and arrow roughly 1,600 to 1,500 years ago, which probably increased the efficiency of Chumash hunters on land and at sea and may also have altered patterns of human violence and warfare. The relatively large *tomol* (plank canoe) may also have been developed about 1,500 years ago (Gamble 2002), significantly improving Chumash marine travel, trade, and hunting capabilities. It is probably no coincidence that relatively specialized and localized craft production—including the appearance of bowl-making, bead-making, and bladelet-production villages among the Island

FIGURE 8.3. Elaborate abalone ornaments with incised edges and concentric rings from SBA-72 (Santa Barbara Museum of Natural History collections; photo by Jon Erlandson).

FIGURE 8.4. Daggers of bear and elk bone from Tecolote Canyon (courtesy of the Santa Barbara Museum of Natural History; photo by Erik Erlandson).

Chumash—and the development of *Olivella* bead currencies intensified about the same time (Kennett and Conlee 2002; Rick 2004). The seaworthy tomol probably made channel crossings faster and safer and allowed substantially more trade goods to be carried between mainland and island villages. This may have provided added impetus for the occupants of Chumash villages to produce a surplus of local specialty goods for export, materials that could be exchanged for key resources not present within their own circumscribed territories.

The Barbareño Chumash traded acorns and other mainland materials to the Island Chumash, for example, in exchange for shell beads, sea otter furs, seal meat, and other materials.

Cooperative trade networks and intermarriage between Chumash towns on the islands, mainland coast, and interior valleys helped redistribute resources, build social alliances, buffer resource shortages during droughts and El Niños, and reduce social stresses that build whenever humans aggregate and interact intensively. Increased trade, craft specialization, population densities, and cultural complexity among the Chumash might be seen as signs of progress, but a variety of evidence shows that such changes came at considerable cost. Like the adoption of agriculture around the world, the increasing complexity of Chumash society appears to have been accompanied by higher levels of violence and other health problems, increased social stress and regulation, greater inequities in the distribution of wealth and power, and increasing impacts on local environments.

The study of Chumash skeletons from Santa Barbara Channel cemeteries shows that Chumash health declined substantially during parts of the Late Holocene, at the same time that violence increased. Evidence for greater violence is seen in increased rates of cranial injuries, parry fractures on the forearms, and projectile wounds from arrow or dart points, spears, or knives (Lambert 1994). The introduction of the bow and arrow about 1,500 years ago may have exacerbated violence and warfare among the Chumash, but a general increase in violence appears to have begun at least 1,000 years earlier. An increase in skeletal pathologies (cribra orbitalia, Harris lines, enamel hypoplasia, etc.) associated with nutritional or metabolic stresses is also seen in some Late Holocene skeletal populations, as well as a gradual reduction in stature (Lambert 1994). This general decline in health can be traced back several thousand years among the Chumash, but it may have peaked between about 1,100 and 600 years ago during the Medieval Climatic Anomaly. After about AD 1350, coastal populations appear to have been healthier and less prone to violence, suggesting that environmental conditions improved, that the Chumash developed social and economic solutions to the problems, or both.

Through more than 13,000 years along the Santa Barbara Coast, Native American cultures changed dramatically through time. Some of the most dramatic changes occurred during the Late Holocene, but the pace of culture change in the area seems to have generally accelerated through time: from the Early Holocene peoples who seem to have changed relatively little, to the somewhat faster developments of the Middle Holocene, to

Late Holocene changes that occurred much more rapidly and seemingly continued to accelerate until European contact. This general acceleration of culture change is found in many parts of the world—and continues to this day—and may be related to the cumulative nature of technological innovations, the expansion of human populations, and the growing amount of cultural interaction that takes place between people.

Although the rapid technological, economic, and social changes of the Late Holocene were crucial to the development of classic Chumash culture, many of the "new" artifact forms emerged from earlier analogues. Circular or j-shaped fishhooks probably evolved from gorges and composite hooks, for instance, the plank tomol emerged from a 13,000-year tradition of seafaring and channel crossings, the bow and arrow improved on earlier projectile technologies, and *Olivella* cup beads emerged from earlier precursors. From this perspective, where change and continuity are given equal weight, many of the Late Holocene technological developments among the Chumash can be seen as incremental rather than revolutionary in nature and the result of a combination of gradual and more punctuated cultural changes.

It is also worth noting that such changes were not solely responses to local population growth or environmental change. During the Late Holocene, and probably much earlier, the Chumash were connected into large interaction networks, through which goods and ideas were traded over much of western North America. This interaction helps explain the appearance of similar styles of manos and metates, mortars and pestles, side-notched dart points, bows and arrows, and bead or ornament types across much of Native California at roughly similar times (Erlandson 1997b:9).

As the Late Holocene came to a close, the Chumash had successfully adapted to a world that had changed dramatically and increasingly rapidly from the natural and cultural landscapes encountered by the people who first settled the Santa Barbara Channel area at least 13,000 years earlier. Their predecessors survived the last gasps of the last glacial, several millennia of rising seas and coastal erosion, and the disappearance of numerous productive estuaries. Their ancestors survived rising human populations, resource shortages, disputes with neighboring tribes or towns, droughts, earthquakes, and El Niños. Despite all this, historical accounts suggest that the Chumash were thriving when Spanish explorers first entered the Santa Barbara Channel area. They would survive the colonial encounter to come, but nothing in more than 10,000 years of experience could prepare the Chumash for the dramatic and devastating changes that came with the arrival of these strangers from distant lands.

AFTER CONTACT: IS THIS THE WAY THE WORLD ENDS?

The world of the Chumash fundamentally changed one fall day in AD 1542, when three Spanish ships commanded by Juan Rodriguez Cabrillo sailed up the California Coast and into the Santa Barbara Channel. For millennia the Chumash had interacted with other tribes in western North America, but their ancestors had been essentially isolated from cultural and biological developments in Eurasia and Africa for 15,000 years or more. Cabrillo's arrival was a harbinger of the emergence of a global economy that would profoundly alter Chumash culture—and all the cultures of the world—forever.

These changes may have begun with the introduction of deadly Old World diseases that devastated the Chumash in the sixteenth century. In the late 1700s, however, Spanish accounts describe a Chumash society that was thriving again, with large coastal populations, an impressive array of maritime and other technologies, extensive trade and occupational specialization, and a rich ceremonial life. With the establishment of the Santa Barbara Presidio and Mission Santa Barbara, however, traditional patterns of Chumash life were changed as they never had been before. The Spanish missionaries, and other colonists who followed them, introduced a pastoral, agrarian, and commercial economy to the region, built on the backs of Chumash labor, by the theft of Chumash land, and at the cost of thousands of Chumash lives. Most of the Chumash were conscripted to live at the missions, where they were required to adopt Euro-

pean customs and forbidden to practice most of their traditional ways. Waves of disease decimated their ranks, while cattle herds expanded exponentially and increasingly affected the wild plant foods that were one of the foundations of the traditional Chumash economy (Dartt and Erlandson 2006). As Chumash population plummeted and their traditional trade networks broke down, the Northern Channel Islands were abandoned in the early 1800s. With the end of Native burning, chaparral and dense riparian thickets encroached on the once open parklands maintained by the Chumash. Marine species such as sea otters, seals, abalones, and fish may have rebounded as Chumash fishing pressures were reduced. Within decades, however, the Spanish hunted grizzly bears to local extinction, and the sea otter, elephant seal, fur seal, great whales, and other animals soon fell under the pressure of emerging global markets and colonial empires.

While they lasted, the Spanish missions administered huge tracts of land—including the Tecolote Canyon area and its beachfront—supposedly held in sacred trust for the Chumash people. In AD 1834, however, the Mexican government secularized the missions and dissolved most of their landholdings. Most of these mission lands were granted to Spanish, Mexican, or other European colonists, including Nicolas Den, who in AD 1842 came to own the Tecolote Canyon area as part of his Rancho Los Dos Pueblos. In a land that was once their own, the Chumash melted into the diverse cultural landscape emerging in Alta California, working in a variety of jobs in Pueblo Santa Barbara or on the ranchos of wealthy landowners.

By the 1850s, in an age of cultural diaspora and gold fever, Santa Barbara and California were transformed into a truly global society of the American melting pot. First, the Chumash were joined by the soldiers, padres, and mission workers from New Spain, people primarily of Spanish and Indian descent. As the pueblos and ranchos of Alta California grew, a steady stream of Spanish, Mexican, and Anglo settlers arrived. With the gold rush, California was flooded by waves of immigrants from America, Mexico, England, Germany, Ireland, Italy, and many nations more. African Americans came to

California, along with Kanakas from Hawaii and other Polynesian kingdoms, thousands of Chinese, and many, many more.

As we ponder the meaning of Santa Barbara, California, and America, we should acknowledge that we are all descended from immigrants. Native Americans established residency here first, however, more than 13,000 years before the Europeans, Africans, Asians, and others who arrived in the last 500 years. And we should never forget that California was stolen from those Indian peoples whose history in this beautiful land dwarfs the heritage of Europeans and Americans. America owes a debt to the Chumash and other Indian peoples that has not yet been paid.

Chumash history has captivated many western scholars and American citizens since the 1800s, when the first geographical surveys of the area began to document the natural and cultural history of the Santa Barbara Channel region. The notion that the extinction of the Chumash and other Indian tribes was inevitable has pervaded the American consciousness since our nation was born and an idea called manifest destiny helped it spread from sea to shining sea. Anthropologists and other scholars have long worked in the shadow of such myths, documenting the history of American Indian cultures even as government policies accelerated their destruction. Prior to the 1970s, archaeologists largely ignored the existence of numerous Chumash descendants, and some anthropologists proclaimed them to be extinct. Even today, remnants of such attitudes linger among some anthropologists and archaeologists (see Haley and Wilcoxon 1997). In a paper titled "This Is the Way the World Ends," the renowned California archaeologist Clement Meighan (1981:65) asked and answered his own rhetorical question:

I wonder whether any of the coastal Indians of California, seeing the arrival of sixteenth-century Spanish and English ships, realized that the world of the Indians was over and that with the coming of the Europeans the Indian culture was fated to disappear?... From all this evidence, we can infer that the Indians of sixteenth-century California saw the arrival of

Europeans as the kind of event that portends the end of the world. In terms of *their* world, they were right.

Although their lives have changed dramatically, the Chumash people never bowed to the inevitable, refusing to join a preordained parade to extinction. More than 5,000 people now identify themselves as Chumash descendants, and their culture has undergone a remarkable revival over the past 40 years (Figure 8.5). In a county that once glorified its Spanish heritage while largely ignoring its much longer Native American past, the Chumash have survived. In a multicultural society now more willing to celebrate its Indian roots and acknowledge the wrongs that were done to the Chumash and other tribes, the Chumash are in the midst of a cultural revival and renaissance. Numerous Chumash people actively participated in protecting, collecting, analyzing, interpreting, illustrating, and preserving the archaeological materials from the Tecolote Canyon Archaeological Project. Recently, for the second year in a row, Chumash people gathered on Santa Cruz Island (Limuw) to celebrate a traditional crossing of the Santa Barbara Channel by paddlers from the Chumash Maritime Association in the tomol 'Elye'wun (*Swordfish*). Illustrating the changing face of anthropology, two Chumash scholars, Michael Cruz and Deana Dartt, also recently earned master's degrees in anthropology from the University of Oregon.

ENVIRONMENTAL IMPACTS AND ECOLOGICAL GHOSTS

The Chumash avoided extinction, but other elements of the Santa Barbara Channel environment have not fared as well. Along with "ending" traditional Chumash culture and ushering in a new era of global markets and cultural diaspora, the European invasion brought new ideas about the natural world and the role humans play in it. Like the Chumash, this new cultural mentality was entrepreneurial and based on production, commerce, and wealth. Unlike the Chumash, European and American invaders saw the natural world as the dominion of man and its natural resources as gifts to be used to generate capital, beat back the wilderness,

FIGURE 8.5. Chumash community members celebrate the dedication of Santa Barbara's Friendship Fountain at Cabrillo Beach in 1985. John Ruiz is at the far right wearing sunglasses (from "The Rainbow Bridge," courtesy of James Bottoms).

and domesticate the landscape. The Chumash supported high population densities and complex sociopolitical and economic structures with local resources and intensive trade with their neighbors, but the newcomers participated in world markets, with furs sent to China, tallow and hides to New Spain; and whale and seal oils to New England and Europe. Within decades of their first settlement, Europeans and Americans engaged in this global commerce were tapping local resources in an unsustainable fashion.

One of the lessons we have learned from the geology and archaeology of the Tecolote area is that Santa Barbara Channel environments are extremely dynamic. In the Monterey, Coldwater, and Sespe formations, this dynamism is written in stone, a story tens of millions of years old. The innocuous tar that washes ashore on the beach tells a simi-

lar tale, the debris of life deposited on an ancient seafloor, buried and transformed into a sealant, a source of energy and wealth, and now a nuisance. Marine terraces and ancient sea cliffs document dramatic swings in global climate and sea level over the past several hundred thousand years. The shells left behind by the ancestors of the Chumash testify to the formation and decline of a productive estuary at the canyon mouth during the Early and Middle Holocene. The thousands of shells and animal bones—a diverse array of fish, land mammals, sea mammals, birds, reptiles, and amphibians—recovered from Chumash sites at the canyon mouth provide evidence for the tremendous natural bounty of the Santa Barbara Coast, as well as the impact the Chumash had on these populations.

The nature of such impacts, however, was fundamentally different from those of the past 200 years or so. Evidence from the Channel Islands and the Santa Barbara Coast suggests that the Chumash and their ancestors harvested either the same or a similar suite of resources for thousands of years. The economic importance of resources like shell-fish, fish, and mammals changed through time, but only one species seems to have disappeared from the archaeological record because of human activity—a flightless duck, *Chendytes lawi*—which co-existed with Native peoples in California for nearly 10,000 years. Despite their high population densities, diversified and sophisticated technologies, and the development of monetary currencies and regional markets, we have no clear evidence that the Chumash caused the extinction of any other local animals during the thousands of years they lived in the area.

This is not to say that they did not affect the local environment around them. The use of fire to promote shrub and grassland and higher populations of terrestrial game and changes in the use of marine fauna through time indicate that they had an impact, as all people do, on the environments of the Santa Barbara Coast. Elsewhere we have argued that the Chumash altered Santa Barbara Channel ecosystems in a variety of ways but that they made a series of economic, technological, and behavioral adjustments that helped maintain a level of sustainability across the millennia (Erlandson et al. 2005; Erlandson, Rick, and Vellanoweth 2004; Rick and Erlandson 2003). Archaeological data from the Tecolote area and the broader Santa Barbara Coast seem to support this idea.

Within a few decades of European settlement, however, California's natural environments were subjected to a series of ecological catastrophes that make the ecological impacts of the Chumash look minor. Shortly after their arrival, Europeans went on a murderous rampage of commercial exploitation unlike anything the California Coast had ever seen. In the process, the ecology of local land-and seascapes was dramatically changed. Beginning with the Spanish and continuing until recent times, most of the large native species were essentially eradicated from local landscapes and seascapes—bears, mountain lions, condors, bald and golden eagles, pelicans, whales, porpoises, seals and

sea lions, sea otters, sharks, swordfish, giant sea bass, and many more. Although a few of these species have recovered (or may recover) under state and federal management, these species haunt the history of the Santa Barbara area like ecological ghosts from the past. In their place, thousands of cattle, horses, pigs, sheep, goats, and other exotic animals were introduced and have further altered the natural balance of California ecosystems. Native plant communities have fared little better, lost or altered by grazing, agriculture, land clearance, fire suppression, the introduction of hundreds of exotic species, and other activities. In recent decades, a litany of ills associated with industrialization and urbanization have afflicted California: overfishing and oil spills; the damming of rivers, channelization of streams, and filling of coastal wetlands; sewage dumping and smog; population growth, pesticides, and pollution. The accumulation of environmental impacts has taken an increasing toll on California's wild and natural resources. The result is a frightening wave of extinctions, fishery closures, the fragmentation and collapse of coastal ecosystems, and an ever more artificial environment.

Current accounts of environmental catastrophe can be deeply depressing, inspiring many not to action but to stick their proverbial heads in the sand. Yet humans are intelligent, and nature is resilient. We must realize the tremendous progress America has made in diagnosing and understanding the ecological effects of our actions. We have some of the strictest environmental and conservation regulations in the world. We have an enlightened and educated populace, many of whom are dedicated to preserving the character and quality of our coastal landscapes. On the brink of extinction just a few decades ago, gray whales, blue whales, seals, sea lions, and even sea otters swim through Santa Barbara Channel waters once again. Although poisoned by pesticides and petrochemicals, brown pelicans lumber over our shorelines again, crashing headlong into the sea. In the Santa Barbara Channel area, there are sizable natural preserves where long-term ecological studies and restoration efforts are under way. And Santa Barbara's coastal landscape remains one of the most beautiful on earth, a refuge that attracts visitors from around the nation and the world. If the history of Tecolote Canyon offers a view of the California Coast in microcosm, there are reasons to be both hopeful and vigilant. Humans have survived for millennia along California's golden shores, and we must learn from their experiences. Ultimately, understanding the long and dynamic history of this amazing coastal landscape—where the mountains meet the sea—offers invaluable insight into the current health of our coast, the sustainability of our own actions, and the gifts we will leave for future generations.

The Power of History

One of the qualities that make humans unique is our keen sense of history. The survival value of recording life experiences is evident in the animal kingdom, where a major investment in memory has been built into the brains of the more complex and social animals. Moving up the evolutionary ladder, as learning replaces instinct, more complex animals increasingly learn from their experiences and pass their wisdom on to their offspring and other community members. Among humans, this capacity for memory, recording history, and learning from the past has been developed to an unprecedented degree. More than any other animal on earth, we are able to analyze the past, anticipate the future, and use these gifts in the present to maximize the chances for the survival of ourselves, our families, and the broader communities of which we are a part.

With such a finely developed sense of history, however, comes great responsibility. It has often been said that those who do not learn from their past are doomed to repeat it. History is littered with the ruins of ancient societies and civilizations led by people who made bad choices, who suffered through difficult circumstances that might have been avoided, or who failed to survive under catastrophic conditions. Others made better choices, avoided disasters, survived, and recorded many of the histories we now hold dear. If we can understand their choices, their failures, successes, and disasters, we can learn something from the past that can help us in the future. If we choose not to preserve our histories, the opportunity to learn from them will be lost from all memory, beyond recall.

In the late 1800s and early 1900s, a few Chumash elders, such as Fernando Librado, Maria Ygnacia, and Juan Justo, worked with several scholars to preserve a wealth of information about their history, geography, languages, and culture. Much of this information, available in numerous fine books that have helped fuel the imagination of the public and build an appreciation for the beauty of Chumash culture, has contributed greatly to the cultural revival of the Chumash today. As demonstrated in this volume, archaeological sites are another important source of information on the history of the cultures and environments in the Santa Barbara Channel area. They are the repository of Chumash and American history, of tangible links between past and present, of objects still sacred to the Chumash, and of information that can guide the protection and restoration of coastal ecosystems.

Yet the archaeological sites of the Chumash, their predecessors and successors, are being lost at an alarming rate. Over the years, thousands of Chumash sites have been damaged or destroyed by development, many of them with little or no scientific study. Although protected by federal, state, and local laws, they are still being lost to development, erosion, vandalism, and looting. Coastal erosion is particularly severe, notoriously difficult to stop, and often dismissed as a natural process that requires no response by agencies or individuals. Such erosion has been exacerbated, however, by the construction of dams, breakwaters, and other structures that rob beaches of protective sediment. Coastal erosion accelerates as sea levels rise, and global warming now poses a largely unrecognized and unmitigated threat to the history and archaeology of the Chumash and other maritime peoples. Erosion of archaeological sites has also been accelerated by the overgrazing of livestock, which encourages soil erosion via wind and water.

Tragically, a misguided fascination with Chumash and other American Indian history leads to widespread illegal looting of Chumash village and camp sites, to the desecration of burial grounds and other sacred areas, and to the destruction of Chumash history. Chumash sites are looted by selfish individuals who seek to profit from the past—

the hoarding of curios in private collections. Ultimately, however, this desecration is fueled by those who buy Chumash artifacts, legally or illegally, and drive the market in Chumash antiquities.

Prior to the construction of Bacara (Figures 8.6 and 8.7), Chumash cemeteries at SBA-71, SBA-72, and SBA-73 were severely damaged by looters over and over again. The bones of a proud people lay shattered and desecrated in the dirt, surrounded by the trash left behind by grave robbers. With the support of the landowner and developers, archaeologists and Chumash tribal members worked together to document the damage done to the archaeological sites. Nothing could fully mitigate the tears and the pain of Chumash elders who struggled to understand yet another insult to their culture and history. American Indian people take such insults very seriously—in at least one case the bodies of grave robbers were found in the bottom of a mine shaft. In the Tecolote case, a fragment of a human jawbone found at SBA-73 was later matched to the other half of a jawbone found by federal investigators and county sheriffs in the home of a grave robber. The perpetrator pleaded guilty and was convicted of violating laws protecting human remains and historical properties. This case and conviction were part of an ongoing monitoring program led by local Chumash and other Indian people, site stewards who work to protect their sacred sites from similar depredations. Chumash descendants are determined that their history will not be lost without a fight.

As we have shown in our chronicle of Tecolote Canyon, archaeological sites are a rich source of information on the long cultural and ecological history of the Santa Barbara area, of California and America, and of humanity itself. Such archaeological histories are more powerful, however, when they are illuminated by the fields of geology, ecology, and traditional history. Histories are most interesting and persuasive, moreover, when they are linked to some of the fundamental issues of the human condition. In this sense, the story of Tecolote is a microcosm that illustrates the irresistible power of the earth itself, the dynamism of coastlines in general, and the ultimate futility of resisting the forces of nature. It is the slow unfolding of human history as reflected in the practices of everyday life. It is a long story of remarkable human ingenuity and innovation and of human struggles to survive and adapt to the challenges posed by environmental changes—some of them of our own making. It is the story of clashing cultures and the powers of cultural persistence and resilience. It is a story of occasional violence, larceny, and greed, the afflictions of all human societies. It is the story of a wealthy "conservationist" who debased his property when oil beckoned, a story of the power of money and the mortality of us all. It is the story of a humiliated Japanese captain who sailed across the Pacific to bombard Tecolote in an act of war and personal revenge. History is not always uplifting; it sometimes sheds light on the darker side of human nature or identifies problems that can no longer be ignored. Ultimately, however, we believe the story of Tecolote Canyon is one of hope—for the protection and restoration of those natural areas and historical sites that remain around us, for the future of the multiethnic society we live in, and for the solutions that science and history will provide for our future.

Where there is history, there is hope. Where there is hope, there is inspiration. And in inspiration, we find the solutions to problems, both large and small. For those who made history before us, from the Amol'amol (ancient ones) to the people of Hel'apunitse, from ranch hands to oil workers and construction crews, to those who reside in the canyon today and the people of many nations who will gather there in years to come, may Tecolote remain a safe haven, an inspiration, and a canyon through time.

POSTSCRIPT

Whether you live in the Santa Barbara area or are just visiting, you are enjoying the beautiful landscape that was occupied and owned solely by the Chumash Indians for thousands of years. For thousands of Chumash descendants, this landscape, its history, and the villages and other sites of their ancestors are sacred ground. Since Europeans arrived in their land, Chumash sites have been heavily affected by farming, urbanization, coastal erosion, and looting.

FIGURE 8.6. The Bacara area in the 1920s (photo courtesy of the Santa Barbara Museum of Natural History and the University of California–Santa Barbara Department of Anthropology).

FIGURE 8.7. The Bacara area today (photo by Erik Erlandson).

If you would like to help preserve and reconstruct Chumash history, tax-deductible contributions can be made to the Santa Barbara Channel Radiocarbon Dating Fund at the University of Oregon's Museum of Natural and Cultural History. During the past 20 years, in cooperation with the Chumash community and a number of agencies and institutions, we have raised more than $70,000 to date threatened archaeological sites and important museum collections from the Chumash area. The results contribute to a better understanding of Chumash history, the protection of Chumash village sites, the study of historical ecology and human impacts in Santa Barbara Channel ecosystems, and marine conservation and management efforts. All contributions to the fund go directly to the dating of key sites with no salary, administrative overhead, or travel costs. Contributions, made out to the Santa Barbara Channel Radiocarbon Dating Fund, should be sent to Dr. Jon Erlandson, Museum of Natural and Cultural History, University of Oregon, Eugene, OR 97403-1224.

Additional Figure and Tables

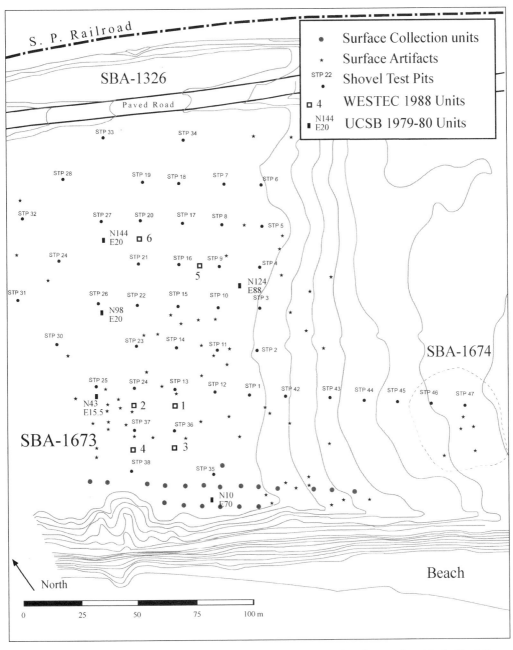

FIGURE A.1. Map of SBA-1673, showing the location of excavations and surface artifacts (drafted by Julia Knowles).

TABLE A.1. Summary of Artifacts from SBA-1326

ARTIFACT TYPE	COUNT
Ground-Stone Tools	
Mano (sandstone)	27
Metate fragment (sandstone)	16
Mortar or bowl fragments (sandstone)	3
Pestle (sandstone)	2
Subtotal	48

ARTIFACT TYPE	COUNT
Chipped-Stone Artifacts	
Core	2
Core tool/chopper	1
Projectile point fragment	1
Biface fragment	1
Hammer stone	1
Flake tools	7
Tool-making debris	76
Subtotal	89
Total	137

Note: Includes shovel test pits, test pits, surface collections, and monitoring finds, including some artifacts from SBA-1673N, which overlaps with SBA-1326.

TABLE A.2. Summary of Artifacts from SBA-75

				TOTAL	
ARTIFACT TYPE	AREA A	AREA B	AREA C	#	%
Mano	3	1	4	11	1.2
Metate	2	1	9	12	1.3
Mortar or bowl	1	—	2	3	.3
Pestle	—	1	—	1	.1
Projectile point	2	1	2	5	.5
Biface	2	4	4	10	1.0
Flake tool	6	2	5	13	1.4
Core	2	—	5	7	.7
Obsidian tool-making debris	—	—	1	1	.1
Fused shale debris	—	—	2	2	.2
Monterey chert debris	131	70	170	371	38.8
Franciscan chert debris	132	34	212	378	39.6
Other tool-making debris	59	17	61	137	14.3
Hammer stone	—	—	—	1	.1
Olivella spire-ground bead	—	—	1	1	.1
Whole *Olivella* shell	—	—	1	1	.1
Quartz crystal	—	—	1	1	.1
Asphaltum	P	—	P	P	—
Red ochre	—	—	P	P	—
Total	340	131	480	955	100.0

Note: Includes surface collection and excavation samples, the latter based on ¼-in screen recovery; P = present. Site totals include three manos from uncertain area, two collected by ARI archaeologists in 1968.

Table A.3. Shellfish Remains from Areas A, B, and C at SBA-75

Type	Area A Weight	%	Area B Weight	%	Area C Weight	%	Total Weight	%
Tivela (Pismo clam)	2,906.8	99.5	103.1	92.8	1,388.4	72.1	4,398.3	88.7
Mytilus (California mussel)	5.8	.2	6.0	5.4	433.0	22.5	444.8	9.0
Saxidomus (Washington clam)	.1	<.1	.4	.4	41.7	2.2	42.2	.9
Chione (Venus clam)	5.5	.2	—	—	35.8	1.9	41.3	.8
Protothaca (littleneck clam)	.4	<.1	1.3	1.2	10.5	.5	12.2	.2
Balanus (acorn barnacle)	—	—	.3	.2	5.6	.3	5.9	.1
Cerithidea (horn snail)	—	—	—	—	2.5	.1	2.5	<.1
Olivella (olive snail)	—	—	—	—	1.4	.1	1.4	<.1
Acanthina (thorn snail)	—	—	—	—	1.0	<.1	1.0	<.1
Ostrea (oyster)	—	—	—	—	1.0	<.1	1.0	<.1
Clinocardium (cockle)	—	—	—	—	.3	<.1	.3	<.1
Polyplacophora (chitons)	—	—	—	—	.3	<.1	.3	<.1
Shell, undifferentiated	2.2	.1	—	—	5.1	.3	7.3	.1
Total	2,920.8		111.1		1,926.6		4,958.5	

Note: All weights in grams; based on ¼-in screen recovery.

TABLE A.4. Vertebrate Remains from Areas A, B, and C at SBA-75

ANIMAL TYPE	AREA A		AREA B		AREA C		TOTAL	
	#	WEIGHT	#	WEIGHT	#	WEIGHT	#	WEIGHT
Deer	3	16.1	—	—	—	—	3	16.1
Ungulate (deer?)	1	.3	—	—	5	5.7	6	6.0
Rabbit	—	—	2	.2	2	.4	4	.6
Gopher	—	—	10	1.7	6	1.5	16	3.2
Sea mammal	6	5.2	1	.6	12	41.1	19	46.9
Large mammal	59	24.2	26	17.2	159	113.8	244	155.2
Medium/large mammal	75	20.9	52	14.5	186	42.5	313	77.9
Medium mammal	8	2.5	1	.4	11	4.5	20	7.4
Small mammal	3	.5	9	2.0	26	5.1	38	7.6
Bird, undifferentiated	1	.2	3	1.0	6	4.2	10	5.4
Pile perch	2	.2	—	—	1	.2	3	.4
Pacific mackerel	—	—	—	—	2	.7	2	.7
Barracuda	—	—	1	.2	2	.5	3	.7
Surfperch?	1	.2	—	—	—	—	1	.2
Giant kelpfish	1	.1	—	—	—	—	1	.1
Sardine?	—	—	—	—	1	<.1	1	<.1
Bony fish, undifferentiated	8	1.7	4	1.3	42	10.0	54	13.0
Bat ray	—	—	—	—	2	.7	2	.7
Soupfin shark?	—	—	—	—	1	1.4	1	1.4
Leopard shark?	—	—	—	—	1	.3	1	.3
Bone, undifferentiated	3	1.4	1	.2	10	3.9	14	5.5
Total	171	73.5	110	39.3	475	236.5	756	349.3

Note: All weights in grams; based on ¼-in screen recovery, except for a sardine vertebra from a column sample.

Table A.5. Shellfish Remains from the Middle Holocene Components at SBA-72N

Type	Clam Midden Unit 97-4		Clam Midden Column 97-4		Mussel Midden Unit 89-8	
	Weight	%	Weight	%	Weight	%
Balanus spp. (acorn barnacle)	185.3	.3	1.4	2.6	4.4	<.1
Chione californiensis (Venus clam)	54.3	.1	—	—	—	—
Chione undatella (Venus clam)	38.1	.1	—	—	—	—
Chione spp. (Venus clam)	19.8	<.1	—	—	—	—
Chitons, undifferentiated	2.4	<.1	—	—	—	—
Decapods (crab)	6.5	<.1	.1	.2	.1	<.1
Gastropods, undifferentiated (snails)	3.0	<.1	—	—	.6	<.1
Haliotis rufescens (red abalone)	118.0	.2	—	—	—	—
Hinnites multirugosus (rock scallop)	4.5	<.1	—	—	—	—
Limpets, undifferentiated	2.6	<.1	—	—	—	—
Megathura crenulata (keyhole limpet)	.9	<.1	—	—	—	—
Mytilus californianus (California mussel)	9,385.5	13.7	16.0	29.6	27,617.4	99.9
Narcissi spp.	.4	<.1	—	—	—	—
Norrissia norrisi (Norris top snail)	.4	<.1	—	—	—	—
Ostrea lurida (oyster)	9.1	<.1	—	—	—	—
Pollicipes polymerus (gooseneck barnacle)	140.8	.2	.4	.7	.1	<.1
Protothaca staminea (littleneck clam)	259.6	.4	<.1	<.1	.2	<.1
Saxidomus nuttalii (Washington clam)	5.5	<.01	—	—	—	—
Septifer bifurcatus (platform mussel)	10.4	<.1	—	—	.3	<.1
Strongylocentrotus spp. (sea urchin)	215.1	.3	.1	.2	—	—
Tegula spp. (turban snail)	4.0	<.1	—	—	—	—
Tivela stultorum (Pismo clam)	57,941.8	84.5	31.5	58.3	—	—
Nacre, undifferentiated	95.1	.1	1.1	2.04	—	—
Shell, undifferentiated	100.2	.1	3.4	6.3	—	—
Total	68,603.3		54.0		27,623.1	

Note: All weights in grams; based on ⅛-in screen recovery.

TABLE A.6. Summary of Chipped-Stone Artifacts from SBA-71

ARTIFACT TYPE	SCREEN RESIDUALS		SURFACE COLLECTION/ MONITORING FIND		TOTAL	
	#	WEIGHT	#	WEIGHT	#	WEIGHT
Biface, excurvate	1	22.0	1	2.7	2	24.7
Biface, preform	—	—	1	11.9	1	11.9
Biface, triangular	—	—	1	5.3	1	5.3
Biface, undifferentiated	2	2.7	2	9.5	4	12.2
Borer/drill, triangular	—	—	2	15.7	2	15.7
Borer/drill, undifferentiated	1	1.3	1	4.9	2	6.2
Core	1	24.5	1	40.7	2	65.2
Flake, retouched/utilized	3	187.7	10	114.8	13	302.5
Flaked cobble	—	—	18	1,615.7	18	1,615.7
Hammer stone	1	368.2	4	2,272.5	5	2,640.7
Scraper	—	—	1	8.5	1	8.5
Debitage, undifferentiated	1,326	305.1	14	289.4	1,340	594.5
Total	1,335	911.5	56	4,391.6	1,391	5,303.1

Note: All weights in grams; based on ⅛-in screen recovery.

TABLE A.7. Summary of Geochemical Data for Obsidian Artifacts from Tecolote Canyon Sites

SITE	CATALOG NUMBER	UNIT: DEPTH (CM)	ARTIFACT TYPE	OBSIDIAN SOURCE	TI	MN	ZN	RB	SR	Y	ZR	NB	PB
SBA-71	447-009a	2: 0–20	Debris	CVF	163±95	91±47	89±12	328±6	10±4	54±7	141±3	51±3	32±7
	447-31a	3: 20–40	Debris	CVF	109±95	77±47	208±19	255±7	9±8	47±5	108±8	31±4	33±9
SBA-71/72	447-73a	STP 97-1	Debris	CVF	134±95	84±47	118±11	284±6	5±8	56±4	128±7	44±3	33±7
	447-73b	STP 97-1	Debris	CVF	129±95	87±47	74±11	286±5	14±7	47±4	138±7	43±3	28±6
	447-106a	STP 97-1	Debris	CVF	130±95	89±47	74±12	303±6	8±8	52±4	136±7	42±3	40±6
	447-106b	STP 97-1	Debris	CVF	108±95	83±47	88±10	308±6	15±7	54±4	147±7	45±3	47±5
	447-106c	STP 97-1	Debris	CVF	90±95	84±47	55±15	301±7	10±8	60±5	130±8	33±4	29±7
	447-179a	STP 97-1	Debris	CD-LM	251±95	99±47	50±11	156±5	98±7	12±4	169±7	11±3	36±5
	447-212a	STP 97-1	Debris	CVF	133±95	117±47	81±10	311±5	9±7	54±4	144±7	49±3	44±4
SBA-72	448-75a	1: 80–100	Debris	CVF-WS	93±95	116±47	107±9	274±4	12±7	54±3	140±7	46±2	34±4
	448-321	5: 0–20	Debris	CVF	183±95	76±47	73±13	266±6	5±9	43±5	114±8	45±4	37±6
	448-350a	5: 20–40	Debris	CVF	163±95	92±47	79±10	267±5	11±7	53±4	141±7	41±3	35±5
	448-350b	5: 0–40	Debris	CVF	87±95	86±47	59±13	243±6	8±8	47±4	106±7	42±3	31±6
	448-380a	5: 40–60	Point	CVF	127±95	73±47	80±14	248±6	ND	54±8	112±4	32±4	32±7
	448-498a	5: 100–120	Debris	CVF-WS	445±95	211±47	60±7	258±4	9±7	53±3	137±7	48±2	37±3
	448-920a	CS 5: 20–40	Debris	CVF	125±95	81±47	84±11	290±6	10±7	52±4	136±7	45±3	28±5
	448-958a	CS 5: 40–60	Debris	CVF	118±95	86±47	87±10	282±6	18±7	53±4	133±7	41±3	36±5
	448-958b	CS 5: 40–60	Debris	CVF	105±95	82±47	57±11	257±5	10±7	42±4	127±7	41±3	18±6
	448-1002a	CS 5: 60–80	Debris	CD-LM	238±95	91±47	69±11	158±5	90±7	19±4	159±8	11±3	38±6
	448-1122a	CS 5: 120–140	Debris	CVF	157±95	93±47	95±11	284±6	9±7	64±4	140±7	42±3	31±5
	448-1123a	CS 5: 120–140	Debris	CVF	134±95	89±47	135±11	305±6	11±7	51±4	131±7	35±4	38±6
	448-1123b	CS 5: 120–140	Debris	CVF	174±95	82±47	58±11	287±6	11±7	49±4	125±7	44±3	44±5
	448-1157a	CS 5:140–160	Debris	CVF	109±95	72±47	96±13	240±6	12±7	41±5	126±8	40±4	42±6
	448-1186a	1: 60–80	Biface	CD-LM	193±95	84±47	60±9	152±4	88±7	13±4	172±7	17±3	31±4

TABLE A.7. (cont'd) Summary of Geochemical Data for Obsidian Artifacts from Tecolote Canyon Sites

SITE	CATALOG NUMBER	UNIT: DEPTH (CM)	ARTIFACT TYPE	OBSIDIAN SOURCE	TI	MN	ZN	RB	SR	Y	ZR	NB	PB
SBA-73	449-467a	11: 0–20	Debris	CD-LM	188 ± 95	83 ± 47	38 ± 13	139 ± 5	85 ± 7	16 ± 4	167 ± 7	10 ± 3	25 ± 6
	449-467b	11: 0–20	Debris	CVF	147 ± 95	73 ± 47	82 ± 12	262 ± 7	13 ± 7	42 ± 5	104 ± 8	40 ± 4	27 ± 6
	449-515a	11: 40–60	Debris	CVF	185 ± 95	114 ± 47	150 ± 10	313 ± 5	13 ± 7	52 ± 4	149 ± 7	58 ± 3	45 ± 4
	449-538a	11: 60–80	Debris	CVF	129 ± 95	92 ± 47	69 ± 12	253 ± 5	13 ± 7	55 ± 4	126 ± 7	43 ± 3	40 ± 6
	449-553a	11: 0–60	Debris	CVF	180 ± 95	111 ± 47	68 ± 10	262 ± 5	14 ± 7	48 ± 4	118 ± 7	48 ± 3	42 ± 5
	449-660a	16: 0–20	Biface	CVF	108 ± 95	102 ± 47	77 ± 8	277 ± 5	11 ± 7	49 ± 3	142 ± 7	54 ± 2	28 ± 4
	449-882a	22: 20–40	Biface	CVF	40 ± 94	101 ± 47	105 ± 9	232 ± 4	9 ± 7	38 ± 3	116 ± 7	41 ± 2	36 ± 4
	449-882b	22: 20–40	Debris	CVF	146 ± 95	84 ± 47	68 ± 11	278 ± 6	10 ± 7	56 ± 4	132 ± 7	51 ± 3	44 ± 5
	449-882c	22:20–40	Debris	CVF	145 ± 95	91 ± 47	59 ± 11	285 ± 6	11 ± 7	55 ± 4	136 ± 7	42 ± 3	45 ± 5
	449-899a	22: 40–60	Debris	CVF	83 ± 95	70 ± 47	63 ± 13	274 ± 7	12 ± 7	51 ± 5	118 ± 8	41 ± 4	33 ± 7
	449-899b	22: 40–60	Debris	CVF	95 ± 95	67 ± 47	85 ± 12	263 ± 6	5 ± 9	48 ± 4	125 ± 7	44 ± 4	37 ± 6
	449-901a	22: 40–60	Point	CVF-WS	191 ± 95	171 ± 47	61 ± 7	269 ± 4	9 ± 7	59 ± 3	147 ± 7	50 ± 2	30 ± 3
	449-1834a	50: 20–40	Debris	CVF-WS	310 ± 95	146 ± 47	74 ± 8	304 ± 5	19 ± 7	58 ± 3	153 ± 7	54 ± 2	43 ± 4
	449-1834b	50: 20–40	Debris	CVF	193 ± 95	118 ± 47	96 ± 8	318 ± 5	13 ± 7	60 ± 4	151 ± 7	51 ± 3	41 ± 4
	449-1834c	50: 20–40	Debris	CVF	159 ± 95	88 ± 47	46 ± 11	203 ± 5	13 ± 7	45 ± 4	143 ± 7	39 ± 3	25 ± 5
	449-1834d	50: 20–40	Debris	CVF	152 ± 95	74 ± 47	103 ± 10	252 ± 6	15 ± 7	45 ± 4	127 ± 7	43 ± 3	32 ± 5
	449-2418a	CS 59: 40–60	Debris	CVF	119 ± 95	88 ± 47	106 ± 12	295 ± 6	9 ± 7	47 ± 4	129 ± 7	37 ± 4	39 ± 6
	449-174		Biface?	CD-LM	837 ± 90	256 ± 27	53 ± 7	158 ± 4	95 ± 9	18 ± 3	182 ± 7	14 ± 1	35 ± 4
SBA-75	?	Trench	Core	Tr-Qu									
SBA-1673	451-475	Surface	Biface	CVF-WS	399 ± 95	238 ± 47	67 ± 7	271 ± 4	9 ± 7	56 ± 3	140 ± 7	48 ± 2	38 ± 3
SBA-1674	452-235a	4: 0–20	Debris	CVF	93 ± 95	70 ± 47	132 ± 16	207 ± 6	16 ± 7	36 ± 4	120 ± 8	32 ± 4	17 ± 8

Note: STP = shovel test pit, CS = column sample, CVF = Coso Volcanic Field, WS = West Sugarloaf; CD-LM = Casa Diablo–Lookout Mountain; Tr-Qu = Truman/Queen.

TABLE A.8. Ground-Stone Artifacts from SBA-71

ARTIFACT TYPE	MATERIAL TYPE	SHOVEL TEST PIT/UNIT	SURFACE COLLECTION	TOTAL
Mortar/bowl fragment	Sandstone	—	11	11
Bowl fragment	Steatite	—	1	1
Pestle or pestle fragments	Sandstone	—	8	8
Metate fragment	Sandstone	4	1	5
Mano	Sandstone	2	13	15
Charm stone	Basalt	—	1	1
Ground stone, undifferentiated	Sandstone	2	3	5
Total		8	38	46

Note: Includes four metate fragments and one mano found in Feature 97-1, a stone cairn that was exposed and then preserved in place.

TABLE A.9. Chipped-Stone Artifacts from Late Holocene Components at SBA-72

ARTIFACT TYPE	INDEX UNITS		NON-INDEX UNITS		SURFACE COLLECTION/ MONITORING FIND		TOTAL	
	#	WEIGHT	#	WEIGHT	#	WEIGHT	#	WEIGHT
Biface, concave base	1	1.9	—	—	—	—	1	1.9
Biface, excurvate	15	73.2	6	8.5	9	70.1	30	151.8
Biface, triangular	1	4.1	1	2	—	—	2	6.1
Biface, undifferentiated	19	30	21	45.4	1	7.3	41	82.7
Borer/drill, triangular	11	30.4	2	3.9	2	11.8	15	46.1
Borer/drill, undifferentiated	16	74.4	11	42.1	1	6.3	28	122.8
Chunk, undifferentiated	4	50	63	388.5	6	107.6	73	546.1
Core	6	255.1	—	—	4	1,157.9	10	1,413
Drill	2	5	—	—	—	—	2	5
Drill/bladelet	1	.1	3	.6	—	—	4	.7
Flake, retouched/utilized	31	271.7	22	382.3	12	359.7	65	1,013.7
Flaked cobble	5	1,601.8	14	589.5	3	1,357.6	22	3,548.9
Hammer stone	1	118	1	14.6	4	1,904.8	6	2,037.4
Debitage, undifferentiated	11,465	3,355.8	9,795	2,122.1	7	3.1	21,267	5,481
Total	11,578	5,871.5	9,939	3,599.5	49	4,986.2	21,566	14,457.2

Note: All weights in grams; based on ⅛-in screen recovery; index units (Units 2 and 5, Column Samples 1, 2, and 5) analyzed in detail (volume 1.54 m³); non-index units had only preliminary analysis.

TABLE A.10. Ground-Stone Tools from Late Holocene Components at SBA-72

ARTIFACT TYPE	MATERIAL TYPE	SHOVEL TEST PIT/UNIT	SURFACE COLLECTION	TOTAL
Mortar or bowl fragments	Sandstone	6	11	17
Pestle	Sandstone	3	4	7
Metate fragments	Sandstone	2	—	2
Mano	Sandstone	2	2	4
Abrader?	Sandstone	2	—	2
Girdled stone/net weight	Sandstone	—	3	3
Pecked stone	Sandstone	2	—	2
Shaft straightener/abrader	Sandstone	1	—	1
Fragment, undifferentiated	Sandstone	10	5	15
Fragment, undifferentiated	Basalt	1	—	1
Fragment, undifferentiated	Shale?	1	—	1
Fragment, undifferentiated	Soapstone	1	—	1
Total		31	25	56

TABLE A.11. Bone Tools from Late Holocene Components at SBA-72

TOOL TYPE	COUNT	WEIGHT (G)
Awl fragment	7	9.76
Gorge, possible	1	.40
Ground/polished fragment		
Edge fragment	5	2.29
Long bone shaft fragment	7	6.30
Mid-body fragment	10	5.20
Near tip fragment	4	.90
Tip fragment	15	2.79
Miscellaneous	3	1.26
Wedge fragment	1	1.28
Total	53	30.18

TABLE A.12. Bone and Stone Beads from SBA-72, SBA-73, and SBA-1674

Site	Unit Type and Number	Bone Tube/ Ornament	Red Shale Disk	Soapstone Barrel	Soapstone Disk	Soapstone Cylinder	Soapstone Ornament	Soapstone Tube	Soapstone Bead in Production	Total
SBA-72N	1	1	—	—	7	1	—	1	3	13
	CS 1	—	—	—	—	—	—	—	1	1
	2	—	—	—	2	1	—	—	—	3
	7	—	—	—	1	—	—	—	—	1
	97-2	—	—	—	1	—	—	—	—	1
	97-3	—	—	—	1	—	—	1	3	5
	STP 97-9	—	—	—	—	—	—	—	1	1
	STP 97-17	—	—	—	1	—	—	—	—	1
SBA-72S	3	—	—	—	—	1	—	—	—	1
	4	—	—	—	5	1	—	—	—	6
	5	—	—	—	8	6	4	—	4	22
	CS 5	—	—	—	5	—	1	—	1	7
	SC #35	—	—	—	1	—	—	—	—	1
	SC #52	—	—	1	—	—	—	—	—	1
Subtotal	—	1	—	1	32	10	5	2	13	64

TABLE A.12. (cont'd) Bone and Stone Beads from SBA-72, SBA-73, and SBA-1674

Site	Unit Type and Number	Bone Tube/ Ornament	Red Shale Disk	Soapstone Barrel	Soapstone Disk	Soapstone Cylinder	Soapstone Ornament	Soapstone Tube	Soapstone Bead in Production	Total
SBA-73N	1	—	1	—	—	—	—	—	—	1
	2	—	—	—	4	2	—	—	—	6
	4	—	—	—	1	3	—	—	—	4
	5	—	—	—	1	—	—	—	—	1
	6	—	—	—	4	1	—	—	—	5
	11	—	—	—	4	—	—	—	2	6
	19	—	—	—	1	—	—	—	—	1
	20	—	—	—	—	—	1	—	—	1
	21	—	—	—	—	—	—	1	—	1
	22	1	—	—	—	1	—	—	—	2
	28	1	—	—	—	—	—	—	1	2
	32	—	—	—	1	—	—	—	1	2
	45	—	—	—	1	—	—	—	—	1
	48	1	—	—	1	—	2	—	—	4
SBA-73S	59	—	—	—	1	—	—	1	—	2
	98-25	1	—	1	3	1	—	—	—	6
Subtotal	—	4	1	1	22	8	3	2	4	44
SBA-1674	6	—	—	—	—	—	—	1	—	1
	9	—	—	—	1	—	—	—	—	1
Total	—	5	1	2	61	19	7	6	19	120

Note: Based on ⅛-in screen recovery; CS = column sample, STP = shovel test pit, SC = surface collection.

TABLE A.13. *Olivella* Beads from Late Holocene Components at Tecolote Canyon Sites

Site	Unit	Volume (M³)	Wall Disk	Callus Cup	Thin Lipped	Spire Lopped	Drilled Rectangle	Bead in Production	Total
SBA-72N	1	.6	57	4	—	4	—	—	65
	CS 1	.075	7	—	—	—	—	1	8
	2	.65	2	—	—	2	—	—	4
	7	.6	1	1	—	—	—	—	2
Subtotal	—		67	5	—	6	—	1	79
SBA-72S	3	.8	4	2	—	—	—	—	6
	4	.75	3	8	—	—	1'	—	12
	5	.80	118	66	—	1	—	6	191
	CS 5	.013	41	27	—	2	—	1	71
	STP 97-25		1	—	—	—	—	—	1
Subtotal	—		167	104	—	3	1	7	281
SBA-73N	2	.6	2	—	—	—	—	—	2
	5	.75	—	—	—	—	—	2	2
	6	.7	—	1	—	—	—	—	1
	11	1.0	2	1	—	2	—	—	5
	CS 11	.063	1	—	—	—	—	—	1
Subtotal	—		5	2	—	2	—	2	11
SBA-73S	59	1.2	10	17	—	—	—	—	27
	CS 59		2	2	—	—	—	1	5
	60		2	2	—	—	—	—	4
	98-25	1.4	25	56	1	1	—	5	88
Subtotal	—		39	77	1	1	—	6	124
SBA-1674	4	.6	—	1	1	—	—	—	2
	10	.4	—	1	—	—	—	—	1
Subtotal	—	1.0	—	2	1	—	—	—	3
Total	—		281	191	2	12	1	20	506

Note: Based on ⅛-in screen recovery; CS = column sample, STP = shovel test pit.

TABLE A.14. Other Shell Beads from Late Holocene Components at Tecolote Canyon Sites

Site	Unit	Volume (m³)	Clam Disk	Dentalium	*Mytilus* Disk	*Mytilus* Cylinder	Red Abalone Disk	Abalone Tube BIP	Bead, Undifferentiated	Total
SBA-72N	CS 1	.075	—	1	—	—	—	—	1	2
SBA-72S	3	.8	—	—	—	—	—	1	—	1
	4	.75	1	—	1	—	—	—	1	3
	5	.80	—	1	8	4	4	—	—	17
	CS 5	.013	—	—	2	1	—	—	2	5
SBA-73N	CS 11	.063	—	1	—	—	—	—	—	1
SBA-73S	CS 59		—	—	1	1	—	—	—	1
	60		—	—	1	1	—	—	—	2
	98-25	1.4	1	—	2	—	1	—	1	5
Total	—		2	3	15	5	5	1	5	37

Note: Based on ⅛-in screen recovery; CS = column sample, BIP = bead in production. Not included in table is one historical abalone button from the surface of SBA-71, and a *Megathura* ring (Unit 1: 40–60 cm), punched *Trivia* shell (Unit 5: 120–140 cm), and punched scallop shell (Unit 5: 140–160 cm) from SBA-72.

TABLE A.15. *Olivella* Bead Detritus from Tecolote Canyon Sites

Site	Unit	Volume (m³)	Whole Shell Weight	Whole Shell #	Base	Callus	Spire	Wall	Other	Total Weight	Total #
SBA-71/72	STP 97-1	—	.43	1	—	—	—	—	—	.43	1
SBA-72N	1	.6	.87	3	—	—	—	—	—	.87	3
	CS 1	.075	—	—	3	5	1	11	—	2.42	20
	2	.65	.83	2	3	13	1	15	—	5.39	34
	7	.6	.52	1	—	—	—	—	—	.52	1
	97-3	.9	—	—	—	—	1	—	—	.01	1
	STP 97-16	.20	.26	1	—	—	—	—	—	.26	1
Subtotal	—		2.48	7	6	18	3	26	—	9.47	60

TABLE A.15. (cont'd) *Olivella* Bead Detritus from Tecolote Canyon Sites

Site	Unit	Volume (M³)	Whole Shell		Base	Callus	Spire	Wall	Other	Total	
			Weight	#						Weight	#
SBA-72S	3	.8	1.15	2	—	—	—	—	—	1.15	2
	4	.75	.90	1	—	7	3	—	1	3.38	12
	5	.80	15.15	19	54	74	16	263	75	83.50	501
	CS 5	.013	5.64	5	12	13	—	56	19	16.17	105
Subtotal	—		22.84	27	66	94	19	319	95	104.20	620
SBA-73N	STP 2	.12	.40	1	—	—	—	—	—	.40	1
	2	.6	—	—	—	—	—	—	1	.35	1
	3	.45	.98	2	—	3	1	—	1	1.51	7
	5	.75	—	—	—	1	—	—	1	.24	2
	6	.7	—	—	—	—	—	—	1	.19	1
	11	1.0	1.91	6	—	—	—	1	—	2.04	7
	CS 11	.063	1.38	1	1	—	—	1	2	1.46	5
	20	1.0	.60	1	—	—	—	—	—	.60	1
Subtotal	—		5.27	11	1	4	1	1	6	6.79	24
SBA-73S	59	1.2	.44	2	8	8	3	28	1	7.29	50
	98-25	1.4	5.47	12	37	26	22	159	29	38.15	285
Subtotal	—		5.91	14	45	34	25	188	30	45.45	336
SBA-1674	4	.6	.27	1	1	—	—	2	—	.97	4
	6	.6	.76	1	—	—	—	—	—	.76	1
	10	.4	—	—	1	—	1	—	—	.58	2
Subtotal	—		1.03	2	2	—	1	2	—	2.31	7
Total	—		37.96	60	120	150	49	533	131	168.65	1,048

Note: All weights in grams; based on ⅛-in screen recovery; STP = shovel test pit, CS = column sample.

Table A.16. Fishhook Fragments from SBA-72, SBA-73, and SBA-1674

Site	Material Type	Grooved Shank	Plain Shank	Midsection	Tip	Blank	Total
SBA-72	California mussel	21	1	44	2	8	76
	Abalone	5	—	3	—	—	8
Subtotal		26	1	47	2	8	84
SBA-73	California mussel	2	—	20	3	5	30
	Abalone	—	—	1	—	—	1
	Bone	1	—	2	—	—	3
Subtotal		3	—	23	3	5	34
SBA-1674	California mussel	—	—	1	—	—	1
Total		29	1	71	5	13	119

Table A.17. Asphaltum-Related Artifacts from Tecolote Canyon Sites

Site	Artifact Type	Test Units	Surface Collection	Total
SBA-71	Asphaltum applicator	0	1	1
SBA-72	Asphaltum basket impression	12	0	12
	Tarring pebble	24	—	24
	Asphaltum applicator	2	1	3
	Cobble with asphaltum	6	—	6
SBA-73	Asphaltum basket impression	4	0	4
	Tarring pebble	62	—	62
	Asphaltum applicator	3	—	3
	Cobble with asphaltum	1	1	2
SBA-1674	Tarring pebble	2	—	2

Note: All values are counts; tarring pebbles and other asphaltum-related artifacts were not systematically collected during construction monitoring.

Table A.18. Shellfish Remains from SBA-72 Index Units

Taxon	Column Sample 1		Unit 2		Unit 5		Column Sample 5		Total			
	Weight	MNI	Weight	MNI	Weight	MNI	Weight	MNI	Weight	% Weight	MNI	% MNI
Amphineura	.97	3	6.92	3	78.73	9	9.83	5	96.45	.3	20	.5
Astraea undosa	24.79	2	.67	2	50.38	4	5.34	2	81.18	.3	10	.3
Balanus sp.	1.36	4	18.93	6	108.95	5	24.10	10	153.34	.5	25	.7
Cardiidae	—	—	—		21.01	3	3.01	4	24.02	.1	7	.2
Chamidae	—	—	—	—	—	—	13.23	1	13.23	.1	1	.1
Chione californiensis	.56	1	24.89	5	12.52	4	1.27	3	39.24	.1	13	.3
Chione undatella	40.17	3	638.64	33	353.50	15	105.33	7	1,137.64	4.0	58	1.5
Chione sp.	6.70	3	1.32	2	18.06	3	11.56	1	37.64	.1	9	.2
Clam, undifferentiated	37.89	5	355.10	7	1,891.07	5	363.95	8	2,648.01	9.3	25	.7
Crab, undifferentiated	3.61	5	12.07	5	734.23	6	269.23	8	1,019.14	3.6	24	.7
Crepidula sp.	.26	1	11.63	17	19.05	65	4.21	12	35.15	.1	95	2.5
Cryptochiton stelleri	—	—	.41	1	11.24	4	.31	2	11.96	.1	7	.2
Cypraea spadica	.04	1	.53	1	11.45	5	2.64	4	14.66	.1	11	.3
Donax gouldii	—	—	—	—	1.76	2	—	—	1.76	.1	2	.1
Donax sp.	—	—	—	—	.60	1	—	—	.60	.1	1	.1
Fissurella volcano	—	—	—	—	1.09	3	.94	4	2.03	.1	7	.2
Gastropod, undifferentiated	1.39	6	6.49	5	31.85	31	4.84	13	44.57	.2	55	1.5
Haliotis rufescens	.69	1	—	—	5.74	3	—	—	6.43	.1	4	.1
Haliotis sp.	.06	1	11.47	5	369.72	4	15.54	7	396.79	1.4	17	.4
Hinnites multirugosus	—	—	.07	1	45.37	2	.30	2	45.74	.2	5	.1
Ischnochiton sp.	2.31	3	18.91	3	31.21	2	9.21	4	61.64	.2	12	.3
Limpet, undifferentiated	—	—	.80	7	.91	4	.04	2	1.75	.1	13	.3
Megathura crenulata	.04	1	.85	4	9.95	4	45.85	3	56.69	.2	12	.3
Mitra idae	—	—	—	—	—	—	7.27	2	7.27	.1	2	.1
Mytilus californianus	90.94	18	500.72	145	2,909.16	600	661.85	81	4,162.67	14.6	844	21.8

TABLE A.18. (cont'd) Shellfish Remains from SBA-72 Index Units

Taxon	Column Sample 1		Unit 2		Unit 5		Column Sample 5		Total			
	Weight	MNI	Weight	MNI	Weight	MNI	Weight	MNI	Weight	% Weight	MNI	% MNI
Nassarius sp.	—	—	—	—	.18	1	—	—	.18	.1	1	.1
Norrissia norrissii	—	—	—	—	34.73	4	—	—	34.73	.1	4	.1
Ostrea lurida	28.88	7	401.09	19	1,087.20	72	176.62	15	1,693.79	5.9	113	2.9
Oyster, undifferentiated	—	—	—	—	—	—	3.74	1	3.74	.1	1	.1
Pectinidae	10.00	6	51.36	26	1,362.38	609	233.46	99	1,657.20	5.8	740	19.1
Polinices lewisii	—	—	—	—	7.90	1	—	—	7.90	.1	1	.1
Polinices sp.	—	—	—	—	—	—	2.88	1	2.88	.1	1	.1
Pollicipes polymerus	.02	2	6.21	5	24.38	5	4.08	7	34.69	.1	19	.5
Protothaca staminea	43.80	6	477.79	45	1,824.42	139	385.53	24	2,731.54	9.6	214	5.5
Psammobiidae	.30	2	3.89	6	21.20	4	19.37	7	44.76	.2	19	.5
Sanguinolaria nuttallii	.26	2	—	—	38.32	16	4.15	2	42.73	.2	20	.5
Saxidomus nuttallii	5.47	5	52.25	7	155.63	5	29.40	2	242.75	.9	19	.5
Septifer bifurcatus	4.49	10	117.05	123	584.54	629	119.94	158	826.02	2.9	920	23.8
Serpulorbis spp.	.01	1	.18	3	34.82	5	.56	3	35.57	.1	12	.3
Siliqua patula?	—	—	—	—	.15	1	—	—	.15	.1	1	.1
Strongylocentrotus spp.	—	—	.05	2	58.56	5	11.45	8	70.06	.2	15	.4
Tagelus californianus	—	—	—	—	7.21	4	.13	2	7.34	.1	6	.2
Tegula sp.	—	—	99.99	8	20.35	5	1.41	1	121.75	.4	14	.4
Tivela stultorum	84.67	6	310.72	16	8,309.11	387	1,350.07	52	10,054.57	35.2	461	11.9
Trachycardium sp.	—	—	—	—	2.89	1	1.57	2	4.46	.1	3	.1
Trivia californiana	—	—	—	—	.12	1	.14	1	.26	.1	2	.1
Undifferentiated shell	13.94	—	78.18	—	643.56	—	154.65	—	890.33	3.1	—	—
Total	403.62	105	3,209.18	512	20,935.20	2,678	4,058.99	576	28,606.99	100.0	3,871	100.0
¹/₁₆-in shell	56.27	—	408.45	—	1,818.56	—	349.49	—	2,632.77	—	—	—

Note: All weights in grams; based on ⅛-in screen recovery; MNI = minimum number of individuals.

TABLE A.19. Fish Remains from SBA-72

TAXON	COLUMN SAMPLE 1		UNIT 2		COLUMN SAMPLE 5		TOTAL			
	WEIGHT	NISP	WEIGHT	NISP	WEIGHT	NISP	WEIGHT	% WEIGHT	NISP	% NISP
Teleosts										
Atherinidae (silversides)	.11	5	.08	3	.09	5	.28	.4	13	1.1
Clinidae (kelpfish)	.06	1	—	—	—	—	.06	.1	1	.1
Clupeidae (herring, sardine)	1.31	113	1.22	111	3.91	356	6.44	9.0	580	47.4
Cottidae (sculpin)	—	—	.01	1	—	—	.01	.1	1	.1
Embiotocidae (surfperch)	.89	29	.62	18	4.44	144	5.95	8.3	191	15.6
Hexagrammidae (greenling)	—	—	.03	2	—	—	.03	.1	2	.2
Labridae (senorita or wrasse)	.13	9	.21	13	.47	26	.81	1.1	48	3.9
Mackerel, undifferentiated	.62	21	1.15	33	2.19	71	3.96	5.5	125	10.2
Merluccius productus (hake)	—	—	—	—	.15	1	.15	.2	1	.1
Paralichthys californicus (halibut)	—	—	—	—	1.2	1	1.20	1.7	1	.1
Pleuronectiformes (flatfishes)	—	—	.05	1	.07	1	.12	.2	2	.2
Porichthys spp. (midshipman)	—	—	—	—	.19	6	.19	.3	6	.5
Sciaenidae (croaker)	.07	4	—	—	.46	30	.53	.7	34	2.8
Scombridae (mackerel, tuna)	—	—	1.45	3	7.19	20	8.64	12.1	23	1.9
Sarda chiliensis (Pacific bonito)	.21	1	—	—	—	—	.21	.3	1	.1
Scomber japonicus (Chub mackerel)	—	—	—	—	.03	1	.03	.1	1	.1
Sebastes spp. (rockfish)	2.13	22	2.11	29	3.6	54	7.84	10.9	105	8.6
Semicossyphus pulcher (sheephead)	.81	2	.86	3	5.79	14	7.46	10.4	19	1.6
Seriola lalandi (yellowtail)	—	—	—	—	13.64	8	13.64	19.0	8	.7
Sphyraena argentea (barracuda)	—	—	.99	2	5.03	10	6.02	8.4	12	1.0
Xiphias gladius (swordfish)	—	—	—	—	2.17	6	2.17	3.0	6	.5
Teleost, undifferentiated	39.64	1,235	52.48	1,423	348.86	10,543	440.98	—	13,201	—
Subtotal	45.98	1,442	61.26	1,642	399.48	11,297	506.72	—	14,381	—

Table A.19. (cont'd) Fish Remains from SBA-72

	Column Sample 1		Unit 2		Column Sample 5		Total			
TAXON	Weight	NISP	Weight	NISP	Weight	NISP	Weight	% Weight	NISP	% NISP
Elasmobranchs										
Carcharinidae (requium sharks)	.47	1	—	—	—	—	.47	.7	1	.1
Galeorhinus galeus (soupfin shark)	—	—	—	—	.03	2	.03	.1	2	.2
Lamma ditropis (salmon shark)	—	—	—	—	.39	1	.39	.5	1	.1
Myliobatis californica (bat ray)	.13	2	.05	2	.42	6	.60	.8	10	.8
Platyrhinoides triseriata (thornback)	.11	3	—	—	—	—	.11	.2	3	.3
Rajidae (thorn or skate)	.02	1	—	—	—	—	.02	.1	1	.1
Rhinobatos productus (guitarfish)	—	—	.08	4	1.13	11	1.21	1.7	15	1.2
Squatina californica (angel shark)	—	—	—	—	.76	4	.76	1.1	4	.3
Stingray	.01	1	—	—	—	—	.01	.1	1	.1
Triakididae (smoothhounds)	.08	1	.40	1	1.85	4	2.33	3.3	6	.5
Elasmobranch, undifferentiated	1.21	17	2.73	25	8.77	106	12.71	—	148	—
Subtotal	2.03	26	3.26	32	13.35	134	18.64	—	192	—
Total	48.01	1,468	64.52	1,674	412.83	11,431	525.36	100.0	14,573	100.0
¹⁄₁₆-in bone	51.67				70.11		121.78			

Note: All weights in grams; based on ⅛-in screen recovery; percentages based on specimens identified to family, genus, and species; NISP = number of identified specimens.

Table A.20. Other Vertebrate Remains from SBA-72

	Column Sample 1		Unit 2		Column Sample 5		Unit 5		Total			
TAXON	Weight	NISP	Weight	NISP	Weight	NISP	Weight	NISP	Weight	% Weight	NISP	% NISP
Artiodactyl	—	—	.53	4	20.47	1	.58	4	21.58	.5	9	.1
Odocoileus spp.	10.64	1	3.49	1	1.48	1	244.86	126	260.47	5.5	129	1.1
Canis spp.	—	—	—	—	25.87	4	2.90	1	28.77	.6	5	.1
Lepus spp.	.81	2	.84	4	.87	3	1.46	4	3.98	.1	13	.1
Procyon lotor	—	—	—	—	—	—	1.94	1	1.94	.1	1	.1

TABLE A.20. (cont'd) Other Vertebrate Remains from SBA-72

Taxon	Column Sample 1		Unit 2		Unit 5		Column Sample 5		Total			
	Weight	NISP	Weight	NISP	Weight	NISP	Weight	NISP	Weight	% Weight	NISP	% NISP
Rodent, undifferentiated	—	—	2.78	47	4.00	29	.30	3	7.08	.2	79	.7
Sea mammal	78.87	538	237.91	727	1,226.41	2,469	387.34	1,467	1,930.53	40.7	5,201	44.2
Pinniped, undifferentiated	—	—	35.89	44	121.46	158	16.15	41	173.50	3.7	243	2.1
Otariid, undifferentiated	7.72	1	34.29	12	343.54	115	41.11	21	426.66	9.0	149	1.3
Arctocephalus	—	—	2.59	2	209.84	21	24.94	7	237.37	5.0	30	.3
Callorhinus ursinus	—	—	—	—	6.31	2	—	—	6.31	.1	2	.1
Zalophus californianus	—	—	—	—	2.69	1	—	—	2.69	.1	1	.1
Phoca vitulina	—	—	—	—	18.09	1	—	—	18.09	.4	1	.1
Enhydra lutris	—	—	—	—	.66	2	—	—	.66	.1	2	.1
Cetacean, undifferentiated	—	—	—	—	29.76	3	—	—	29.76	.6	3	.1
Large mammal	127.08	678	167.40	242	623.81	631	245.58	609	1,163.87	24.5	2,160	18.4
Medium mammal	17.42	349	98.58	485	127.13	551	87.41	870	330.54	7.0	2,255	19.2
Mammal, undifferentiated	—	—	—	—	2.00	5	—	—	2.00	.1	5	.1
Reptile/amphibian	1.06	19	.77	15	8.11	165	.96	23	10.90	.2	222	1.9
Turtle	—	—	—	—	5.54	15	—	—	5.54	.1	15	.1
Bird, undifferentiated	1.52	27	1.47	14	22.62	171	4.31	63	29.92	.6	275	2.3
Phalacrocorax spp.	—	—	3.72	2	.72	2	—	—	4.44	.1	4	.1
Larus spp.	—	—	—	—	.67	1	—	—	.67	.1	1	.1
Uria aalge	—	—	—	—	.21	1	—	—	.21	.0	1	.1
Small fauna, undifferentiated	6.29	190	3.64	54	27.33	434	10.53	274	47.79	1.01	952	8.1
Tooth, undifferentiated	.05	1	3.53	36	9.65	75	1.58	23	14.81	—	135	—
Bone, undifferentiated	32.88	1,226	496.58	9,122	1,822.63	18,701	160.76	5,385	2,512.85	—	34,434	—
Total	284.34	3,032	1,094.01	10,811	4,864.92	23,689	1,029.66	8,795	7,272.93	—	46,327	—
$\frac{1}{16}$-in bone	38.32	—	—	—	300.15	—	266.71	—	605.18	—	—	—

Note: All weights in grams; based on ⅛-in screen recovery; NISP = number of identified specimens.

Table A.21. Dietary Reconstruction for Faunal Remains from Column Sample 1 at SBA-72N

Faunal Category	Shell/Bone Weight (g)	Meat Yield Multiplier	Estimated Meat Yield	% Meat Yield
Scallop (*Argopecten* spp.)	10.0	.4	4.0	.1
Wavy top shell (*Astraea undosa*)	24.79	.365	9.0	.2
Venus clam (*Chione* spp.)	47.43	.171	8.1	.2
Chitons	2.31	1.15	2.7	.05
Clam, undifferentiated	37.89	.356	13.5	.3
Red Abalone (*Haliotis rufescens*)	.69	1.36	.9	.02
California mussel (*Mytilus californianus*)	90.94	.298	27.1	.5
Oyster (*Ostrea lurida*)	28.88	.292	8.4	.2
Littleneck clam (*Protothaca staminea*)	43.8	.61	26.7	.5
Purple clam (*Sanguinolaria nuttalli*)	.26	1.25	.3	.01
Washington clam (*Saxidomus nuttallii*)	5.47	.463	2.5	.05
Platform mussel (*Septifer bifurcatus*)	4.49	.364	1.6	.03
Pismo clam (*Tivela stultorum*)	84.67	.254	21.5	.4
Shell Subtotal			126.5	2.5
Fish	48.01	27.7	1,329.9	25.9
Bird	1.52	15	22.8	.4
Land Mammals	155.95	10	1,559.5	30.4
Sea Mammal	86.59	24.2	2,095.5	40.8
Vertebrate subtotal	292.07		5,007.7	97.5
Total			5,134.1	

Note: Based on corrected ¹⁄₁₆-in screen recovery; meat yield multiplier for undifferentiated clam averages *Tivela* and *Saxidomus*; percent meat yield values for shellfish taxa are contribution to total shellfish yield.

Table A.22. Dietary Reconstruction for Faunal Remains from Column Sample 5 at SBA-72S

Faunal Category	Shell/Bone Weight (g)	Meat Yield Multiplier	Estimated Meat Yield	% Meat Yield
Scallop (*Argopecten aequisulcatus*)	233.46	.4	93.4	.3
Wavy top shell (*Astraea undosa*)	5.34	.365	1.9	.01
Venus clam (*Chione undatella*)	118.16	.171	20.2	.1
Chitons	9.52	1.15	10.9	.04
Clam, undifferentiated	363.95	.356	129.6	.5
Abalone (*Haliotis* spp.)	15.54	1.15	17.9	.1
California mussel (*Mytilus californianus*)	661.85	.298	197.2	.7
Oyster (*Ostrea lurida*)	180.36	.292	52.7	.2
Littleneck clam (*Protothaca staminea*)	385.53	.61	235.2	.8
Purple clam (*Sanguinolaria nuttalli*)	4.15	1.25	5.2	.02
Washington clam (*Saxidomus nuttallii*)	29.4	.463	13.6	.05
Platform mussel (*Septifer bifurcatus*)	119.94	.364	43.7	.2
Sea urchin (*Strongylocentrotus* spp.)	11.45	.583	6.7	.02
Black turban snail (*Tegula funebralis*)	1.41	.365	.5	<.01
Pismo clam (*Tivela stultorum*)	1,350.07	.254	342.9	1.2
Shellfish Subtotal			1,171.6	4.2
Fish	412.83	27.7	11,435.4	41.1
Bird	4.31	15.0	64.7	.2
Land Mammals	381.68	10.0	3,816.8	13.7
Sea Mammal	469.54	24.2	11,362.9	40.8
Vertebrate subtotal			26,679.7	95.8
Total			27,851.3	

Note: Based on corrected ¹⁄₁₆-in screen recovery; meat yield multiplier for undifferentiated clam averages *Tivela* and *Saxidomus*; percent meat yield values for shellfish taxa are contribution to total shellfish yield.

TABLE A.23. Chipped-Stone Artifacts from SBA-73

ARTIFACT TYPE	INDEX UNITS		NON-INDEX UNITS		SURFACE COLLECTION/ MONITORING FIND		TOTAL	
	#	WEIGHT	#	WEIGHT	#	WEIGHT	#	WEIGHT
Biface, excurvate	12	34.1	39	110.9	54	443.6	105	588.6
Biface, triangular	8	4.9	5	4.9	4	39.2	17	49
Biface, undifferentiated	11	8.2	73	133.5	19	147.5	103	289.2
Borer/drill, triangular	1	1.4	3	1.5	1	11.3	5	14.2
Borer/drill, undifferentiated	12	57.8	59	151.3	11	50.2	82	259.3
Core	2	417.7	7	704	3	127.7	12	1,249.4
Drill/bladelet	3	1.9	6	1.1	1	2.3	10	5.3
Flake, retouched/utilized	23	549.4	128	927.1	43	910.3	194	2,386.8
Flake, undifferentiated	708	1,334.8	3,237	742.3	17	203.2	3,962	2,280.3
Flaked cobble	6	1,348.8	14	2,817	7	2,748.2	27	6,914
Hammer stone	2	676	10	918.8	8	3,907.6	20	5,502.4
Debitage, undifferentiated	6,600	3,580.5	57,968	11,515.3	21	263.5	64,589	15,359.3
Total	7,388	8,015.5	61,549	18,027.7	189	8,854.6	69,126	34,897.8

Note: All weights in grams; based on ⅛-in screen recovery; index units (Column Sample 11 and Units 22, 59, 98-25) analyzed in detail (volume 3.26 m³); non-index units had only preliminary analysis.

TABLE A.24. Ground-Stone Artifacts from SBA-73

ARTIFACT TYPE	MATERIAL TYPE	SHOVEL TEST PIT/UNIT	SURFACE COLLECTION	TOTAL
Mortar/bowl fragment	Sandstone	16	16	32
Mortar/bowl fragment	Mudstone	—	1	1
Bowl fragment	Soapstone	—	2	2
Pestle or pestle fragments	Sandstone	4	25	29
Pestle	Basalt?	—	1	1
Mano	Sandstone	1	5	6
Metate	Sandstone	3	5	8
Abrader	Sandstone	2	—	2
Anvil	Sandstone	1	—	1
Donut stone, fragment	Mudstone	1	—	1
Donut stone fragment	Sandstone	1	—	1
Pecked cobble	Sandstone	—	1	1
Fragment, battered	Sandstone	—	1	1
Fragment, pecked	Sandstone	6	2	8
Fragment, undifferentiated	?	1	1	2
Fragment, undifferentiated	Sandstone	45	14	59
Pitted stone	Sandstone	1	—	1
Total		82	74	156

TABLE A.25. Bone Tools and Modified Bones from SBA-73

BONE TOOL TYPE	COUNT	WEIGHT (G)
Awl fragment	13	9.2
Barb, composite harpoon	1	.9
Flaker	1	11.7
Gorge	2	.4
Ground/polished fragments		
Base fragment	1	1.4
Edge fragment	5	2.6
Long bone shaft fragment	3	1.5
Mid-body fragment	24	14.2
Near tip fragment	7	1.3
Tip fragment	12	5.6
Miscellaneous	14	4.4
Cut sea mammal bone	1	27.0
Notched fish spine	1	.1
Point, diamond shape	1	.5
Radially fractured deer bone	1	5.9
Rib with asphaltum	1	1.6
Tube or whistle, bird bone	1	.4
Wedge fragment	1	5.0
Total	90	93.7

Note: Three fishhook fragments were not included.

TABLE A.26. Shellfish Remains from SBA-73 Index Units

Taxon	Column Sample 11 Weight	MNI	Unit 22 Weight	MNI	Unit 59 Weight	MNI	Unit 98-25 Weight	MNI	Total Weight	% Weight	MNI	% MNI
Astraea undosa	—	—	—	—	15.27	4	193.15	7	208.42	1.8	11	1.1
Balanus sp.	1.68	4	.14	1	20.72	5	31.34	7	53.88	.5	17	1.7
Cardiidae	—	—	—	—	—	—	.91	1	.91	.1	1	.1
Chione californiensis	.16	1	—	—	16.01	5	61.81	5	77.98	.7	11	1.1
Chione undatella	100.07	6	1.05	1	197.83	17	1,317.01	92	1,615.96	13.7	116	11.8
Chione sp.	—	—	—	—	108.44	2	434.94	3	543.38	4.6	5	.5
Chitons, undifferentiated	2.39	3	—	—	11.95	4	15.58	4	29.92	.3	11	1.1
Clam, undifferentiated	46.55	5	6.98	2	199.46	6	677.91	6	930.90	7.9	19	1.9
Crepidula sp.	3.25	6	—	—	3.96	10	15.45	44	22.66	.2	60	6.1
Cypraea spadica	—	—	—	—	3.27	3	3.07	3	6.34	.1	6	.6
Cryptochiton stelleri	.27	1	—	—	—	—	—	—	.27	.0	1	.1
Crab, undifferentiated	1.26	4	—	—	96.98	6	329.97	7	428.21	3.6	17	1.7
Gastropod, undifferentiated	.62	4	—	—	6.34	5	59.72	11	66.68	.6	20	2.0
Haliotis rufescens	.08	1	—	—	38.94	1	—	—	39.02	.3	2	.2
Haliotis sp.	.45	1	—	—	10.06	4	70.69	6	81.20	.7	11	1.1
Hinnites sp.	—	—	—	—	10.65	5	38.14	5	48.79	.4	10	1.0
Ischnochiton sp.	1.05	2	—	—	7.57	4	32.22	5	40.84	.6	11	1.1
Limpet, undifferentiated	—	—	—	—	.23	2	1.98	9	2.21	.1	11	1.1
Megathura crenulata	—	—	—	—	4.00	4	.54	2	4.54	.1	6	.6
Mytilus californianus	69.48	23	.33	1	134.49	16	290.26	41	494.56	4.2	81	8.3
Norrisia norrissii	—	—	—	—	—	—	10.74	6	10.74	.1	6	.6
Ostrea lurida	77.26	6	1.18	1	238.39	9	712.42	37	1,029.25	8.7	53	5.4
Pododesmus sp.	—	—	—	—	1.32	2	—	—	1.32	.1	2	.2
Polinices lewisii	—	—	—	—	—	—	2.24	1	2.24	.1	1	.1

Table A.26. (cont'd) Shellfish Remains from SBA-73 Index Units

Taxon	Column Sample 11		Unit 22		Unit 59		Unit 98-25		Total			
	Weight	MNI	Weight	MNI	Weight	MNI	Weight	MNI	Weight	% Weight	MNI	% MNI
Pollicipes polymerus	.76	2	—	—	.71	3	4.56	5	6.03	.1	10	1.0
Protothaca laciniata	—	—	—	—	—	—	14.76	3	14.76	.1	3	.3
Protothaca staminea	133.54	8	1.04	1	618.09	39	3,247.48	169	4,000.15	33.9	217	22.1
Psammobiidae	.08	1	—	—	—	—	25.28	5	25.36	.2	6	.6
Sanguinolaria	—	—	—	—	10.86	6	2.60	5	13.46	.1	11	1.1
Saxidomus nuttallii	4.41	5	—	—	220.08	5	209.00	5	433.49	3.7	15	1.5
Scallop, undifferentiated	.48	4	.03	1	40.49	15	352.22	107	393.22	3.3	127	13.0
Septifer bifurcatus	9.56	13	—	—	5.88	6	23.14	17	38.58	.3	36	3.7
Serpulorbis spp.	14.35	1	—	—	.13	3	1.19	4	15.67	.1	8	.8
Strongylocentrotus spp.	.03	1	—	—	7.87	5	27.34	6	35.24	.3	12	1.2
Tegula sp.	14.03	1	—	—	12.57	2	34.66	5	61.26	.5	8	.8
Tivela stultorum	32.70	5	1.20	2	195.65	18	413.55	12	643.10	5.5	37	3.8
Trachycardium sp.	—	—	—	—	—	—	.38	1	.38	.0	1	.1
Undifferentiated shell	10.30	—	.75	—	74.65	—	299.05	—	384.75	3.3	—	—
Total	524.81	108	12.70	10	2,312.86	216	8,955.30	646	11,805.67	100.0	980	100.0
$\frac{1}{16}$-in shell	150.09	—	—	—	256.32	—	574.99	—	981.40	—	—	—

Note: All weights in grams; based on ⅛-in screen recovery; MNI = minimum number of individuals.

TABLE A.27. Fish Remains from SBA-73 Index Units

TAXON	COLUMN SAMPLE 11 WEIGHT	NISP	UNIT 22 WEIGHT	NISP	UNIT 59 WEIGHT	NISP	UNIT 98-25 WEIGHT	NISP	TOTAL WEIGHT	% WEIGHT	NISP	% NISP
Teleosts												
Atherinidae (silversides)	—	—	—	—	.25	10	.50	18	.75	.42	28	.56
Clinidae (kelpfish)	—	—	—	—	.18	4	.18	8	.36	.20	12	.24
Clupeidae (herring, sardine)	.08	11	.03	3	6.14	529	28.20	2,654	34.45	19.13	3,197	64.20
Cottidae (sculpin)	—	—	—	—	.10	2	.18	3	.28	.16	5	.10
Embiotocidae (surfperch)	—	—	.18	4	3.14	86	10.24	308	13.56	7.53	398	7.99
Hexagrammidae (greenling, lingcod)	—	—	—	—	—	—	.08	5	.08	.04	5	.10
Labridae (senorita or wrasse)	.04	3	—	—	.65	55	2.86	229	3.55	1.97	287	5.76
Mackerel, undifferentiated	.02	1	—	—	3.69	90	20.45	452	24.16	13.41	543	10.90
Mola mola (ocean sunfish)	—	—	—	—	—	—	1.81	3	1.81	1.00	3	.06
Ophiodon elongatus (lingcod)	—	—	—	—	—	—	.18	1	.18	.10	1	.02
Paralabrax clathratus (kelp bass)	—	—	—	—	—	—	.10	1	.10	.06	1	.02
Paralichthys californicus (halibut)	—	—	—	—	—	—	1.22	2	1.22	.68	2	.04
Platyrhinoidis triseriata (thornback)	—	—	—	—	.03	3	—	—	.03	.02	3	.06
Pleuronectiformes (flatfishes)	—	—	—	—	—	—	.01	1	.01	.01	1	.02
Porichthys spp. (midshipman)	—	—	—	—	—	—	.42	6	.42	.23	6	.12
Sarda chiliensis (bonito)	—	—	—	—	1.56	4	1.70	6	3.26	1.81	10	.20
Sciaenidae (croaker)	—	—	—	—	.27	17	2.02	92	2.29	1.27	109	2.19
Scombridae (mackerel, tuna)	—	—	—	—	.66	3	6.81	15	7.47	4.15	18	.36
Thunnus alalunga (albacore)	—	—	—	—	—	—	2.72	4	2.72	1.51	4	.08
Sebastes spp. (rockfish)	.03	2	—	—	5.21	64	8.15	138	13.39	7.43	204	4.10
Semicossyphus pulcher (sheephead)	.26	1	.90	7	4.98	11	7.55	16	13.69	7.60	35	.70
Seriola lalandi (yellowtail)	—	—	—	—	2.96	4	22.88	13	25.84	14.35	17	.34

TABLE A.27. (cont'd) Fish Remains from SBA-73 Index Units

TAXON	COLUMN SAMPLE 11		UNIT 22		UNIT 59		UNIT 98-25		TOTAL			
	WEIGHT	NISP	WEIGHT	NISP	WEIGHT	NISP	WEIGHT	NISP	WEIGHT	% WEIGHT	NISP	% NISP
Sphyraena argentea (barracuda)	—	—	—	—	4.32	8	9.03	19	13.35	7.41	27	.54
Teleost, undifferentiated	2.20	124	3.50	83	284.63	8,077	877.58	26,438	1,167.91	—	34,722	—
Subtotal	2.63	142	4.61	97	318.77	8,967	1,004.87	30,432	1,330.88	—	39,638	—
Elasmobranchs												
Carcharhinidae (requium sharks)	—	—	—	—	1.44	3	7.67	12	9.11	5.06	15	.30
Galeorhinus galeus (soupfin shark)	—	—	—	—	.03	1	3.81	6	3.84	2.13	7	.14
Lamma ditropis (salmon shark)	—	—	—	—	—	—	.22	2	.22	.12	2	.04
Myliobatis californica (bat ray)	.02	1	—	—	1.53	6	1.51	15	3.06	1.70	22	.44
Prionace glauca (blue shark)	—	—	—	—	—	—	.16	1	.16	.09	1	.02
Squatina californica (angel shark)	—	—	—	—	.04	1	.14	7	.18	.10	8	.16
Rhinobatos productus (guitarfish)	—	—	—	—	.14	3	.34	5	.48	.27	8	.16
Triakididae	—	—	—	—	.08	1	—	—	.08	.04	1	.02
Elasmobranch, undifferentiated	—	—	.44	8	2.63	30	5.01	70	8.08	—	108	—
Subtotal	.02	1	.44	8	5.89	45	18.86	118	25.21	—	172	—
Total	2.65	143	5.05	105	324.66	9,012	1,023.73	30,550	1,356.09	—	39,810	—
1/16-in bone	4.46	—	—	—	—	—	121.36	—	125.82	—	—	—

Note: Based on ⅛-in screen recovery; percentages based on specimens identified to family, genus, and species.

TABLE A.28. Other Vertebrate Remains from SBA-73 Index Units

Taxon	Column Sample 11		Unit 22		Unit 59		Unit 98-25		Total			
	Weight	NISP	Weight	NISP	Weight	NISP	Weight	NISP	Weight	% Weight	NISP	% NISP
Artiodactyl	—	—	—	—	—	—	12.06	2	12.06	.5	2	.1
Odocoileus spp.	—	—	—	—	—	—	11.75	11	11.75	.5	11	.2
Lepus spp.	—	—	—	—	1.63	7	—	—	1.63	.1	7	.1
Rodent, undifferentiated	.35	7	2.56	24	3.10	47	1.77	42	7.78	.3	120	1.7
Sea mammal	34.33	64	99.57	408	224.78	899	697.50	1,534	1,056.18	43.4	2,905	42.1
Pinniped, undifferentiated	9.50	10	.12	1	6.61	22	95.72	101	111.95	4.6	134	1.9
Otariid, undifferentiated	.87	2	—	—	14.78	14	117.71	40	133.36	5.5	56	.8
Arctocephalus	—	—	—	—	2.26	1	54.58	7	56.84	2.3	8	.1
Phocidae	—	—	—	—	—	—	.62	1	.62	.1	1	.1
Cetacean, undifferentiated	—	—	—	—	—	—	25.24	3	25.24	1.0	3	.1
Large mammal	42.77	76	153.61	650	223.49	568	384.95	556	804.82	33.1	1,850	26.8
Medium mammal	9.19	52	17.17	231	33.95	305	99.80	524	160.11	6.6	1,112	16.1
Mammal, undifferentiated	—	—	—	—	—	—	10.52	3	10.52	.4	3	.1
Bird, undifferentiated	—	—	1.51	23	6.39	91	7.82	60	15.72	.7	174	2.5
Gavia spp.	—	—	—	—	—	—	.59	1	.59	.1	1	.1
Larus spp.	—	—	—	—	—	—	.61	1	.61	.1	1	.1
Podiceps spp.	—	—	—	—	.24	1	.18	1	.42	.1	2	.1
Tytonidae	—	—	—	—	—	—	.58	2	.58	.1	2	.1
Reptile/amphibian	.01	1	.09	1	.78	20	.89	32	1.77	.1	54	.8
Small fauna, undifferentiated	.42	11	3.07	67	9.22	211	8.58	170	21.29	.9	459	6.7
Tooth, undifferentiated	.22	6	—	—	—	—	—	—	.22	—	6	—
Bone, undifferentiated	87.78	1,745	85.69	2,134	204.66	5,027	764.14	13,324	1,142.27	—	22,230	—
Total	185.44	1,974	363.39	3,539	731.89	7,213	2,295.61	16,415	3,576.33	—	29,141	—
1/16-in bone	32.15	—	—	—	—	—	—	—	32.15	—	—	—

Note: All weights in grams; based on ⅛-in screen recovery.

TABLE A.29. Dietary Reconstruction for Faunal Remains from Column Sample 11 at SBA-73N

FAUNAL CATEGORY	SHELL/BONE WEIGHT (G)	MEAT YIELD MULTIPLIER	ESTIMATED MEAT YIELD	% MEAT YIELD
Venus clam (*Chione undatella*)	100.23	.171	17.1	.9
Chiton (Polyplacophora)	1.32	1.15	1.5	.1
Clam, undifferentiated	46.55	.356	16.6	.9
Abalone (*Haliotis* spp.)	.53	1.36	.7	.04
California mussel (*Mytilus californianus*)	69.48	.298	20.7	1.1
Oyster (*Ostrea lurida*)	77.26	.292	22.6	1.2
Littleneck clam (*Protothaca staminea*)	133.54	.61	81.5	4.4
Washington clam (*Saxidomus nuttallii*)	4.41	.463	2.0	.1
Platform mussel (*Septifer bifurcatus*)	9.56	.364	3.5	.2
Black turban snail (*Tegula funebralis*)	14.03	.365	5.1	.3
Pismo clam (*Tivela stultorum*)	32.7	.254	8.3	.4
Shell Subtotal			179.6	9.7
Fish	2.65	27.7	73.4	4.0
Bird	0	15.0	0	.0
Land Mammals	51.96	10.0	519.6	28.0
Sea Mammal	44.7	24.2	1,081.7	58.3
Vertebrate subtotal			1,674.7	90.3
Total			1,854.4	

Note: Based on ⅟₁₆-in screen recovery; meat multiplier for undifferentiated clam is an average for *Tivela* and *Saxidomus*; percent meat yield values for shellfish taxa are contribution to total shellfish yield.

Table A.30. Dietary Reconstruction for Faunal Remains from Unit 98-25 at SBA-73S

Faunal Category	Shell/Bone Weight (g)	Meat Yield Multiplier	Estimated Meat Yield	% Meat Yield
Scallop (*Argopecten aequisulcatus*)	352.22	.4	140.9	.2
Wavy top shell (*Astraea undosa*)	193.15	.365	70.5	.1
Venus clam (*Chione undatella*)	1,813.76	.171	310.2	.5
Chiton (Polyplacophora)	32.22	1.15	37.1	.1
Clam, undifferentiated	677.91	.356	241.3	.4
Abalone (*Haliotis* spp.)	70.69	1.15	81.3	.1
California mussel (*Mytilus californianus*)	290.26	.298	86.5	.1
Oyster (*Ostrea lurida*)	712.42	.292	208.0	.3
Littleneck clam (*Protothaca staminea*)	3,262.24	.61	1,990.0	3.3
Washington clam (*Saxidomus nuttallii*)	209.0	.463	96.8	.2
Platform mussel (*Septifer bifurcatus*)	23.14	.364	8.4	.01
Sea urchin (*Strongylocentrotus* spp.)	27.34	.583	15.9	.03
Black turban snail (*Tegula funebralis*)	34.66	.365	12.7	.02
Pismo clam (*Tivela stultorum*)	413.55	.254	105.0	.2
Shell Subtotal			3,404.5	5.6
Fish	1,023.73	27.7	28,357.3	46.5
Bird	9.78	15.0	146.7	.2
Land Mammals	508.56	10.0	5,085.6	8.3
Sea Mammal	991.37	24.2	23,991.2	39.3
Vertebrate subtotal			57,580.8	94.4
Total			60,985.3	

Note: Based on 1/16-in screen recovery; meat multiplier for undifferentiated clam is an average for *Tivela* and *Saxidomus*; percent meat yield values for shellfish taxa are contribution to total shellfish yield.

TABLE A.31. Ground-Stone Artifacts from SBA-1674

ARTIFACT TYPE	MATERIAL TYPE	SHOVEL TEST PIT/UNIT	SURFACE COLLECTION	TOTAL
Pestle	Sandstone	—	1	1
Mano	Sandstone	3	1	4
Abrader?	Sandstone	1	—	1
Ground stone, undifferentiated	Sandstone	3	1	4
Total		7	3	10

TABLE A.32. Summary of Chipped-Stone Artifacts from SBA-1674

ARTIFACT TYPE	INDEX UNITS		NON-INDEX UNITS		SURFACE COLLECTION/ MONITORING FIND		TOTAL	
	#	WEIGHT	#	WEIGHT	#	WEIGHT	#	WEIGHT
Biface, excurvate	1	3.6	1	3.4	1	12	3	19
Biface, triangular	1	.2	1	3.9	1	2.4	3	6.5
Biface, undifferentiated	0	0	6	4.6	0	0	6	4.6
Borer/drill, triangular	—	—	1	8.3	1	11	2	19.3
Borer/drill, undifferentiated	0	0	3	3.1	1	18.2	4	21.3
Core—chert, undifferentiated	—	—	—	—	1	174.1	1	174.1
Flake, retouched/utilized	1	1.3	5	20.3	3	64.6	9	86.2
Flaked cobble	—	—	—	—	1	251.9	1	251.9
Hammer stone	—	—	—	—	1	126.8	1	126.8
Debitage, undifferentiated	381	68.1	1,969	615.1	2	.7	2,352	683.9
Total	384	73.2	1,986	658.7	12	661.7	2,382	1,393.6

Note: All weights in grams; based on ⅛-in screen recovery; index units (Unit 4, Column Sample 4) analyzed in detail (volume .64 m^3); non-index units had only preliminary analysis.

Table A.33. Shellfish Remains from Unit 4 at SBA-1674

Scientific and Common Names	Weight (g)	% Weight	MNI	% MNI
Astraea undosa (wavy top shell)	2.21	1.1	1	1.7
Balanus sp. (barnacle, undifferentiated)	.12	.1	1	1.7
Chione californiensis (California Venus clam)	.13	.1	1	1.7
Chione undatella (Venus clam)	25.3	12.6	2	3.4
Crepidula sp. (slipper shell)	.08	<.1	1	1.7
Haliotis spp. (abalone, undifferentiated)	4.07	2.1	4	6.9
Ischnochiton conspicuous (chiton)	.19	.1	2	3.4
Mytilus californianus (California mussel)	21.55	10.8	8	13.8
Ostrea lurida (Pacific oyster)	31.18	15.6	6	10.4
Pectinidae (scallop, undifferentiated)	.03	<.1	2	3.4
Pollicipes polymerus (gooseneck barnacle)	.28	.1	3	5.2
Protothaca staminea (littleneck clam)	38.23	19.1	9	15.5
Saxidomus nuttallii (Washington clam)	1.45	.7	1	1.7
Septifer bifurcatus (platform mussel)	.13	.1	1	1.7
Strongylocentrotus spp. (sea urchin)	.04	<.1	1	1.7
Tivela stultorum (Pismo clam)	32.99	16.5	3	5.2
Amphineura (chiton, undifferentiated)	.18	.1	1	1.7
Clam, undifferentiated	29.24	14.6	6	10.4
Decapoda (crab, undifferentiated)	.32	.2	2	3.4
Gastropoda (snail, undifferentiated)	.84	.4	2	3.4
Psammobiidae (sunset clam)	.57	.3	1	1.7
Shell, undifferentiated	11.24	5.6	—	—
Total	200.37	100.0	58	100.0
¹⁄₁₆-in shell (unidentified)	20.19	—	—	—

Note: Based on ⅛-in screen recovery; MNI = minimum number of individuals.

Table A.34. Fish Remains from Unit 4 at SBA-1674

Scientific and Common Names	Unit 4		Column Sample 4		All			
	Weight	NISP	Weight	NISP	Weight	% Weight	NISP	% NISP
Teleosts								
Clupeidae (herring, sardine)	.56	5	.01	1	.57	23.65	6	30.0
Embiotocidae (surfperch)	.15	1	.02	1	.17	7.05	2	10.0
Mackerel, undifferentiated	.82	6	.04	1	.86	35.68	7	35.0
Sebastes sp. (rockfish)	.15	1	—	—	.15	6.22	1	5.0
Semicossyphus pulcher (sheephead)	.61	2	.01	1	.62	25.73	3	15.0
Teleost, undifferentiated	8.87	131	1.38	38	10.25	—	169	—
Subtotal	11.16	146	1.46	42	12.62	—	188	95.0
Elasmobranchs								
Myliobatus californica (bat ray)	—	—	.04	1	.04	1.66	1	5.0
Elasmobranch, undifferentiated	.37	2	—	—	.37	—	2	—
Subtotal	.37	2	.04	1	.41	—	3	—
Total	11.53	148	1.50	43	13.03	—	191	—

Note: All weights in grams; based on ⅛-in screen recovery; percentages based on specimens identified to family, genus, or species. Includes soil from rock cluster in 20–40 cm level but not rodent tailings (one teleost otolith, .17 g; one undifferentiated shark tooth, .15 g).

Table A.35. Other Vertebrate Remains from Unit 4 at SBA-1674

Taxon	Unit 4		Column Sample 4		Total			
	Weight	NISP	Weight	NISP	Weight	% Weight	NISP	% NISP
Sea mammal	13.61	20	1.90	4	15.51	26.08	24	13.56
Pinniped	2.11	2	—	—	2.11	3.55	2	1.13
Otariid seal	1.03	2	—	—	1.03	1.73	2	1.13
Large mammal	29.77	64	2.84	8	32.61	54.84	72	40.68
Medium mammal	3.98	27	.96	4	4.94	8.31	31	17.51
Rodent, undifferentiated	.97	7	—	—	.97	1.63	7	3.95
Reptile/amphibian	.17	2	—	—	.17	.29	2	1.13
Small fauna, undifferentiated	2.06	34	.06	3	2.12	3.57	37	20.90
Undifferentiated bone	44.12	620	6.01	121	50.13	—	741	—
Total	97.82	778	11.77	140	109.59	—	918	—
¹⁄₁₆-in bone	—	—	11.16	—	11.16	—	—	—

Note: All weights in grams; based on ⅛-in screen recovery; includes soil from rock cluster in Unit 4 level 20–40 cm. Rodent back dirt from 20–40 cm level not included consists of 36 fragments (10.74 g) of undifferentiated bone.

Glossary

Accelerator mass spectrometry (AMS). A method of directly and precisely measuring the types of atoms a material contains, AMS is used in radiocarbon dating small organic samples.

A-horizon. The upper (topsoil) and relatively organic-rich layers of a soil horizon.

Alta California. Upper California of the Spanish and Mexican period, corresponding to the modern state of California.

American period. The time period beginning in AD 1848, when Mexico ceded California to America under the terms of the Treaty of Guadalupe Hidalgo, until the present.

Artifact. A portable object manufactured by humans. Artifacts include tools or tool-making debris made from stone, bone, shell, wood, plant fibers, glass, metals, and other raw materials. Artifacts are the primary method by which archaeologists reconstruct past technologies, trade patterns, and other human activities.

Asphaltum. Also known as tar or bitumen, asphaltum is a weathered crude-oil product that occurs naturally in the Santa Barbara Channel area, where it seeps from underground reservoirs through faults and other fissures. Asphaltum was widely used by the Chumash as a glue or sealant.

Atlatl. A "throwing board" used to launch darts, widely used by Native American people before the introduction of the bow and arrow.

Awl. A small pointed artifact, usually made from animal bone in the Chumash area, commonly used in basket making and other tasks.

Barbareño Chumash. Chumash residents of the Santa Barbara Coast, living from approximately the Rincon to the Gaviota areas. The Barbareño, whose name derives from the fact that most of them were affiliated with Mission Santa Barbara after Spanish conquest, had their own distinctive dialect of the Chumash language.

Bipoint. A small and cylindrical bone tool pointed on both ends—sometimes called a gorge—used in hook-and-line fishing by Santa Barbara Channel peoples from about 10,000 years ago into historic times.

Bitumen. See *Asphaltum*.

^{14}C Dating. See *Radiocarbon (^{14}C) dating*.

Calendar years before present (cal BP). Contrasted with radiocarbon years and RYBP, calendar years are expressed in real solar years, either on the AD/BC scale of the Christian calendar or in calendar years before present (cal BP), whereby international convention the reference point (BP) is AD 1950.

Caliche. A calcium carbonate ($CaCO_3$) deposit that precipitates out of soil or groundwater and can build up as small soil concretions or as thin coatings on archaeological materials (shells, bones, artifacts). In many shell midden soils, especially older soils with relatively impermeable clay-rich B-horizons, calcium carbonate often weathers out of shells and bones in the upper portions of a soil horizon and is deposited in the lower soil horizons.

Canaliño. The "People of the Channel," a term defined by David Banks Rogers in the 1920s to describe the ancestors of the Chumash people. The Canaliño culture includes many of the traits attributed to the complex maritime Chumash. Radiocarbon dating has shown that the Canaliño culture developed between about 4,000 and 3,000 years ago.

Chert. A hard, highly siliceous, flintlike sedimentary rock widely used by Indian people in the Santa Barbara Channel area to make a variety of chipped-stone artifacts. Tool-quality cherts were found in a variety of geological formations (Monterey, Franciscan, Cico, etc.) in the Chumash region and can be used to help reconstruct trade networks among various tribal groups in the area.

Chipped stone. A type of artifact that fractures conchoidally, generally consisting of both tools and tool-making debris, manufactured by chipping or flaking of siliceous rocks such as chert, quartzite, obsidian, and siliceous shale.

Chumash Indians. A group of linguistically related tribes that historically occupied the coast and interior valleys of southern California, from north of San Luis Obispo to the Topanga and Malibu Canyon areas of northern Los Angeles County, including the Northern Channel Islands.

Early Holocene. A general division of the Holocene (10,000 years ago to the present) geological period, ranging from about 10,000 to 7,000 years ago. The Early Holocene encompasses portions of the archaeological cultures known as the Paleocoastal and Milling Stone horizons.

Ecofact. A nonartifactual object, such as unmodified bone, shell, charcoal, and other natural materials, from which archaeologists and their colleagues reconstruct past environments.

Egalitarian. Societies in which no formal status differences exist (see *Hierarchical*), where people are relatively equal and where status differences are earned by individual effort rather than inherited.

Elasmobranchs. Cartilaginous fishes, including sharks and rays, underrepresented in the archaeological record where only their teeth, vertebrae, and denticles generally preserve.

Faunal remains. The remains of vertebrate and invertebrate animals—usually consisting of hard parts such as shells, bones, teeth, and antler preserved in archaeological sites—used by archaeologists to reconstruct past environments and human subsistence activities.

Feature. A group of spatially related objects (artifacts and ecofacts) found in an archaeological site that are associated by a common function and age, including fire hearths, burials, house floors, historic building foundations, and others.

Fused shale. A glass-like metamorphic rock, formed by the intense heat of burning in oil shales, which is found in relatively few and localized outcrops in Ventura and Santa Barbara counties. Fused shale was used by the Chumash to make projectile points and other chipped-stone tools.

Gorge. See *Bipoint.*

Ground stone. A type of artifact manufactured principally by pecking, grinding, or polishing of rocks such as sandstone or soapstone.

Hammer stone. A battered stone, generally made from hard and waterworn cobbles, used as a hammer to make chipped-stone tools and ground-stone tools or in other tasks.

Hunting people. The intermediate culture in David Banks Rogers's 1929 cultural chronology for the Santa Barbara Coast. Subsequent work has shown sites of the Hunting people to have been occupied between about 6,500 and 3,000 years ago.

Hydration. The gradual absorption of water by the external surfaces of obsidian artifacts. By measuring the thickness of hydration bands, the approximate age of obsidian artifacts can sometimes be determined. The method has produced mixed results in the Santa Barbara Channel area, where alkaline soils and wildfires appear to affect hydration rates.

Late Holocene. A portion of the Holocene (~10,000 years ago to the present) geological period encompassing the last 3,000 to 3,500 years. The Late Holocene is the time period during which many of the recognizable traits of Chumash culture developed.

Mano. A common ground-stone tool, consisting of a handheld and cobble-sized stone, used to grind small seeds or other materials (paints etc.) on a metate. Mostly made of sandstone in the Santa Barbara area, manos have one or more surfaces that are polished (and often faceted) by use and may also be intentionally roughened or "pecked" to facilitate grinding.

Metate. A large ground-stone artifact used in combination with a mano to grind small seeds or other materials. Usually made of sandstone in the Santa Barbara area, metates were either flat or basin-shaped platforms on which materials were ground.

Mexican period. The period from AD 1822 to 1848, when the Mexican government ruled Alta California.

Midden. A culturally produced soil strewn with the debris (animal bones and shells, charcoal, ash, discarded tools, and tool-making refuse) left by ancient peoples.

Middle Holocene. A portion of the Holocene (10,000 years ago to the present) geological period, encompassing the time between about 7,000 and 3,500 years ago.

Milling Stone. A ground-stone tool (see mano or metate), as well as an early archaeological culture (see Oak Grove) defined in the Santa Barbara area and the wider southern/central California Coast.

Minimum number of individuals (MNI). A quantitative and comparative measure of abundance used by archaeologists to analyze the skeletal remains of shellfish, fish, mammals, and other animals. Based on the analysis of repetitive elements (i.e., shellfish hinges or spires), MNI values estimate the minimum number of individual animals represented by the remains of a particular species or other taxon.

Miocene. A period of geological time, extending from about 15 million to five million years ago.

Mission (Spanish) period. The period in California history, from AD 1769 to 1822, when Alta California was actively ruled by the Spanish through a combination of religious (Franciscan missions) and secular (military presidios) institutions, sometimes referred to as the "sword and the cross."

Mortar. A bowl-shaped ground-stone tool generally believed to be used primarily in the processing of acorns, other fleshy foods, and other materials (pigments etc.) that required grinding. Mostly made of sandstone or soapstone in the Chumash area, they were used in combination with pestles.

Number of individual specimens (NISP). A quantitative and comparative measure of abundance used by archaeologists to analyze faunal assemblages. Unlike MNI, NISP measures the total number of shell or bone fragments identified to a particular species or other taxonomic category.

Oak Grove people. An early archaeological culture defined by D. B. Rogers (1929), essentially synonymous with the Milling Stone horizon, that ranges in age between about 9,000 and 3,000 years ago and is characterized by an abundance of manos and metates (milling stones).

Obsidian sourcing. The geochemical fingerprinting of volcanic glasses (obsidian) that allows an artifact to be traced to its original geological source, allowing archaeologists to reconstruct trade patterns and how they changed through time. The Chumash obtained obsidian primarily from the eastern Sierras by trading with neighboring tribes.

Olivella biplicata. A common olive-shaped marine snail found along many sandy beaches of the Santa Barbara Channel area, their shells were the principal source of shell beads made and traded by the Chumash and their ancestors for about 10,000 years.

Ochre. Iron-rich minerals that have been oxidized, producing bright red colors used as pigments or dyes, as medicines, and for other purposes by a wide variety of ancient peoples.

Pestle. A cylinder-shaped ground-stone artifact used in combination with a bowl or mortar to grind plant foods, minerals, and other materials. Normally, only the small distal end of a pestle was used for grinding.

Pinniped. A general faunal category that includes all seals and sea lions.

Projectile point. A common chipped-stone artifact type that includes spear points, dart points, and arrow points. Changes in projectile point styles through time provide an important chronological tool for archaeologists.

Protohistoric. A period of sporadic and poorly documented contacts between Native American peoples and early European explorers, prior to the Historic period. Coastal California's Protohistoric period begins with Cabrillo's voyage of AD 1542 and ends with Spanish settlement in AD 1769.

Quartzite. A relatively hard metamorphic rock, generally a sandstone fused under great heat or pressure, that was relatively common along the Santa Barbara Coast and was used by the Chumash and their predecessors to make chipped-stone tools.

Radiocarbon (^{14}C) dating. A relatively precise dating method based on measuring the amount of the radioactive carbon isotope (^{14}C) present in all living organisms. Because ^{14}C has a relatively short half-life (5,730 years), it can be used to date organic (wood or charcoal, shell, bone, etc.) samples from archaeological or geological sites dating between about 40,000 years ago and the present.

Radiocarbon years before present (RYBP). Age estimates developed by radiocarbon (^{14}C) laboratories that measure the ratio of radioactive and stable carbon isotopes in organic samples. For a variety of reasons, ^{14}C ages vary systematically from calendar ages. After the careful ^{14}C dating of thousands of samples (tree rings etc.) of known age, radiocarbon dates can now be calibrated to calendar years, providing a more precise estimate of the age of archaeological samples.

Shell midden. A midden or refuse deposit in which marine shell is one of the primary constituents.

Shovel test pit (STP). A small (c. 40-cm-wide) cylindrical test hole excavated to determine whether archaeological materials are present in an area and to chart variation in the density of artifacts or ecofacts through space. Usually dug in 20- or 25-cm levels, with excavated soils water screened and processed in the lab, STPs allow archaeologists to relatively quickly establish if archaeological materials are present in an area and gather data on the size and nature of sites.

Siliceous shale. A sedimentary rock common along the Santa Barbara Coast, generally derived from the white or buff Monterey Formation that forms many coastal cliffs in the area, that contains a mixture of clay, lime, and siliceous particles. The more siliceous variants, sometimes referred to as porcelainite, were used by the Chumash to make certain chipped-stone tools.

Site. A concentration of archaeological materials consisting of some combination of artifacts, ecofacts, and features. In the United States, archaeological sites are often recorded and referred to by trinomials representing the state (CA-), county (SBA-), and number (1, 2, 3, etc.).

Survey. An examination of surface exposures (including road cuts, stream banks, and other subsurface exposures) by archaeologists in search of artifacts or other evidence of human activity. Also known as archaeological reconnaissance, survey work normally does not include subsurface excavations.

Teleosts. The bony fish, distinctive from the cartilaginous sharks and rays (elasmobranchs), that have skeletons dominated by bony elements. The teleosts include many common fish in Santa Barbara Channel waters, from tuna to rockfish and sardines.

Terminal Pleistocene. A geological time period corresponding to the last several millennia of the Pleistocene epoch, from about 15,000 to 10,000 years ago. Most archaeologists believe that the Americas were first settled by humans during the terminal Pleistocene, and the earliest well-documented archaeological sites in the Santa Barbara Channel date to this time period.

Test unit. An excavation unit, often .5-×-1.0-m or 1.0-×-1.0-m wide, used by archaeologists to systematically collect information on the structure, contents, stratigraphy, and nature of an archaeological site or feature. Individual test units, generally excavated in 10- or 20-cm levels, can also be combined to excavate larger areas.

Tongva. Also known as the Gabrielino, the Tongva were a group of Uto-Aztecan-speaking peoples who occupied the wider Los Angeles Basin and the Southern Channel Islands.

References Cited

Anderson, K., and D. Stone

1999   *Phase 3 Archaeological Investigation of CA-SBA-69 and CA-SBA-70 for the Winchester Common Residential Development Project and Extension of Cathedral Oaks Road.* Science Applications International Corporation, Santa Barbara.

Applegate, R.

1975   An Index of Chumash Place Names. In *Papers on the Chumash.* San Luis Obispo County Archaeological Society Occasional Paper 9:19–46. San Luis Obispo.

Arnold, J. E.

1987   *Craft Specialization in the Prehistoric Channel Islands, California.* University of California Publications in Anthropology 18. University of California Press, Berkeley.

1992a   Complex Hunter-Gatherer-Fishers of Prehistoric California: Chiefs, Specialists, and Maritime Adaptations of the Channel Islands. *American Antiquity* 57:60–84.

1992b   Cultural Disruption and the Political Economy in Channel Islands Prehistory. In *Essays on the Prehistory of Maritime California,* edited by T. L. Jones, pp. 129–144. Center for Archaeological Research at Davis Publication 10. University of California, Davis.

1997   Bigger Boats, Crowded Creekbanks: Environmental Stresses in Perspective. *American Antiquity* 62:337–339.

2001   *The Origins of a Pacific Coast Chiefdom: The Chumash of the Channel Islands.* University of Utah Press, Salt Lake City.

Arnold, J. E., R. Colten, and S. Pletka

1997   Contexts of Cultural Change in Insular California. *American Antiquity* 62:157–168.

Axelrod, D. L.

1967   Geologic History of the Californian Insular Flora. In *Proceedings of the Symposium on the Biology of the California Islands,* edited by R. N. Philbrick, pp. 267–315. Santa Barbara Botanical Garden, Santa Barbara.

Bennyhoff, J. A., and R. E. Hughes

1987   *Shell Bead Ornament Exchange Between California and the Western Great Basin.* Anthropological Papers of the American Museum of Natural History 64(2).

Benson, A.

1997   *The Noontide Sun: The Field Journals of the Reverend Stephen Bowers, Pioneer California Archaeologist.* Ballena Press Anthropological Papers 44. Menlo Park.

Berger, R.

1982   The Wooley Mammoth Site, Santa Rosa Island, California. In *Peopling of the New World,* edited by J. Ericson, R. E. Taylor, and R. Berger, pp. 163–170. Ballena Press Anthropological Papers 23. Menlo Park.

Blackburn, T. C.

1975   *December's Child: A Book of Chumash Oral Narratives Collected by J. P. Harrington.* University of California Press, Berkeley.

Braje, T. J., J. M. Erlandson, and J. Timbrook

2005   An Asphaltum Coiled Basket Impression, Tarring Pebbles, and Middle Holocene Water Bottles from San Miguel Island, California. *Journal of California and Great Basin Anthropology* 25(2):61–67.

Carter, G. F.

1980a   The Metate: An Early Grain-Grinding Implement in the New World. In *Early Native*

Americans: Prehistoric Demography, Economy, and Technology, edited by D. L. Browman, pp. 21–39. Mouton, The Hague.

1980b   *Earlier Than You Think*. Texas A&M University Press, College Station.

Castillo, E. D.

1978   The Impact of Euro-American Exploration and Settlement. In *California*, edited by R. F. Heizer, pp. 99–127. Handbook of North American Indians Vol. 8, Smithsonian Institution, Washington, D.C.

Colten, R. H.

1993   Prehistoric Subsistence, Specialization, and Economy in a Southern California Chiefdom. Unpublished Ph.D. dissertation, University of California, Los Angeles.

Connolly, T., J. Erlandson, and S. Norris

1995   Early Holocene Basketry and Cordage from Daisy Cave, San Miguel Island, California. *American Antiquity* 60:309–318.

Cook, S. F.

1978   Historical Demography. In *California*, edited by R. F. Heizer, pp. 91–98. Handbook of North American Indians Vol. 8, Smithsonian Institution, Washington, D.C.

Cooley, T. G., and J. Erlandson

1989   *Results of Phase I/II Archaeological Testing at CA-SBa-1673, Hyatt Regency Santa Barbara Project*. WESTEC Services, Santa Barbara.

Dartt, D., and J. M. Erlandson

2006   Little Choice for the Chumash? Colonialism, Cattle, and Coercion in Mission Period California. *American Indian Quarterly* 30(3–4):416–430.

Davenport, D., J. R. Johnson, and J. Timbrook

1993   The Chumash and the Swordfish. *Antiquity* 67:257–272.

DuBarton, A.

1991   From Hunters to Fisherman? Developing Marine Resource Specialization on the Santa Barbara Channel. Analysis of the Artifacts and Midden Constituents from CA-SBA-71. Unpublished Master's thesis, Anthropology Department, University of Nevada, Las Vegas.

Engelhardt, Z.

1923   *Santa Barbara Mission. Missions and Missionaries of California: Local History*. James H. Barry, San Francisco.

Erlandson, J. M.

1986   Cultural Resources Management Plan: Hyatt Goleta Resort Development, Santa Barbara County, California. Manuscript on file, Central Coast Archaeological Information Center, University of California, Santa Barbara.

1987   *Boundary Definition and Significance Evaluation of Low and Moderate Sensitivity Areas at CA-SBa-73, Tecolote Canyon, Santa Barbara County, California*. Center for Archaeological Studies, University of California, Santa Barbara.

1988a   Cultural Evolution and Paleogeography on the Santa Barbara Coast: A 9600-Year ^{14}C Record from Southern California. *Radiocarbon* 30:25–39.

1988b   The Role of Shellfish in Prehistoric Economies: A Protein Perspective. *American Antiquity* 52:102–109.

1991   Shellfish and Seeds as Optimal Resources: Early Holocene Subsistence on the Santa Barbara Coast. In *Hunter-Gatherers of Early Holocene Coastal California*, edited by J. M. Erlandson and R. H. Colten, pp. 89–101. Institute of Archaeology, University of California, Los Angeles.

1993   Summary and Conclusions. In *Archaeological Investigations at CA-SBA-1731: A Transitional Middle to Late Period Site on the Santa Barbara Channel*, edited by J. M. Erlandson and J. Gerber, pp. 187–196. Dames and Moore, Santa Barbara.

1994   *Early Hunter-Gatherers of the California Coast*. Plenum, New York.

1997a   The Middle Holocene on the Western Santa Barbara Coast. In *Archaeology of the California Coast During the Middle Holocene*, edited by J. M. Erlandson and M. A. Glassow, pp. 91–109. Institute of Archaeology, University of California, Los Angeles.

1997b   The Middle Holocene Along the California Coast. In *Archaeology of the California Coast During the Middle Holocene*, edited by J. M. Erlandson and T. L. Jones, pp. 1–10. Institute of Archaeology, University of California, Los Angeles.

2001   The Archaeology of Aquatic Adaptations: Paradigms for a New Millennium. *Journal of Archaeological Research* 9:287–350.

2002   Anatomically Modern Humans, Maritime Voyaging, and the Pleistocene Colonization of the Americas. In *The First Americans: The Pleistocene Colonization of the New World*, edited by N. Jablonski, pp. 59–92. Memoirs of the California Academy of Sciences 27. San Francisco.

2007   Sea Change: The Paleocoastal Occupations of Daisy Cave. In *Seeking Our Past: An Introduction to North American Archaeology*, edited by S. W. Neusius and G. T. Gross, pp. 135–143. Oxford University Press, Oxford.

Erlandson, J. M., and K. Bartoy

1995   The Chumash, Cabrillo, and Old World Dis-
        eases. *Journal of California and Great Basin An-
        thropology* 17:153–173.

Erlandson, J. M., T. Braje, R. L. Vellanoweth, and
T. C. Rick

2006   Chumash Features at SBA-73N: Managing and
        Mitigating Under Fire. *Proceedings of the Society
        for California Archaeology* 19:191–196.

Erlandson, J. M., and T. G. Cooley

1988a   *Results of Archaeological Testing at CA-SBa-1326,
        Hyatt Regency Santa Barbara Project.* WESTEC
        Services, Santa Barbara.

1988b   *Archaeological Test Excavations at CA-SBa-72,
        Hyatt Regency Hotel Project, Santa Barbara
        County, CA.* WESTEC Services, Santa Barbara.

1988c   *Archaeological Test Excavations at CA-SBa-73N
        for the Access Road and Bridge Construction Dur-
        ing the Hyatt Regency Hotel Project, Santa Bar-
        bara County, California.* WESTEC Services,
        Santa Barbara.

Erlandson, J. M., T. Cooley, and R. Carrico

1987   A Fluted Projectile Point from the Southern Cal-
        ifornia Coast: Chronology and Context at CA-
        SBA-1951. *Journal of California and Great Basin
        Anthropology* 9:120–129.

Erlandson, J. M., and J. Gerber (editors)

1993   *Archaeological Investigations at CA-SBA-1731:
        A Transitional Middle-to-Late Period Site on
        the Santa Barbara Channel.* Dames and Moore,
        Santa Barbara.

Erlandson, J. M., and M. A. Glassow (editors)

1997   *Archaeology of the California Coast During the
        Middle Holocene.* Institute of Archaeology, Uni-
        versity of California, Los Angeles.

Erlandson, J. M., and T. L. Jones (editors)

2002   *Catalysts to Complexity: Late Holocene Societies of
        the California Coast.* Cotsen Institute of Archae-
        ology, University of California, Los Angeles.

Erlandson, J. M., D. J. Kennett, R. J. Behl, and I. Hough

1997   The Cico Chert Source on San Miguel Island,
        California. *Journal of California and Great Basin
        Anthropology* 19:124–130.

Erlandson, J. M., D. J. Kennett, B. L. Ingram, D. A. Guthrie,
D. P. Morris, M. A. Tveskov, G. J. West, and P. L. Walker

1996   An Archaeological and Paleontological Chronol-
        ogy for Daisy Cave (CA-SMI-261), San Miguel
        Island, California. *Radiocarbon* 38:355–373.

Erlandson, J. M., J. Pjerrou, T. K. Rockwell, and
P. L. Walker

1988   *Cultural Ecology on the Southern California
        Coast at 5500 BP: A Comparative Analysis of CA-*

SBA-75. Archives of California Prehistory No. 15.
Coyote Press, Salinas, California.

Erlandson, J. M., and T. C. Rick

2002   Late Holocene Cultural Developments Along
        the Santa Barbara Coast. In *Catalysts to Com-
        plexity: Late Holocene Societies of the California
        Coast,* edited by J. M. Erlandson and T. L. Jones,
        pp. 166–182. Cotsen Institute of Archaeology,
        University of California, Los Angeles.

Erlandson, J. M., T. C. Rick, J. A. Estes, M. H. Graham,
T. Braje, and R. L. Vellanoweth

2005   Sea Otters, Shellfish, and Humans: 10,000 Years
        of Ecological Interaction on San Miguel Island.
        In *Proceedings of the Sixth California Islands Sym-
        posium, Ventura, California,* edited by D. K. Gar-
        celon and C. A. Schwemm, pp. 58–69. Institute
        for Wildlife Studies and National Park Service,
        Arcata, California.

Erlandson, J. M., T. C. Rick, D. J. Kennett, and
P. L. Walker

2001   Dates, Demography, and Disease: Cultural Con-
        tacts and Possible Evidence for Old World Epi-
        demics Among the Island Chumash. *Pacific Coast
        Archaeological Society Quarterly* 37(3):11–26.

Erlandson, J. M., T. C. Rick, and R. Vellanoweth

2004   Human Impacts on Ancient Environments: A
        Case Study from California's Northern Channel
        Islands. In *Voyages of Discovery: The Archaeology
        of Islands,* edited by S. M. Fitzpatrick, pp. 51–83.
        Praeger, New York.

Erlandson, J. M., T. C. Rick, R. L. Vellanoweth, and
D. J. Kennett

1999   Marine Subsistence at a 9300 Year-Old Shell
        Midden on Santa Rosa Island, California. *Jour-
        nal of Field Archaeology* 26:255–265.

Erlandson, J. M., and T. K. Rockwell

1987   Radiocarbon Reversals and Stratigraphic Discon-
        tinuities: Natural Formation Processes in Coastal
        California Archaeological Sites. In *Natural For-
        mation Processes of the Archaeological Record,*
        Vol. 352, edited by D. Nash and M. Petraglia, pp.
        51–73. BAR International Series, Oxford.

Eschmeyer, W. N., E. S. Herald, and H. Hammann

1983   *A Field Guide to Pacific Coast Fishes of North
        America.* Houghton Mifflin, Boston.

Fenenga, G. L.

1984   *A Typological Analysis of the Temporal and Geo-
        graphic Distribution of the "Eccentric" Crescent in
        Western North America.* Department of Anthro-
        pology, University of California, Berkeley.

Fitzgerald, R. T., Terry L. Jones, and A. Schroth

2005   Ancient Long Distance Trade in Western North

America: New AMS Radiocarbon Dates from Southern California. *Journal of Archaeological Science* 32:423–434.

Fuller, T., and G. King
1980   Historical Background. In *Cultural Resources Technical Report: Proposed Embarcadero Residential Development*, edited by J. B. Serena, pp. 95–124. Social Process Research Institute, University of California, Santa Barbara.

Gallegos, D.
1991   Antiquity and Adaptation at Agua Hedionda, Carlsbad, California. In *Hunter-Gatherers of Early Holocene Coastal California*, edited by J. M. Erlandson and R. H. Colten, pp. 19–41. Institute of Archaeology, University of California, Los Angeles.

Gamble, L. H.
2002   Evidence for the Origin of the Plank Canoe in North America. *American Antiquity* 67:301–315.

Gibson, R. O.
1991   *The Chumash*. Chelsea House Publishers, New York.

Glassow, M. A.
1980   Subsistence Strategies at Tecolote Canyon, Coastal Santa Barbara County, California. Paper presented at the Society for California Archaeology Annual Meeting.
1996   *Purismeño Chumash Prehistory: Maritime Adaptations Along the Southern California Coast*. Harcourt Brace College Publishers, Fort Worth.
1997   Middle Holocene Cultural Developments in the Central Santa Barbara Channel Region. In *Archaeology of the California Coast During the Middle Holocene*, edited by J. M. Erlandson and M. A. Glassow, pp. 73–90. Institute of Archaeology, University of California, Los Angeles.

Glassow, M. A., and L. Wilcoxon
1988   Coastal Adaptations near Point Conception, California, with Particular Regard to Shellfish Exploitation. *American Antiquity* 53:35–51.

Glassow, M. A., L. Wilcoxon, and J. Erlandson
1988   Cultural and Environmental Change During the Early Period of Santa Barbara Channel Prehistory. In *The Archaeology of Prehistoric Coastlines*, edited by G. Bailey and J. Parkington, pp. 64–77. Cambridge University Press, New York.

Graham, M. H., P. K. Dayton, and J. M. Erlandson
2003   Ice Ages and Ecological Transitions on Temperate Coasts. *Trends in Ecology and Evolution* 18(1):33–40.

Guthrie, D. A.
1980   Analysis of Avifaunal and Bat Remains from Midden Sites on San Miguel Island. In *The Cal-ifornia Channel Islands: Proceedings of a Multidisciplinary Symposium*, edited by D. Power, pp. 689–702. Santa Barbara Museum of Natural History, Santa Barbara.

Haley, B. D.
1980   Historical Archaeology. In *Cultural Resources Technical Report: Proposed Embarcadero Residential Development*, edited by J. B. Serena, pp. 259–265. Social Process Research Institute, University of California, Santa Barbara.

Haley, B. D., and L. R. Wilcoxon
1997   Anthropology and the Making of Chumash Tradition. *Current Anthropology* 38(5):761–777.

Harrison, W.
1964   Prehistory of the Santa Barbara Coast, California. Unpublished Ph.D. dissertation, University of Arizona.

Harrison, W. M., and E. S. Harrison
1966   An Archaeological Sequence for the Hunting People of Santa Barbara, California. *University of California Archaeological Survey Annual Report* 8:1–89. Los Angeles.

Hawley, W. A.
1987   *Early Days of Santa Barbara*. 3rd ed. Santa Barbara Heritage, Santa Barbara.

Heizer, R.
1974   Were the Chumash Whale Hunters? Implications for Ethnography in 1974. *Journal of California Anthropology* 1(1):26–32.

Hess, S., and D. Stone
1997   *Phase 2 Testing of CA-SBA-2499 APN 70-120-54 and 70-120-68 Mountain View Residential Development Santa Barbara County, California*. Science Applications International Corporation, Santa Barbara.

Heusser, L. E.
1978   Pollen in Santa Barbara Basin, California: A 12,000 Year Record. *Geological Society of America Bulletin* 89:673–678.

Heye, G. G.
1921   *Certain Artifacts from San Miguel Island, California*. Indian Notes and Monographs 7(4). Museum of the American Indian, New York.

Holliday, J. S.
1981   *The World Rushed In: The Gold Rush Experience*. Simon and Schuster, New York.

Howard, W. J., and L. M. Raab
1993   *Olivella* Grooved Rectangle Beads as Evidence of an Early Period Southern Channel Islands Interaction Sphere. *Pacific Coast Archaeological Society Quarterly* 29(3):1–11.

Hudson, D. T.
1976   *Marine Archaeology Along the Southern Cali-*

fornia Coast. San Diego Museum Papers 9. San Diego Museum of Man, San Diego.

Hudson, T., and T. C. Blackburn

1982   *The Material Culture of the Chumash Interaction Sphere, Vol. I: Food Procurement and Transportation*. Ballena Press Anthropological Papers No. 25. Ballena Press and Santa Barbara Museum of Natural History, Menlo Park and Santa Barbara.

1983   *The Material Culture of the Chumash Interaction Sphere, Vol. II: Food Preparation and Shelter*. Ballena Press Anthropological Papers No. 27. Ballena Press and Santa Barbara Museum of Natural History, Menlo Park and Santa Barbara.

1985   *The Material Culture of the Chumash Interaction Sphere, Vol. III: Clothing, Ornamentation, and Grooming*. Ballena Press Anthropological Papers No. 28. Ballena Press and Santa Barbara Museum of Natural History, Menlo Park and Santa Barbara.

1986   *The Material Culture of the Chumash Interaction Sphere, Vol. IV: Ceremonial Paraphernalia, Games, and Amusements*. Ballena Press Anthropological Papers No. 30. Ballena Press and Santa Barbara Museum of Natural History, Menlo Park and Santa Barbara.

1987   *The Material Culture of the Chumash Interaction Sphere, Vol. V: Manufacturing Processes, Metrology, and Trade*. Ballena Press Anthropological Papers No. 31. Ballena Press and Santa Barbara Museum of Natural History, Menlo Park and Santa Barbara.

Hudson, T., J. Timbrook, and M. Rempe

1978   *Tomol: Chumash Watercraft as Described in the Ethnographic Notes of John P. Harrington*. Ballena Press Anthropological Papers 9. Menlo Park.

Hudson, T., and E. Underhay

1978   *Crystals in the Sky: An Intellectual Odyssey Involving Chumash Astronomy, Cosmology and Rock Art*. Ballena Press Anthropological Papers No. 10. Santa Barbara Museum of Natural History, Santa Barbara.

Imwalle, M. H.

1997   Historic Feature at CA-SBA-73N/Santa Barbara Club Resort and Spa Project. Manuscript on file, Central Coast Archaeological Information Center, University of California, Santa Barbara.

Inman, D.

1983   Application of Coastal Dynamics to the Reconstruction of Paleocoastlines in the Vicinity of La Jolla, California. In *Quaternary Coastlines and Marine Archaeology*, edited by P. Masters and N. Flemming, pp. 1–49. Academic Press, New York.

Jackson, R. H.

1994   *Indian Population Decline: The Missions of Northwestern New Spain*. University of New Mexico Press, Albuquerque.

Jenkins, D. L., and J. M. Erlandson

1996   *Olivella* Grooved Rectangle Beads from a Middle Holocene Site in the Fort Rock Valley, Northern Great Basin. *Journal of California and Great Basin Anthropology* 18(2):296–306.

Johnson, D. L.

1989   Subsurface Stone Lines, Stone Zones, Artifact-Manuport Layers, and Biomantles Produced by Bioturbation via Pocket Gophers (*Thomomys bottae*). *American Antiquity* 54:370–389.

Johnson, J. R.

1980   Analysis of Fish Remains. In *Cultural Resources Technical Report: Proposed Embarcadero Residential Development*, edited by J. B. Serena, pp. 216–223. Social Process Research Institute, University of California, Santa Barbara.

1988   Chumash Social Organization: An Ethnohistorical Perspective. Unpublished Ph.D. dissertation, University of California, Santa Barbara.

Johnson, J. R., T. W. Stafford, H. O. Ajie, and D. P. Morris

2002   Arlington Springs Revisited. In *Proceedings of the Fifth California Islands Symposium*, edited by D. Browne, K. Mitchell, and H. Chaney, pp. 541–545. Santa Barbara Museum of Natural History and U.S. Department of the Interior Minerals Management Service, Pacific Outer Continental Shelf Region, Santa Barbara.

Johnson, J. R., C. N. Warren, and S. E. Warren

1982   Ethnohistoric Overview of Native American Culture. In *Intensive Cultural Resources Survey for the Goleta Flood Protection Program, Santa Barbara County, California*, by L. R. Wilcoxon, J. M. Erlandson, and D. F. Stone, pp. 12–48. Archaeological Systems Management, San Diego.

Jones, T., G. M. Brown, L. M. Raab, J. L. McVickar, W. G. Spaulding, D. J. Kennett, A. York, and P. Walker

1999   Environmental Imperatives Reconsidered: Demographic Crises in Western North America During the Medieval Climatic Anomaly. *Current Anthropology* 40(2):137–170.

Kelsey, H.

1985   European Impact on the California Indians, 1530–1830. *The Americas* 41(4):494–511.

Kennett, D. J.

1998   Behavioral Ecology and Hunter-Gatherer Societies of the Northern Channel Islands, California. Unpublished Ph.D. dissertation, University of California, Santa Barbara.

2005   *The Island Chumash: Behavioral Ecology of a*

Maritime Society. University of California Press, Berkeley.

Kennett, D. J., and C. Conlee

2002   Emergence of Late Holocene Sociopolitical Complexity on Santa Rosa and San Miguel Islands. In *Catalysts to Complexity: Late Holocene Societies of the California Coast*, edited by J. M. Erlandson and T. L. Jones, pp. 147–165. Cotsen Institute of Archaeology, University of California, Los Angeles.

Kennett, D. J., and J. P. Kennett

2000   Competitive and Cooperative Responses to Climatic Instability in Coastal Southern California. *American Antiquity* 65:379–396.

Kennett, D. J., J. P. Kennett, J. M. Erlandson, and K. G. Cannariato

2007   Human Responses to Middle Holocene Climate Change on California's Channel Islands. *Quaternary Science Reviews* 26:351–367.

King, C. D.

1967   The Sweetwater Mesa Site (LAn-267) and Its Place in Southern California Prehistory. *Archaeological Survey Annual Report (Los Angeles)* 9:27–104.

1971   Chumash Inter-Village Economic Exchange. *Indian Historian* 4(1):30–43.

1980   Prehistoric Background. In *Cultural Resources Technical Report: Proposed Embarcadero Residential Development*, edited by J. B. Serena, pp. 23–93. Social Process Research Institute, University of California, Santa Barbara.

1990   *Evolution of Chumash Society: A Comparative Study of Artifacts Used for Social System Maintenance in the Santa Barbara Channel Region Before AD 1804*. Garland, New York.

King, C. D., and T. P. Rudolph

1991   Ethnohistoric Resource Use. In *Western Chumash Prehistory: Resource Use and Settlement in the Santa Ynez River Valley*, edited by C. F. Woodman, J. L. Rudolph, and T. P. Rudolph, pp. 103–135. Science Applications International Corporation, Santa Barbara.

King, C. D., and J. B. Serena

1980   Temporally Sensitive Artifacts from 1979 Excavations. In *Cultural Resources Technical Report: Proposed Embarcadero Residential Development*, edited by J. B. Serena, pp. 179–182. Social Process Research Institute, University of California, Santa Barbara.

Kinlan, B. P., Michael H. Graham, and Jon M. Erlandson

2005   Late Quaternary Changes in the Size, Shape, and Isolation of the California Islands: Ecological and Anthropological Implications. In *Proceedings of the Sixth California Islands Symposium, Ventura, California*, edited by D. K. Garcelon and C. A. Schwemm, pp. 119–130. Institute for Wildlife Studies and National Park Service, Arcata, California.

Kornfeld, M.

1980   Analysis of Chipped Stone Artifacts. In *Cultural Resources Technical Report: Proposed Embarcadero Residential Development*, edited by J. B. Serena, pp. 225–249. Social Process Research Institute, University of California, Santa Barbara.

Kornfeld, M., and J. Erlandson

1980   Summary of Field Work Results. In *Cultural Resources Technical Report: Proposed Embarcadero Residential Development*, edited by J. B. Serena, pp. 157–178. Social Process Research Institute, University of California, Santa Barbara.

Kornfeld, M., C. D. King, T. Fuller, G. King, J. B. Serena, P. E. Snethkamp, J. Erlandson, B. D. Haley, J. D. Moore, K. R. Lawson, and J. R. Johnson

1980   *Cultural Resources Technical Report: Proposed Embarcadero Residential Development*. Edited by J. B. Serena. Social Process Research Institute, University of California, Santa Barbara.

Kowta, M.

1969   The Sayles Complex: A Late Milling Stone Assemblage from Cajon Pass and the Ecological Implications of Its Scraper Planes. *University of California Publications in Anthropology* 6:1–101.

Lambert, P. M.

1993   Health in Prehistoric Populations of the Santa Barbara Channel Islands. *American Antiquity* 58:509–522.

1994   War and Peace on the Western Front: A Study of Violent Conflict and Its Correlates in Prehistoric Hunter-Gatherer Societies of Coastal Southern California. Unpublished Ph.D. dissertation, University of California, Santa Barbara.

Lambert, P. M., and P. L. Walker

1991   Physical Anthropological Evidence for the Evolution of Social Complexity in Coastal Southern California. *Antiquity* 65:963–973.

Landberg, L. C. W.

1965   *The Chumash Indians of Southern California*. Southwest Museum Papers 19. Los Angeles.

Lantis, D. W., R. Steiner, and A. E. Karinen

1973   *California: Land of Contrast*. 2nd ed. Kendall/Hunt Publishers, Dubuque.

Lawson, K. R., Brian D. Haley, and Jeffery B. Serena

1980   Analysis of Osseus Faunal Remains. In *Cultural Resources Technical Report: Proposed Embarca-*

dero Residential Development, edited by J. B. Serena, pp. 209–216. Social Process Research Institute, University of California, Santa Barbara.

Librado, F.

1979   *Breath of the Sun: Life in Early California as Told by a Chumash Indian, Fernando Librado, to John P. Harrington.* Edited by T. Hudson. Malki Museum Press, Banning, California.

1981   *Eye of the Flute: Chumash Traditional History and Ritual as Told by Fernando Librado Kitsepawit to John P. Harrington.* Edited by T. Hudson, T. Blackburn, R. Curletti, and J. Timbrook. Malki Museum Press and Santa Barbara Museum of Natural History, Banning and Santa Barbara, California.

Lightfoot, K.

1993   Long-Term Developments in Complex Hunter-Gatherer Societies: Recent Perspectives from the Pacific Coast of North America. *Journal of Archaeological Research* 1(3):167–201.

Macko, M.

1987   *Results of Boundary Testing at Sites CA-SBA-69 and CA-SBA-70 Within the Winchester Common Residential Development and Cathedral Oaks Road Extension Project Sites.* Report on file, Central Coast Archaeological Information Center, University of California, Santa Barbara.

McLendon, S., and J. R. Johnson

1999   *Cultural Affiliation and Lineal Descent of Chumash Peoples in the Channel Islands and the Santa Monica Mountains.* Santa Barbara Museum of Natural History and Hunter College, Santa Barbara and New York.

Meehan, B.

1982   *Shell Bed to Shell Midden.* Australian Institute of Aboriginal Studies, Canberra.

Meighan, C. W.

1981   "This Is the Way the World Ends": Native Responses to the Age of Exploration in California. In *Early California: Perception and Reality*, by H. J. Bruman and C. W. Meighan, pp. 43–74. Andrews Clark Memorial Library, Los Angeles.

Moore, J. D.

1980   Analysis of Non-Ornamental Ground Stone. In *Cultural Resources Technical Report: Proposed Embarcadero Residential Development*, edited by J. B. Serena, pp. 251–257. Social Process Research Institute, University of California, Santa Barbara.

Moore, J. D., J. A. English, J. Hudson, T. Rudolph, and J. B. Serena

1982   *Archaeological Excavations: SBA-73 North, Santa Barbara County, California.* Office of Public Archaeology, Social Process Research Institute, University of California, Santa Barbara.

Moratto, M. J.

1984   *California Archaeology.* Academic Press, New York.

Moss, M. L., and J. M. Erlandson

1995   Reflections on North American Pacific Coast Prehistory. *Journal of World Prehistory* 9:1–45.

Mulroy, T., R. Thompson, M. Hochberg, P. Collins, and P. Lehman

1984   *Draft Technical Appendix J: Terrestrial and Freshwater Biology.* Point Arguello Field and Gaviota Processing Facility Area Study and Chevron/Texaco Development Plans Environmental Impact Report/Environmental Impact Statement. Arthur D. Little, San Francisco.

Norris, R. M.

1968   Seacliff Retreat near Santa Barbara, California. *Mineral Information Service* 21:87–91.

2003   *The Geology and Landscape of Santa Barbara County, California and Its Offshore Islands.* Santa Barbara Museum of Natural History, Santa Barbara.

Norris, R. M., and R. W. Webb

1990   *Geology of California.* John Wiley and Sons, New York.

Olson, R.

1930   Chumash Prehistory. *University of California Publications in American Archaeology and Ethnology* 28:1–21.

O'Neill, O. H.

1939   *History of Santa Barbara County.* Union Printing, Santa Barbara.

Orr, P. C.

1943   Archaeology of Mescalitan Island and the Customs of the Canaliño. *Santa Barbara Museum of Natural History Occasional Papers* 5:1–61.

1968   *Prehistory of Santa Rosa Island.* Santa Barbara Museum of Natural History, Santa Barbara.

Orr, P. C., and R. Berger

1966   The Fire Areas on Santa Rosa Island, California. *Proceedings of the National Academy of Sciences* 56(5):1409–1416.

Owen, R. C.

1964   Early Milling Stone Horizon (Oak Grove), Santa Barbara County, California: Radiocarbon Dates. *American Antiquity* 30(2):233–241.

Owen, R. C., F. Curtis, and D. S. Miller

1964   The Glen Annie Canyon Site, SBA-142: An Early Horizon Coastal Site of Santa Barbara County. *Archaeological Survey Annual Report* 6:435–503.

Paez, J.
1968   *Cabrillo's Log 1542–1543: A Voyage of Discovery.* Translated by J. R. Moriarity and M. Keistman. The Western Explorer 5(2/3). Cabrillo Historical Association, San Diego.

Pisias, N. G.
1978   Paleoecology of the Santa Barbara Basin During the Last 8,000 Years. *Quaternary Research* 10: 366–384.
1979   Model for Paleoceanographic Reconstructions of the California Current During the Last 8,000 Years. *Quaternary Research* 11(3):373–386.

Preston, W.
1996   Serpent in Eden: Dispersal of Foreign Diseases into Pre-Mission California. *Journal of California and Great Basin Anthropology* 18:2–37.

Priestley, H. I. (editor)
1937   *A Historical, Political, and Natural Description of California by Pedro Fages, Soldier of Spain.* 1st ed. University of California Press, Berkeley.

Raab, L. M. and D. O. Larson
1997   Medieval Climatic Anomaly and Punctuated Cultural Evolution in Coastal Southern California. *American Antiquity* 62:319–336.

Rick, T. C.
2004   Daily Activities, Community Dynamics, and Historical Ecology on California's Northern Channel Islands. Unpublished Ph.D. dissertation, University of Oregon, Eugene.
2007   *The Archaeology and Historical Ecology of Late Holocene San Miguel Island.* Perspectives in California Archaeology 8. Cotsen Institute of Archaeology, University of California, Los Angeles.

Rick, T. C., and J. M. Erlandson
2000   Early Holocene Fishing Strategies on the California Coast: Evidence from CA-SBA-2057. *Journal of Archaeological Science* 27:621–633.
2003   Archeology, Ancient Human Impacts on the Environment, and Cultural Resource Management on Channel Islands National Park, California. *CRM: The Journal of Heritage Stewardship* 1: 86–89.

Rick, T. C., J. M. Erlandson, and R. L. Vellanoweth
2001   Paleocoastal Marine Fishing on the Pacific Coast of the Americas: Perspectives from Daisy Cave, California. *American Antiquity* 66:595–613.

Rick, T. C., J. M. Erlandson, R. L. Vellanoweth, and T. J. Braje
2005   From Pleistocene Mariners to Complex Hunter-Gatherers: The Archaeology of the California Channel Islands. *Journal of World Prehistory* 19: 169–228.

Rick, T. C., D. J. Kennett, and J. M. Erlandson
2005   Archaeology and Paleoecology of the Abalone Rocks Estuary, Santa Rosa Island, California. In *Proceedings of the Sixth California Islands Symposium, Ventura, California*, edited by D. K. Garcelon and C. A. Schwemm, pp. 237–245. Institute for Wildlife Studies and National Park Service, Arcata, California.

Rick, T. C., C. E. Skinner, J. M. Erlandson, and R. L. Vellanoweth
2001   Obsidian Source Characterization and Human Exchange Systems on California's Channel Islands. *Pacific Coast Archaeological Society Quarterly* 37(3):27–44.

Rick, T. C., R. L. Vellanoweth, J. M. Erlandson, and D. J. Kennett
2002   On the Antiquity of the Single-Piece Fishhook: AMS Radiocarbon Evidence from the Southern California Coast. *Journal of Archaeological Science* 29:933–942.

Robinson, W. W.
1948   *Land in California: The Story of Mission Lands, Ranchos, Squatters, Mining Claims, Railroad Grants, Land Scrip, Homesteads.* University of California Press, Berkeley.

Rogers, D. B.
1926   Original field notes. On file, Santa Barbara Museum of Natural History, Santa Barbara.
1929   *Prehistoric Man on the Santa Barbara Coast.* Santa Barbara Museum of Natural History, Santa Barbara.

Salls, R. A.
1988   Prehistoric Fisheries of the California Bight. Unpublished Ph.D. dissertation, University of California, Los Angeles.

Santoro, L. J., T. Hazeltine, and A. G. Toren
1995   *Phase II Archaeological Excavations at CA-SBA-2499.* ISERA Group, Santa Barbara. Report on file, Central Coast Archaeological Information Center, University of California, Santa Barbara.

Schoenherr, A. A.
1992   *A Natural History of California.* University of California Press, Berkeley.

Schumacher, P.
1875   Ancient Graves and Shell-Heaps of California. In *Annual Report, 1875*, pp. 335–350. Smithsonian Institution, Washington, D.C.

Serena, J. B.
1980   Analysis of Shellfish Remains. In *Cultural Resource Technical Report: Proposed Embarcadero Residential Development*, edited by J. B. Serena, pp. 183–208. Social Process Research Institute, University of California, Santa Barbara.

Smith, C. F.

1976   *A Flora of the Santa Barbara Region.* Santa Barbara Museum of Natural History, Santa Barbara.

Smith, W. E.

1983   The Reverend Stephen Bowers: "Curiousity Hunter of the Santa Barbara Channel Islands." *California History*, Spring:26–37.

Stannard, D. E.

1989   *Before the Horror: The Population of Hawaii on the Eve of Western Contact.* Social Sciences Research Institute and University of Hawaii Press, Honolulu.

Stine, S.

1994   Extreme and Persistent Drought in California and Patagonia During Medieval Time. *Nature* 369:546–549.

Stuiver, M., and P. J. Reimer

1993   Extended ^{14}C Data Base and Revised CALIB 3.0 ^{14}C Age Calibration Program. *Radiocarbon* 35(1):215–230.

Thornton, R.

1987   *American Indian Holocaust and Survival: A Population History Since 1492.* University of Oklahoma Press, Norman.

Timbrook, J.

1990   Ethnobotany of the Chumash Indians, California, Based on the Ethnographic Notes of John P. Harrington. *Economic Botany* 44:236–253.

Timbrook, J., J. Johnson, and D. Earle

1982   Vegetation Burning by the Chumash. *Journal of California and Great Basin Anthropology* 4:163–186.

Tompkins, W. A.

1960   *Santa Barbara's Royal Rancho.* Howell-North, Berkeley.

1966   *Goleta the Good Land.* Pioneer Publishing, Fresno.

1975   *Santa Barbara: Past and Present.* Tecolote Books, Santa Barbara.

1976   *It Happened in Old Santa Barbara.* Santa Barbara National Bank, Santa Barbara.

Vellanoweth, R. L.

2001   AMS Radiocarbon Dating and Shell Bead Chronologies: Middle Holocene Exchange and Interaction in Western North America. *Journal of Archaeological Science* 28:941–950.

Vellanoweth, R. L., and J. M. Erlandson

2000   Notes on a "Pleistocene" Milling Stone Site at Tecolote Canyon, Santa Barbara, California. *Current Research in the Pleistocene* 17:85–87.

2004   Coastal Paleogeography and Human Land Use at Tecolote Canyon, Santa Barbara County, California, USA. *Geoarchaeology* 19(2):141–165.

Wagner, H. R.

1929   *Spanish Voyages to the Northwest Coast of North America in the Sixteenth Century.* California Historical Society, San Francisco.

Walker, P. L., and T. Hudson

1993   *Chumash Healing: Changing Health and Medical Practices in an American Indian Society.* Malki Museum, Banning, California.

Walker, P. L., and P. Lambert

1989   Skeletal Evidence for Stress During a Period of Cultural Change in Prehistoric California. In *Advances in Paleopathology,* edited by L. Capasso, pp. 207–212. Journal of Paleopathology Monographic Publication 1. Marino Solfanelli, Chieti, Italy.

Wallace, W.

1955   Suggested Chronology for Southern California Coastal Archaeology. *Southwest Journal of Anthropology* 11:214–230.

Warren, C.

1968   Cultural Tradition and Ecological Adaptation on the Southern California Coast. *Eastern New Mexico University Contributions to Anthropology* 1(3):1–14.

Yatsko, A.

2000   Late Holocene Paleoclimatic Stress and Prehistoric Human Occupation on San Clemente Island. Unpublished Ph.D. dissertation, University of California, Los Angeles.